T0355507

The Presidential Expectations Gap

For several decades, political observers have noted that public expectations of the U.S. president are becoming increasingly excessive and unreasonable. Today, all presidents confront an expectations gap—the difference between what the public expects them to accomplish and what is actually possible for them to accomplish. Despite the abundance of anecdotal evidence and conventional wisdom regarding the expectations gap, few scholars have attempted to test the expectations gap thesis empirically. Richard Waterman, Carol L. Silva, and Hank Jenkins-Smith conduct the first systematic study to determine whether the expectations gap does in fact exist and to identify the factors that contribute to the public's disappointment in a given president. Using data from five original surveys, they confirm that the expectations gap is manifest in public opinion, that it leads to lower approval ratings, and that it lowers the chance that a president will be reelected. The gap even contributes to the success of the political party that does not hold the White House in congressional midterm elections. More broadly, the authors find that the expectations gap is entangled with the effects of partisanship, as well as with declining levels of trust in leadership. This study provides important insights not only on the American presidency and public opinion but also on trust in government.

Richard Waterman is Professor of Political Science at the University of Kentucky.

Carol L. Silva is Associate Professor of Political Science and Director of the Center for Risk and Crisis Management at the University of Oklahoma.

Hank Jenkins-Smith is Professor of Political Science and Associate Director of the Center for Applied Social Research at the University of Oklahoma.

The Presidential Expectations Gap

Public Attitudes Concerning the Presidency

Richard Waterman, Carol L. Silva, and
Hank Jenkins-Smith

University of Michigan Press
Ann Arbor

First paperback edition 2016
Copyright © by the University of Michigan 2014

Published in the United States of America by the
University of Michigan Press
Printed and bound by CPI Group (UK) Ltd, Croydon, CR0 4YY

2019   2018   2017   2016   5   4   3   2

A CIP catalog record for this book is available from the British Library.

Library of Congress Cataloging-in-Publication Data

Waterman, Richard W.
    The presidential expectations gap : public attitudes concerning the
presidency / Richard Waterman, Carol L. Silva, Hank Jenkins-Smith.
        pages   cm
    Includes bibliographical references and index.
        ISBN 978-0-472-11914-1 (hardback) — ISBN 978-0-472-02971-6 (e-book)
        1. Presidents—United States—Public opinion.   2. United States—
Politics and government.   I. Silva, Carol L.   II. Jenkins-Smith, Hank
C.   III. Title.
    JK516.W377   2014
    352.230973—dc23

                                                              2013036410

ISBN 978-0-472-03659-2 (pbk. : alk. paper)

Contents

Acknowledgments   vii

Chapter 1   The Role of Public Expectations   1

Chapter 2   Public Expectations in a Historical Perspective   6

Chapter 3   Comparing Incumbent and Retrospective Evaluations
of Presidential Performance   16

Chapter 4   Analyzing Public Expectations   29

Chapter 5   Testing the Expectations Gap Thesis:
The Presidency of Bill Clinton   51

Chapter 6   The Economy, Ethical Standards, and Partisanship   72

Chapter 7   Presidential Scandal and the Expectations Gap:
Why Did Clinton Survive the Impeachment Crisis?   84

Chapter 8   George W. Bush: War and the Economy   104

Chapter 9   Barack Obama: The Candidate/Incumbent
Expectations Gap   120

Chapter 10   Micro- and Macro-Level Models of the
Expectations Gap   133

Chapter 11   The Expectations Gap in a Broader Theoretical Context   161

Appendix A   *Survey Methodology*   177

Appendix B   *Measurement of Our Independent Variables*   187

Notes   191

References   195

Index   204

Acknowledgments

This book is unusual in that the research it describes was undertaken over three decades, for which data were collected in 5 nationwide or statewide surveys, and in the course of which all three of us changed institutions (some of us twice). The seeds of the idea for a valid and reliable measure of the gap between citizens' expectations of a president and their perceptions of presidential performance grew from conversations among the authors at the Institute for Public Policy (IPP) at the University of New Mexico in the early 1990s. Most of the data utilized here were collected by the IPP's Survey Research Center. We then moved on to other universities—with Silva and Jenkins-Smith relocating to Texas A&M's GBS School of Public Service, and Waterman joining the faculty at the University of Kentucky, where he served as Chair of the Department of Political Science. The data collection efforts continued in this period, and the 2007 nationwide survey was fielded with the able assistance of Texas A&M's Public Policy Research Institute (PPRI). Jenkins-Smith and Silva moved once more, landing at the University of Oklahoma, splitting their time between the Department of Political Science and the Center for Applied Social Research.

Over the course of our academic migrations, we accumulated many debts, intellectual and otherwise. At the University of New Mexico, several of our colleagues provided both suggestions and encouragement. Neil Mitchell, Joe Stewart, and Kerry Herron all helped us think through the measurement options and model development. Amy Goodin, at the UNM IPP's Survey Research Center, managed the data collection efforts, and Carol Brown provided excellent institutional and logistical support. Funding for the surveys came from the IPP, based on the institutional support made possible by Dr. Paul Risser (then Vice President for Research at UNM). At Texas A&M University, James Dyer at the PPRI undertook the data collection effort, and

George Edwards provided excellent recommendations for the modeling and analysis. The GBS also provided funding for the 2007 survey. The University of Kentucky provided sabbatical time release to work on this project. Walt Smith and Arvind Raichur, both graduates of the University of New Mexico also provided intellectual contributions to this work. We also owe thanks to the editors and reviewers of the journals that published various parts of this project as articles, including the *Journal of Politics* and the *Presidential Studies Quarterly.* The reviews, and the patience of the editors, provided valuable opportunities to improve those articles and the chapters of this book. And at the University of Michigan Press, we are particularly indebted to Melody Herr, Susan Cronin, Shaun Manning, and Kevin Rennells. We thank them for making this a better book.

In short, this book could not have been written without the support of many friends, colleagues, administrators, editors, and reviewers. We are deeply grateful for that support.

We would like to acknowledge the following: An earlier version of chapter 7 appeared in the *Presidential Studies Quarterly.* See Carol L. Silva, Richard W. Waterman, and Hank C. Jenkins-Smith, "Why Did Clinton Survive the Impeachment Crisis? A Test of Three Explanations," *Presidential Studies Quarterly* 37 (3) (2007): 468–85.

An earlier version of chapter 10 appeared in the *Journal of Politics.* See Hank C. Jenkins-Smith, Carol L. Silva, and Richard W. Waterman, "Micro and Macro Models of the Presidential Expectations Gap," *Journal of Politics* 67 (August 2005): 690–715.

All of the quotes at the beginning of the chapters in this book derive from John T. Woolley's The American Presidency Project at http://www.presidency.ucsb.edu/ws/?pid=90174.

Hank C. Jenkins-Smith   **Carol L. Silva**   **Richard Waterman**
University of Oklahoma   University of Oklahoma   University of Kentucky

CHAPTER I

The Role of Public Expectations

William H. Lawrence: As you look back upon your first 2 years in office, sir, has your experience in the office matched your expectations? You had studied a good deal the power of the Presidency, the methods of its operations. How has this worked out as you saw it in advance?

President John Kennedy: Well, I think in the first place the problems are more difficult than I had imagined they were. Secondly, there is a limitation upon the ability of the United States to solve these problems."

American Broadcasting Company television and radio interview,
December 17, 1962

In the American political system, presidents deal with a wide variety of difficult issues. Yet as President Kennedy's response indicates, presidents soon discover that they have only a limited ability to solve many of the nation's most intractable problems. Put another way, presidents quickly discover that their own expectations of what they can accomplish may very well be excessive and unrealistic. Further complicating matters, the public expects presidential action on a broad range of policy issues and its expectations are often contradictory. For instance, while many people demand that the president produce a balanced budget, they also support increased funding for an ever-escalating number of federal programs including national defense, Medicare, and education. Consequently, presidents find themselves overwhelmed, without the vital constitutional or legal resources necessary to satisfy escalating demands for immediate action. The end result is that all presidents, at some point in their term of office, fail to satisfy public expectations.

In this book we examine what presidential scholars often refer to as the expectations gap: the difference between public expectations and the realities of presidential performance. The expectations gap is of particular importance because political scientists, historians, journalists, pollsters, presidential advisers, bloggers, pundits of sundry ideological stripes, and even presidents themselves regularly discuss its implications. On any given day one is liable to read a story about how the incumbent president did not satisfy expectations (e.g., by failing to lower gas prices) and as a result faces the prospect of lower approval ratings and an increased probability of electoral defeat. What is often missing from these stories is a discussion of the very real limits of presidential power and whether what the public demands is even feasible. Instead, the primary focus generally is on the president's inability to satisfy basic public expectations.

For more than half a century presidential scholars have made the expectations gap one of the defining concepts of the presidential literature. Yet for all the attention it has received there has been little attempt to define what is meant by an expectations gap or to systematically analyze its actual effects. Still, in a field that is often criticized as devoid of theory, the expectations gap represents a key theoretical concept that may help us to better understand the power and influence of the modern presidency.

This book uses a variety of techniques (quantitative, qualitative, and historical) to examine the nature and impact of the expectations gap, not merely during the era of the modern presidency (roughly 1933 to the present) but also throughout American history. We examine how the expectations gap evolved, its short-term beneficial effects, and its hypothesized long-term detrimental consequences. At the centerpiece of our work are five surveys we conducted especially for this book. They allowed us to develop several empirical measures of the expectations gap and to examine the gap in relation to two incumbent presidents, Bill Clinton and George W. Bush. We also include a case study of the presidency of Barack Obama, as well as retrospective evaluations of nine past presidents. We focus on six basic questions:

1. What is the expectations gap?
2. Is there evidence that a gap exists between public expectations and presidential performance?
3. If so, what impact does the gap exert on incumbent presidents of different political parties?
4. Do the gap and public expectations vary over time?
5. What are the expectations gap's key determinants?
6. Are expectations related only to the presidency or is the expecta-

tions gap related to the wider phenomena of political polarization and lower levels of trust in our governmental system?

What Are Public Expectations?

One of the first scholars to specifically address the concept of an expectations gap was Louis Brownlow, the head of Franklin Delano Roosevelt's 1937 Committee on Administrative Management. In his 1949 book, the *President and the Presidency*, published by the Public Administration Service, Brownlow asserted that the public expects more from its presidents than presidents can reasonably be expected to deliver, thus creating a gap between expectations and presidential performance. In 1960 Richard Neustadt argued that the public believes "the man inside the White House [can] do something about everything" (Neustadt 1980 [1960], 7). By the end of that decade the idea of an expectations gap was well established, with Seligman and Baer (1969, 18–19) positing that public expectations take the form of specific policy demands (on the economy or foreign policy) and personal presidential attributes (such as leadership ability and personal comportment). The concept is now regularly cited in the presidential literature.

What makes the expectations paradigm important and potentially treacherous for incumbent presidents is not merely that the public expects action but rather that it expects action on an increasingly broad and escalating range of issues. Furthermore, public expectations are excessive, often contradictory, and therefore unrealistic (see Edwards and Wayne 1999, 101–7). These expectations are then posited to exhibit long-term detrimental consequences in the form of lower presidential approval ratings, an increased likelihood of electoral failure, and a greater propensity for presidential scandal, as presidents push the limits of the law in an attempt to satisfy public demands. The expectations gap also is important because, as Stephen Wayne (1982, 185) writes, expectations "shape evaluations, and evaluations, in turn, affect the capacity [of presidents] to get things done."

The impact of the gap is even broader than these scholars suggest. Cronin and Genovese (1998) have isolated nine different paradoxes of the presidency that are related to the expectations gap. These include the idea that the public wants powerful presidents but is suspicious of a strong, national government; the public seeks out a common person, yet it wants a president who is charismatic and larger than life; the public seeks presidents who are above politics, but it also wants them to be master politicians; and the skills that are necessary for a candidate to get elected may not be the same skill sets presidents require to govern effectively once they are in office. Lammers and Genovese (2000, 3) also posit that "citizens expect their presidents to accomplish great things. . . . Yet all occupants of the White House face a series of roadblocks, checks, and balances that inhibit behavior and make governing difficult." In other words, presidents often lack the necessary constitutional or legal authority, or the practical political resources, to accomplish the many tasks that the public expects from them. And even if they had that power, public expectations are so contradictory and unrealistic that satisfying public demands is often impossible. As a result, the "nation expects more of the President than he can possibly do, more than we give him either the authority or the means to do. Thus, expecting from him the impossible, inevitably we shall be disappointed in his performance" (Brownlow 1969, 35).

This in turn can translate into a pattern of presidential failure. In his highly influential book *The Personal Presidency,* Theodore Lowi (1985, 11) argued that because of these excessive and unrealistic public expectations, the "probability of [presidential] failure is always tending toward 100 percent. . . . Given the exalted rhetoric and high expectations surrounding the presidency, a partial success is defined by the mass public as a failure." More recently, William Howell (2003, 8–9) wrote, "The public now expects presidents to accomplish far more than their formal powers permit . . . Armed with little more than the powers to propose and veto legislation and recommend appointment of bureaucrats and judges, however, modern presidents appear doomed to failure from the very beginning." And Steven Schier (2011, 793) notes that no president since 1965 has solved the political authority dilemma, which involves satisfying "the expectations that surround the exercise of power at a given moment."

Presidential scholars thus consider public expectations to be a systemic problem that affects all modern presidents. Furthermore, the trend over the twentieth and the twenty-first centuries reflects an even greater expansion of public expectations. As Seligman and Baer (1969, 18) warned us nearly half a century ago, "A major political trend of our time is the growth in public expectations of the presidency and the expanding scope of presidential action." Other major presidential scholars have echoed these warnings. Cronin (1980, 76) stated, "Nothing is more evident in the twentieth century than the steady accumulation of presidential responsibilities. Less evident but equally important are the heightened public expectations of the president." Hargrove and Nelson (1984, 59) added, "The constitutional nature of the presidency assures that to the extent that the federal government is the object of public demands for political change, the presidency will be at the center of the American political system." And in his preface to *Presiden-*

tial Power and the Modern Presidents, Richard Neustadt (1990, ix) wrote: "Weakness is still what I see: weakness in the sense of a great gap between what is expected of a man (or someday woman) and assured capacity to carry through. Expectations rise and clerkly tasks increase, while prospects of sustained support from any quarter worsen as foreign alliances loosen and political parties wane."

And there appears to be no end in sight to the expectations gap dilemma. During the heat of a presidential campaign candidates are likely to promise whatever is necessary to secure votes. Candidates promise voters that they will be job creators, without offering specific proposals. They denounce high crime rates, drug abuse, and the lack of progress in the Middle East peace process. The public therefore consumes a steady diet of campaign promises that further expand their expectations.

Yet despite its prominence in the presidential literature, the expectations gap has rarely been subjected to a broad-based empirical analysis (though see Waterman, Jenkins-Smith, and Silva 1999). As Dennis Simon (2009, 35) writes, "Unlike the research on topics such as presidential approval, there is no corpus of work that constitutes the normal science on public expectations." This book addresses Simon's critique. We begin in the next chapter with a focus on the historical foundations of the expectations gap. In chapter 3 we then include a comparison of the retrospective approval ratings for past presidents with evaluations of two sitting presidents. In chapters 4–8 we turn our attention to a test of various measures of the expectations gap derived specifically for this book from five surveys we conducted between 1996 through 2007. The main body of this work is dedicated to an analysis of public attitudes of two incumbent presidents: Bill Clinton and George W. Bush. In studying these presidents our goal is to place the expectations gap within the empirical reach of quantitative presidential scholars, taking it from an amorphous and often abstract concept and translating it into a quantifiable construct. In chapter 9 we then examine whether presidents themselves have unrealistic expectations upon entering office, as suggested by John Kennedy's response, which opened this chapter. Our method here is a case study of the presidency of Barack Obama. In chapter 10 we examine the determinants of the expectations gap thesis. Finally, in chapter 11 we tie the expectations gap thesis to the larger issue of trust in government.

CHAPTER 2

Public Expectations in a
Historical Perspective

We know that history is ours to make. And if there is great danger,
there is now also the excitement of great expectations.

Lyndon Johnson, State of the Union, January 4, 1965

When they discuss the expectations gap presidential scholars generally relate
it only to the modern presidency. We tend to ignore a discussion of expectations in the period prior to the modern presidency because the presidential
office was then much weaker. It is therefore assumed that expectations were
not important. Yet, even at this earlier period in American history, expectations helped to define the power and influence of the American presidency.

For example, in 1819, when the U.S. economy suffered a serious economic
retrenchment or panic, President James Monroe argued that Congress, not
the president, was expected to take the lead on economic matters (Waterman 2010, 18). Monroe then was reelected without opposition the next year.
It is inconceivable that a modern president could successfully claim that he
is not responsible for the state of the U.S. economy. For example, when in
1992 George H. W. Bush suggested that the worst of the recession was over
and that ameliorative governmental action actually would result in increased
deficits and other negative economic consequences, scores of angry primary
voters in New Hampshire rejected their incumbent president. National elec-
torates also rejected other presidents (Herbert Hoover, Gerald Ford, and
Jimmy Carter) because they failed to provide an environment of economic
prosperity; George W. Bush saw his approval ratings fall to historic lows
during his second term and by 2008 his approval ratings were in the low
20 percent range. Even popular presidents, such as Ronald Reagan, suffered

low approval ratings during hard economic times. Reagan's approval ratings fell into the 40 percent and even the 30 percent range during 1981 and 1982, before rebounding with the healthy economy in 1983. It is clear then that during the era of the modern presidency, no president would dare follow Monroe's 1819 example of placing the blame and responsibility for action on Congress. Why then did he do it? The straightforward answer is that public and elite expectations of presidential performance have changed markedly over time. Prior to the advent of the modern presidency, the public did not expect presidents to act aggressively in times of economic peril, a pattern of presidential reticence that was repeated throughout the nineteenth century (see Waterman 2010).

In the twentieth century, particularly with the advent of the Great Depression, but even during the presidency of Theodore Roosevelt and the Panic of 1907, presidents began to take a more activist approach to economic calamities. Why did presidents adopt a more aggressive leadership approach? Why did the public come to expect the president to take the lead on economic policy? To answer these questions we must first understand why public expectations of presidential performance changed throughout American history.

An Ambiguous Constitution

One reason why expectations of presidential performance have been so malleable over time is because the president's Article II powers are exceedingly vague. Public expectations are important because our constitution does not provide a clear articulation of the powers of the presidency (Waterman, Wright, and St. Clair 1999, 152). Only 38 percent of the words in Article II of the U.S. Constitution deal with the presidency's enumerated powers. While the Founders understood what the powers of the legislative branch should be, they did not have a clear idea of which powers they wanted to delegate to the presidency (Thach 1969, 140).

What then are the ramifications of an ambiguous constitutional delegation of presidential power? Barbara Hinckley (1985, 22) notes, "In an office left undefined, public expectations can be critically important." In effect, the "office is undefined: thus presidents become what people want them to be." In this way, expectations "shape action; action leads to further expectations" (Hinckley 1990, 8–9).

Because of a high level of constitutional ambiguity, then, presidents have wide latitude to define and redefine the powers and functions of the presidential office, in both domestic and foreign affairs. Presidential powers are "vast and vague" (Thomas, Pika, and Watson 1993, 12). Thus, when George Washington became our first president, "ambiguity reigned" (Phelps 1989, 259) and it was necessary for our first president to begin defining the new presidential office.

Initially, the ambiguity of constitutional power limited presidential power. As respected presidential scholar Fred Greenstein (2009, 80) writes, "The capacity of early presidents to respond . . . was reduced by the prevailing view of their responsibilities." The early expectation was that "the president should be an arbiter of the other forces in the nation rather than a policy maker." The president's limited role had much to do with perceptions of the role of the federal government. During the first decade of the nineteenth century, when Thomas Jefferson was president, "[a]lmost all of the things that republican governments do which affect the daily lives and fortunes of their citizens, and therefore engage their interest were . . . not done by the national government," but rather by state and local governments (Young 1966, 31–32).

And in these early days of the republic, even when the public did look to the nation's capital for leadership, it tended to look first to Congress, not the presidency (Lowi 1985, 28). Congress, and not the president, was therefore the most powerful of the three branches of government for most of the nineteenth century. These public and elite expectations were powerful factors establishing the initial parameters of presidential power. As a result, expectations shaped the presidential office as much at the beginning of our nation's history as they do today, but until the end of the nineteenth century they mostly served to constrain presidential power.

It is not surprising then that the presidents of this earlier era, with a few notable exceptions, were often colorless and undistinguished politicians. Presidents often were referred to as the "chief magistrate," a term signifying limited power. Few early presidents were so bold as to advocate their own policy agendas; when they did (e.g., John Quincy Adams), Congress simply ignored them. In fact, expectations of presidential power were so limited, and the powers of that office so vaguely defined that, as late as the 1840s and the presidency of John Tyler, the president's right to use the constitutional veto power was still a subject of considerable controversy. When Tyler issued three legal vetoes, the House of Representatives voted to impeach him. Though the effort fell short, it demonstrates that presidential power was still evolving against a backdrop of limited expectations (see Waterman 2010, chap. 9).

It is not a mere coincidence that the presidents of the antebellum period were weak and ineffectual, generally rated by historians as among the worst presidents of all time. Presidents Zachary Taylor, Franklin Pierce, and James Buchanan were nominated, not because they promised strong leadership, but because the political parties at the time desired presidential candidates who could win a crucial state and would not threaten the equilibrium of the existing political order. Following Abraham Lincoln's activist presidency during the Civil War, the political parties again selected weak candidates for the nation's highest office. In fact, after the Civil War, particularly with the presidencies of Andrew Johnson and Ulysses S. Grant, the presidency reached its nadir, with presidents even temporarily losing the right to nominate and fire their own political appointees. The presidencies of Rutherford Hayes and Grover Cleveland represented an incremental increase in the president's power and prestige, but a strong presidency was still nowhere in sight.

Yet even as the presidency reached its low point in terms of power and influence, expectations were changing. Directly following the Civil War a series of economic and social factors stimulated a veritable transformation in the American way of life (see Wiebe 1967). Instrumental was the revolution occurring within the expanding and centralizing American economy. By the 1870s America was undergoing a period of "radical social change" (Croly 1989, 101). With the rapid centralization of the economy, the rise of powerful corporations and trusts, from the cities to rural America the public demanded new and more vigorous and accountable institutions of government. More important, having discovered that their state and local governments were incapable of standing up to the powerful new corporations and monopolies that were centralizing the nation's economic interests, the public incrementally turned its attention toward the nation's capital to seek a redress of grievances (see White 1958, 2–3). V. O. Key (1958, 84) writes, "In a gross sense the roots of the remaking of the political order may be traced to the growth of the place of business in the national economy." Not only did the newly emerging economy place new public demands on government, ironically the rise of a new class of powerful business executives also provided a new model for a more activist American presidency.

Consequently, as the nineteenth century came to an end, a vast series of disparate economic transformations provided the basis for a new set of public expectations that focused attention on the national government and the presidency in particular. At the same time, the United States first assumed an important position on the world stage with the Spanish-American War of 1898. All of the pieces were coming together for a new focus on presidential power.

Consequently, by the time Theodore Roosevelt became president in 1901 the political environment was ripe for a more activist presidency and new public expectations were leading the way. With an instinctive understanding of the changing political dynamic, Roosevelt played a critical role in the evolution of the presidency, both during his almost eight years in the White House and then during his remarkable third party run for the presidency in 1912 (see Milkis 2009). As president, Theodore Roosevelt introduced his own presidential agenda (the Square Deal), put pressure on members of Congress to acquiesce in adopting presidential initiatives, embarked on a more activist role in foreign affairs, threatened to use the national military to protect the rights of labor over capital, and actively intervened during the Panic of 1907. He also initiated what he called the "bully pulpit," elevated the significance of the Washington press corps, and reached out through them directly to the American public. Roosevelt (1913, 357) concluded, "I did not usurp power, but I did greatly broaden the use of executive power." Theodore Roosevelt's expansive view of presidential power, though it was criticized by his critics as monarchical and dictatorial, would have been unthinkable had it not been for the fact that the American public at the turn of the twentieth century was looking for stronger and more energetic leadership from its federal executive. Roosevelt's reinterpretation of the presidency's powers therefore fit with and cultivated the public's desire for a more activist presidency.

Expectations Change

Theodore Roosevelt's successors took note of this new leadership style. Woodrow Wilson also actively used the techniques of the rhetorical presidency to advance his political agenda (see Canes-Wrone 2006). As Whitford and Yates (2009, 14–15) write, since these early days of the twentieth century "presidents have made varying use of rhetorical leadership, but all have governed with the tacit understanding that public rhetoric is not only a resource for them to use but is also to some degree an expected component of executive performance." Consequently, decades before Franklin Delano Roosevelt is given credit for establishing the modern presidency, expectations already were shifting and the contours of a more personal relationship between the public and the presidency already had emerged. With Franklin Roosevelt's elevation to the presidency in 1933, this governmental transformation was further institutionalized.

In 1933, as the effects of the Great Depression deepened, FDR addressed the nation and asked his radio listeners to share their concerns with him. The public overwhelmingly responded. Prior to Franklin Roosevelt's presidency, only one clerk was required to process the president's mail. The "daily grist of letters and telegrams [to the White House] frequently" ran "as high as 2,000 or 3,000," and only one clerk at the Executive Office was required to classify all the incoming mail (Haskin 1923, 54–55). Under FDR a staff of fifty had to be hired to handle his correspondence. His mail averaged 5,000 letters per day, increasing at times to a daily receipt of 150,000 letters (Leuchtenburg 1988, 7). The increased correspondence is evidence that the public now looked directly to the White House for leadership.

Technological advances greatly facilitated FDR's closer relationship with the public. Radio allowed him to simultaneously and directly enter the homes of millions of Americans, to converse with the public and to advocate his own personal presidential political agenda (the New Deal). Later advances in scientific polling and improved transportation forged an even closer and stronger bond between the American people and their president, long before television, cable news, the Internet, or Twitter became staples of American politics. FDR's presidency, therefore, fueled by a series of political and technological innovations, promoted a thorough and fundamental transformation in public expectations of presidential performance. As James (2005, 24–25) writes, "For better or worse, the president was now the acknowledged centerpiece in politics—its prime mover—and the exaggerated expectations placed upon executive leadership sent presidents on an extended search for new tools of influence to justify their newfound preeminence."

To accommodate this personal connection between the public and its president and the heightened expectations that came with it, Roosevelt found it necessary to expand the presidency's institutional apparatus. In the famous words of the president's 1937 Committee on Administrative Management, "the president needs help." As a result, new institutions including the Executive Office of the President were established and over time and the size and functions of the White House Office and the other components of the institutional presidency expanded and evolved, providing presidents with copious new mechanisms to perform outreach to a seemingly ever-growing group of citizens, the press, as well as both public and private interest groups. Expanded public expectations therefore had the ancillary effect of promoting a permanent transformation in the scope and size of the president's personal bureaucracy. Still, as Moe (1985, 269) cautions, "the expectations surrounding presidential performance far outstrip the institutional capacity of presidents to perform." As a result, as Howell (2003) convincingly argues, presidents continue to develop new unilateral powers (such as an expanded use of executive orders, presidential signing statements, and presidential memoranda and directives) in an attempt to satisfy escalating public demands for action.

While many of Franklin Roosevelt's successors decried the evils of big government (in particular Ronald Reagan and the two Bush presidents), and while Jimmy Carter and George H. W. Bush actually attempted through their rhetoric and their actions to lower public expectations, each of FDR's successors increased the federal government's role in some consequential policy area. Dwight Eisenhower, a moderate Republican, established the interstate highway program. Kennedy and Johnson then initiated a wide-ranging agenda that expanded civil rights protection, while LBJ created a broad antipoverty agenda that included such programs as Medicaid, Medicare, and Head Start. Richard Nixon created the Environmental Protection Agency and even instituted wage and price controls to deal with runaway inflation. Jimmy Carter shepherded major federal energy legislation through Congress. George H. W. Bush signed the Americans with Disabilities Act and his son advocated such major federal programs as "No Child Left Behind" and an expensive federal prescription drug program. Harry Truman, Richard Nixon, Bill Clinton, and Barack Obama made national health care a centerpiece of their policy agendas. And even under the anti-big-government policies of the Reagan administration, there was an exponential increase in military spending. Consequently, since Franklin Roosevelt's time both Democratic and Republican presidents have promoted activist policies that substantially increased the size of government and focused the public's attention directly on both the federal government and the White House.

Yet while expanding expectations provided presidents with electoral benefits and with some policy successes, these very same developments also represented something of a double-edged sword. While the reach and power of the presidency expanded, so too did the nature of public expectations. As Lowi (1985, 151) concludes, "Here in a nutshell is the dilemma: The more the presidents holds to the initiative and keeps it personal, the more he reinforces the mythology that there actually exists in the White House a 'capacity to govern'." In time, then, public expectations would both fuel presidential power and provide an impediment for each of the modern presidents.

In sum, throughout American history public expectations of presidential performance have been enhanced and transformed. The public now focuses its "demands and expectations on the President" (Seligman and Baer 1969, 18). Lowi (1985, 20) refers to this heightened relationship between the public and the presidency as a "pathology" because "it escalates the rhetoric at home, ratcheting up expectations notch by notch, and fuels adventurism abroad" as presidents seek yet another venue where they can attempt to satisfy public expectations. Why then is it so hard for presidents to satisfy escalating expectations?

The Outsider Presidents

One source of Lowi's "pathology" is the tendency for the American public to elect outsiders to the White House. Outsiders are presidents who do not come directly from the Washington establishment—that is, they are not insiders—and who therefore lack both the experience and the expertise to govern in Washington. Rather, they require a long learning curve before they can effectively tackle the increasingly complex presidential job. Typically, during the election campaign the outsider candidates treat Washington with a measure of scorn. They campaign on the theme that only someone who is not from Washington will be capable of fixing Washington's problems. The outsider trend began at least with George Wallace's failed 1968 third-party run for the White House, but the anti-Washington spirit has become a central theme of various presidential candidates of both political parties.

The first successful outsider candidate in the modern presidential age was Jimmy Carter, a Democrat, who was narrowly elected to the White House in 1976. A one-term Georgia governor, Carter had held no federal office. He ran against the moral corruption of the Nixon White House, promising Americans that he would never lie to them. He also promised to fundamentally change the way Washington worked by introducing a series of structural reforms such as zero-based budgeting. Yet, when Carter arrived in Washington, he found that it did not work the way he expected (Carter 2010, 14). Partisanship was more pronounced than he expected, even from his own partisans in Congress, who often rebelled against his legislative initiatives (e.g., cuts in federal water projects).

Following Carter's lead, Reagan, Clinton, and George W. Bush were former governors who campaigned against the Washington system. Barack Obama, though he was a sitting U.S. senator, had only been in office for two years when he announced his intention to run for president and then ran against the party establishment candidate, Hillary Rodham Clinton. In 2012, Republican presidential candidate Mitt Romney argued that he was qualified to be president in part because he was not part of the Washington establishment. Of the successfully elected presidents since the 1976 election, only George Herbert Walker Bush can be described as an insider, with vast experience inside the Washington community.

Running as an outsider has political advantages. Like Carter, it is possible to disavow any blame for the current political mess. It is possible to employ the rhetoric of someone who, like the voters themselves, is disgusted with the Washington political game and intent on changing it. The rhetoric of the outsider candidates is therefore filled with boilerplate bromides about the evils of Washington, its innate corruption, and the necessity for ameliorative action. Promising change is easy, but, as Carter discovered, effectuating change is an entirely different and much more difficult matter. What is surprising is that, with the exception of Reagan, who came to office with a skilled White House team largely derived from the Nixon and Ford administrations, the outsider presidents have had to learn the realities of inside-the-beltway Washington politics the hard way—as they governed. These presidents then exhibited an expectations gap of their own. As they moved from running for office to governing, they discovered that the political world they had inherited looked vastly different from 1400 Pennsylvania Avenue than it did from the campaign trail. Later in this book, when we examine the presidency of Barack Obama, we refer to this phenomenon as the candidate/incumbent expectations gap.

The prevalence of outsider candidates, then, combined with the public's own inflated and unrealistic expectations, fueled by the tendency of presidential candidates to promise the moon in order to get elected, creates what presidential scholars recognize as a systemic dilemma for the modern presidency. How can presidents satisfy public expectations when they do not have the expertise or experience to govern affectively once they are elected? The consensus within the presidential literature is that they cannot. The expectations gap therefore is posited to have several deleterious effects:

- The gap means that the incumbent president will be subject to a high level of scrutiny and criticism.
- Incumbent presidents also will be unfavorably compared to an ideal president, often the ideal image of Franklin Delano Roosevelt.
- The expectations gap leads to lower presidential approval ratings and an increased likelihood that the incumbent president will not be reelected.
- The gap also increases the likelihood that presidents will misuse their power in an attempt to satisfy public demands, thus resulting in an increased propensity for scandals, as well as congressional and criminal investigations.
- And since presidents run against the system to secure election, and then find it difficult to satisfy public demands for action, the expectations gap translates into lower levels of trust in government and its leaders.

In the chapters that follow we use a variety of quantitative and qualitative techniques to examine whether an expectations gap exists. To do so we created multiple measures of the expectations gap. We then examine whether the gap exerts deleterious consequences such as lower approval ratings and an increased likelihood of rejection at the polls. We also examine the president's own expectations gap upon entering office. Finally, we examine the determinants of the gap and whether it is related to other trends in American politics, in particular declining public trust in our governmental system and its leaders. We turn in the next chapter to how the approval ratings of two incumbent presidents fare in comparison to their immediate predecessors in office.

CHAPTER 3

Comparing Incumbent and Retrospective Evaluations of Presidential Performance

I think it would be good for special interest groups of all kinds—
labor, business, environment, and others—to cooperate and to
express a partnership in things that are accomplished for the good,
instead of concentrating on the negative things that fail to measure
up to their own very high expectations.

President Jimmy Carter, news conference, May 12, 1977

Not only is the president's job difficult, according to one of our nation's top presidential experts, George Edwards (1983, 191), "the president's job is more difficult than [it was] in the past." Since the birth of the modern presidency the policy demands on the presidency have expanded exponentially, with presidents currently expected to resolve virtually every societal problem including such highly intractable and diverse issues as managing the economy, controlling the spread of nuclear weapons, confronting international terrorists and drug traffickers, reversing the trend toward global climate change, as well as ameliorating the scourges of crime, teenage promiscuity, and the more mundane propensity of American's to eat, drink, curse, and smoke too much.

Consequently, when Barack Obama assumed the presidency in January 2009 he inherited not only a collapsing economy and two wars (in Afghanistan and Iraq) but also a broken health care system, a burgeoning international trade deficit, a pressing need for serious immigration reform, a rapidly deteriorating infrastructure, as well as the contradictory needs to stimulate the economy and balance the budget. These, plus myriad other divisive issues, confronted Obama from the very first moment that he took the presidential oath of office. Given his message of hope and change in the 2008 campaign, public demands and expectations for action were stratospherically high.

Although Obama entered the White House under what may be considered the most egregious economic, national security, and political circumstances since the days of the Great Depression and World War II, most previous presidents likewise faced daunting and contradictory policy agendas when they were elected. Nixon was elected at the height of the Vietnam War and the Cold War. Ford assumed office upon the resignation of a sitting president. Carter became president during a time of runaway inflation, unemployment, and interest rates, and declining American prestige abroad. Reagan also had to handle a crushing recession, as well as the follow-up to the Iranian hostage crisis and the repercussions of the Soviet invasion of Afghanistan. George H. W. Bush had crises in Panama and the Persian Gulf, as well as a recession. Clinton faced a poor economy and an escalating budget deficit. George W. Bush came to the presidency in a disputed election, his very legitimacy as president questioned, only to face the tragedies of September 11, 2001, followed by two wars, Hurricane Katrina, and the collapse of the U.S. economy. As for the public, having invested its hopes and dreams in each of these particular candidates, American voters expected direct and effective action, often immediately, and exhibited very little patience for the glacial pace of actual policymaking in Washington, nor the increasingly negative tone of Washington politics.

In addition to these concerns, presidents also must deal with issues that arise suddenly. Who expected that in 2009 Barack Obama would have to deal with a threat from Somali pirates or that in 2011 Congress might actually push the nation to the brink of default for the first time in modern history? The way that issues crowd onto the presidential agenda virtually guarantees that some citizens will be displeased with the president's performance, especially since progress on many of these issues (e.g., the war on drugs, the war on child pornography, the war on terror, the war on poverty) is a protracted and incremental process, with few benchmarks likely to satisfy political skeptics. The reality that presidents must try to maneuver their preferred legislation through an arcane and complex constitutional and legislative process, one that has become increasingly ossified and vituperative in recent decades (as exemplified by the health care debate of 2009–10 and its claims that Obama supported "Death Panels" that would "pull the plug on Grandma"), also guarantees that presidential initiatives will be a compromise (in itself an increasingly dirty word in Washington's current political vernacular), watered down, rejected, or outright neglected. In this process, presidents can appear ineffectual or even incompetent, even when they actually achieve major reforms. It should come as little surprise then that Theodore Lowi (1985) argues that presidential failure rates are approaching 100 percent.

But the increasing difficulty of the art of governance is not the only reason scholars believe the presidency today is an exponentially more demanding office than it was in the past. For during the previous century the entire Washington political environment became a more complex and treacherous political terrain for presidents to navigate. For example, according to George Edwards (1983, 191), presidents find it more difficult to govern today because there is an increased likelihood that they will "receive more criticism in the press" than the presidents of the past (see also Brody 1991; Cohen 2008). With networks pandering to the Right (FOX News), the Left (MSNBC), and with talk show hosts such as Glenn Beck and Rush Limbaugh repeatedly making outrageous and incendiary claims, combined with a blogosphere that reports virtually any rumor as fact, it is difficult for even informed citizens to determine the dividing line between news, entertainment, and pure fiction. This increased scrutiny by argumentative reporters, bloggers, and talking heads is just one more symptom of a much more broad-based adversarial political relationship in Washington. For not only is the press more critical of incumbent presidents, the public is also more skeptical of its leaders.

Like the press, it is increasingly difficult for presidents to manage their relations with Congress. The likelihood that divided government will occur has increased to a probability of about 80 percent since Richard Nixon became president in 1969 (Cameron 2000; see also Jones 1994, 1995). Of the presidents from Richard Nixon to Barack Obama, only Jimmy Carter enjoyed the benefit of unified government for one full term.

In addition to divided government, Congress has become more ideologically polarized and less amenable to cooperating with an incumbent president. In his first three years in office, Barack Obama faced an unprecedented number of filibuster threats, secret holds on nominees, and other obstructionist techniques that allowed Republicans, particularly in the Senate, to bring the president's ambitious domestic agenda to a near standstill. Appointments were regularly delayed or scuttled, even when there was overwhelming support across the aisle for the individual appointee. And the opposition party appears more willing to press its case against an incumbent president, even during the so-called honeymoon period, a time when both parties and the media generally once found a measure of common ground. Although there are a multitude of explanations for the deteriorating relationship between presidents and their political environment, one thing is clear: modern presidents interact with a far more diverse, dispersed, and adversarial governmental system than did the presidents of the traditional presidential era (Kernell 1997). As a result, the president's job has become more difficult to perform (Buchanan 1978), inducing presidential scholars to raise the specter of a public that expects far more from its presidents than any president can possibly deliver, resulting in a permanent *expectations gap.* As Genovese (1995, 27) comments, "In the United States, the gap between expectations and resources, image and reality of power, is enormous. In effect, there is a huge gap between what is expected of a president and what he can realistically deliver."

While much has been written about the expectations gap, is there any evidence the gap actually exists? In this chapter we first address this question by comparing the approval ratings of two incumbent presidents (Bill Clinton and George W. Bush) with retrospective evaluations of their immediate predecessors. The reason we do so is because one means of conceptualizing the expectations gap thesis posits that *incumbent presidents are held to a higher evaluative standard than are even their immediate predecessors in office.* Once presidents leave office, with the burdens of the office now lifted from their shoulders and with unrealistic expectations now shifted onto a new incumbent, the past presidents' approval ratings should improve. We therefore hypothesize that an incumbent president should have a lower approval rating than their predecessors. This should be the case whether the incumbent is a Democrat or a Republican.

To empirically test this hypothesis, we examine data from two surveys on public perceptions of the president taken a decade apart. The first survey was conducted among citizens of an electoral swing state, New Mexico, in early 1996. The second one was a nationwide survey conducted during 2007 (details on how the various data sets were collected are presented in appendix A). In both cases respondents were asked to evaluate an incumbent president, a Democrat, Bill Clinton (in 1996), or a Republican, George W. Bush (in 2007). They were then subsequently asked to evaluate the performance of several of the incumbent's preceding presidents.

The remainder of this chapter unfolds in two sections. In the first part we compare incumbent president William Jefferson Clinton with eight of his predecessors. In the second section we compare evaluations of incumbent president George Walker Bush with his immediate predecessors.

Bill Clinton and His Predecessors

The expectations gap thesis posits that the public has unrealistically high expectations of presidential performance, which in turn translates into lower approval ratings for the incumbent president. To test this possibility in January and February of 1996 we asked respondents to a statewide New Mexico survey to evaluate incumbent president Bill Clinton's performance in office. Each of our respondents was asked, "Using a scale of excellent, good, fair, or poor how would you rate the job Bill Clinton is doing as President of the United States?" We then posed the following question: "We would like to evaluate the performance of past presidents of the United States. Even if you are not sure, we would like you to answer to the best of your ability. Using a scale of excellent, good, fair, and poor how would you rate the following past presidents of the United States?" The past presidents were presented in reverse order: George H. W. Bush, Ronald Reagan, Jimmy Carter, Gerald Ford, Richard Nixon, Lyndon Johnson, John Kennedy, and Dwight Eisenhower. The responses to these questions provide us with data on incumbent and retrospective evaluations of eight presidents spanning the entire period from 1953 to 1993. There were a greater number of nonresponders as we move back in time; that is, more people answered Don't Know/No Answer for Presidents Eisenhower and Kennedy than for Bush and Reagan. Still, the sample size was robust for all presidents, with the number of cases ranging from 564 for Bill Clinton to 510 for Eisenhower.

As can be seen in table 3.1, the two earliest presidents in our sample, John Kennedy and Dwight Eisenhower, received the highest percentage of excellent responses of the nine presidents we examined. Almost 30 percent of our respondents ranked the job Kennedy did as president as excellent, while 21 percent ranked Eisenhower at the same level. The next two highest-ranked presidents were of more recent vintage. Ronald Reagan's job performance was ranked as excellent by almost 16 percent of our respondents, while George H. W. Bush's job performance was ranked as excellent by

TABLE 3.1. Retroactive Evaluations of Past Presidents Compared to the Incumbent Bill Clinton's Evaluations, Jan/Feb 1996 Survey

	Excellent	Good	Fair	Poor	Ranking (Exc. + Good)
Clinton	6.4%	27.8%	37.6%	28.2%	8
GHW Bush	12.6%	46.6%	32.0%	8.9%	3
Reagan	15.9%	38.6%	27.8%	17.7%	4
Carter	6.8%	30.9%	40.5%	21.7%	5
Ford	4.1%	31.5%	49.9%	14.4%	7
Nixon	5.9%	27.0%	33.7%	33.3%	9
Johnson	4.4%	32.2%	40.6%	22.8%	6
Kennedy	29.7%	46.3%	20.0%	3.9%	1
Eisenhower	21.0%	50.2%	24.9%	3.9%	2

slightly less than 13 percent of our respondents. The lowest-ranked presidents on this dimension were Gerald Ford at just 4.1 percent and Lyndon Johnson at 4.4 percent. Nixon and Carter fared only marginally better at 5.9 and 6.8 percent, respectively. How then does the incumbent, Bill Clinton, compare? He received an excellent rating of just 6.4 percent. Thus, Clinton ranks slightly ahead of Ford, Nixon, and Carter, but far behind the other presidents, including his predecessor, George H. W. Bush.

At the other extreme, Clinton receives the second highest poor rating. Only Nixon at 33.3 percent has a larger poor rating than Clinton at 28.2 percent. Johnson has a poor rating of 22.8 percent, Carter 21.7 percent, and Reagan 17.7 percent. The lowest poor evaluations are for Kennedy and Eisenhower at 3.9 percent.

If we combine the excellent and good responses for each president they ranked as follows: (1) Kennedy, 76.0 percent; (2) Eisenhower, 71.2 percent; (3) George Herbert Walker Bush, 59.2 percent; (4) Ronald Reagan, 54.5 percent; (5) Jimmy Carter, 37.7 percent; (6) Gerald Ford, 35.6 percent; (7) Bill Clinton, 34.2 percent; and (8) Richard Nixon, 32.9 percent. Kennedy and Eisenhower remain the two most popular presidents. Somewhat surprisingly, given his electoral defeat in 1992 (and his loss of the state of New Mexico to Bill Clinton that year), George H. W. Bush ranks third. As for the other four past presidents, each had combined ratings of less than 40 percent. These findings suggest that the public does not hold all past presidents in high regard. Of these lowest-rated presidents, two are Democrats (Johnson and Carter) and two are Republicans (Nixon and Ford). Thus the partisan identification of the president does not appear to explain why these low ratings exist. What does?

Interestingly, the four lowest rated presidents are all from the so-called *Vietnam Watergate era*. Johnson escalated America's involvement in the Vietnam War, after having run for president in 1964 on a theme that the war should be left to Asian and not American boys. Before the war was ended, Nixon escalated military involvement, expanding the war into other contiguous countries, such as the controversial bombing of Cambodia. Gerald Ford was president when Americans hastily departed South Vietnam in ignominy in 1975 and Carter used his pardon power to try to heal the nation's wounds.

The various Watergate era scandals raised direct concerns about trust in our nation's leaders. Prior to Watergate, Johnson was viewed through the prism of a generation gap. He was a president who misled the nation on its way to war in Vietnam. At the same time the nation's urban fabric was coming apart, with riots in many of America's major cities. Following Johnson with a strong message of law and order, Nixon subsequently was removed from office because of his involvement in a series of Watergate related crimes. Nixon was designated as "an unindicted co-conspirator" and eventually accepted a pardon for his breaches of conduct. Ford, Nixon's handpicked vice president and eventual successor, after promising not to pardon Nixon, did so, which led to yet another crisis of confidence in America's leadership. It also contributed to Ford's electoral defeat in 1976. Carter then was elected on the promise that he would never lie to the American people—in essence he presented himself as the very antithesis of Richard Nixon. When the Bert Lance affair exploded in seedy headlines, and Carter stood by his OMB director despite serious ethical charges, the new president's poll numbers collapsed and his image for decency was never fully restored. In the end, the taking of the hostages in Iran and the Soviet invasion of Afghanistan raised the specter that Carter was the steward of a weak and ineffectual presidency, a man who, like his predecessor, was decent but not quite up to the job.

These four presidents, then, historically have much in common. Each governed at times of crisis, and their leadership choices served to undercut American's trust in government and its leaders. It is therefore particularly interesting that our respondents evaluated these four presidents more critically than their two immediate predecessors or their two successors. It suggests that the public is still highly critical of the presidents from the Vietnam-Watergate period, an era that brought considerable shame to the institution of the presidency. Seen in this light, our respondents' rating of the eight past presidents is understandable. The VietnamWatergate era presidents are rated poorly, while the presidents before and after this period, representing more of a perceived innocence of the presidency (Eisenhower and Kennedy) and the renewal of its power and authority (Reagan and G. H. W. Bush), are rated much more positively.

To understand what the public thought of Bill Clinton's leadership at the commencement of his reelection contest, then, we have two distinctly different groups of past presidents with which to compare him: the VietnamWatergate era presidents and what we can call the innocence/renewal presidents. How then does the incumbent president, Bill Clinton, compare to these past presidents? Again, only 6.4 percent of all respondents ranked Clinton's performance as excellent, ranking him lower than all but Carter at 6.8 percent. In contrast, nearly twice as many respondents ranked George H. W. Bush's performance as excellent as they did for Bill Clinton. With regard to poor ratings, Clinton's performance ranks at the low end of the distribution with Johnson and Nixon. The evidence from the survey suggests, then, that the Clinton ranking falls squarely within those of the four VietnamWatergate era presidencies.

The evidence on this point is even clearer when we turn to the combined excellent and good ratings. Clinton's combined rating is only 34.2 percent, which ranks him only 1.3 percentage points ahead of Richard Nixon, a president who left office in disgrace. Clinton's approval ratings also are in the same range as Carter, Ford, and Johnson. On the other hand, Bill Clinton's rating trails George H. W. Bush's by 25 percentage points—remember that Clinton handily defeated Bush in New Mexico less than four years before this survey was conducted. Furthermore, he trails John Kennedy (a president that Clinton idolized) by 41.8 percentage points. When we compare Clinton to his predecessors, the incumbent does not fare well.

To find out whether these perceptions are driven by any particular characteristic of presidential leadership we next asked our respondents the following question: "Thinking about four qualities of presidential leadership (sound judgment in a crisis, experience in foreign affairs, high ethical standards, and the ability to work well with Congress), which one of these qualities is the most important quality for an excellent president to have?" Thirty-eight percent of respondents identified high ethical standards as the most important quality; 35 percent identified an ability to work well with Congress; 23 percent sound judgment in a crisis; and just 4 percent experience in foreign affairs. Table 3.2 provides the frequencies and percentages for each president according to how our respondents ranked the four leadership questions.

With regard to those respondents who identified high ethical standards as the most important quality of presidential leadership the rankings are Eisenhower, 75.2 percent; Kennedy, 73.3 percent; G. H. W. Bush, 58.9 percent; Reagan, 56.4 percent; Ford, 37.8 percent; Carter, 36.6 percent; Johnson, 31.9 percent; Nixon, 29.5 percent; and Clinton, 29 percent. Consequently, Clinton ranks dead last (recall that this survey was conducted before the

TABLE 3.2. Approval Ratings—Combined Percentage of Excellent and Good Responses, by the Importance of Presidential Qualifications for the Jan/Feb 1996 Survey

High Ethical Standards		Works Well with Congress		Sound Judgment in a Crisis		Experience in Foreign Affairs	
Eisenhower	75.2%	Kennedy	80.0%	Kennedy	73.8%	Kennedy	75.8%
Kennedy	73.3%	Eisenhower	69.5%	Eisenhower	67.2%	Eisenhower	75.0%
GHW Bush	58.9%	Bush	58.1%	Bush	58.0%	Bush	67.7%
Reagan	56.4%	Reagan	52.2%	Reagan	53.0%	Reagan	58.0%
Ford	37.8%	Johnson	36.4%	Johnson	44.0%	Ford	46.3%
Carter	36.6%	Clinton	36.0%	Carter	39.6%	Carter	43.3%
Johnson	31.9%	Carter	34.6%	Nixon	38.6%	Nixon	40.0%
Nixon	29.5%	Ford	31.7%	Clinton	36.7%	Johnson	32.1%
Clinton	29.0%	Nixon	29.9%	Ford	33.4%	Clinton	29.0%

onset of the Monica Lewinsky scandal and his subsequent impeachment). Only 29 percent of these respondents gave Clinton an excellent or good rating. Thus, Clinton ranks behind even Richard Nixon (29.5%), a president who repeatedly lied to the American people about his involvement in the Watergate scandal, was named by a grand jury as an unindicted coconspirator in a criminal investigation, and was finally forced to resign from office rather than face the almost certain judgment of impeachment and removal from office. Clinton also ranks behind Lyndon Johnson (31.9%), who also had serious image problems, including a perception that he was averse to telling the truth.

From a historical perspective the most interesting finding is that 73.3 percent of our respondents who identified high ethical standards as the most important quality ranked John Kennedy as either excellent or good, which ranks him second only to Eisenhower (75.2%). This is surprising since there has been a constant parade of books and television programs documenting Kennedy's sexual adventures, his dependence on prescription drugs, the fact that he hid serious illnesses from the public, and various other ethical lapses in judgment. One might therefore have expected people who consider high ethical standards to be an important criterion to have had more critical evaluations of Kennedy's performance. Yet he ranks second from the top on this dimension. Clearly, then, Kennedy's well-documented lapses in moral etiquette did not damage his retrospective performance evaluations. That Clinton, who is often compared to Kennedy regarding his comportment in office, ranks last is therefore even more striking.

In fact, Bill Clinton ranked last in three out of the four categories. Surprisingly, given that in 1996 he faced divided government and an openly hostile Republican Congress, only with regard to an ability to work well with Congress was Clinton rated as performing better than any one of our cohort of eight past presidents. On this dimension he ranks slightly ahead of Carter, Ford, and Nixon, but again far behind his predecessor George H. W. Bush (22.1 points behind). Consequently, our respondents rendered extremely low evaluations of Bill Clinton's performance in office, across four leadership dimensions. Is this then evidence that Clinton was held to a higher standard than his predecessors or is it evidence that Clinton was a fundamentally unpopular president? To answer this question we then asked for our respondents' evaluations of two other contemporary incumbents, Senate Majority Leader Bob Dole and the Speaker of the House Newt Gingrich. The results are presented in table 3.3.

As of January-February 1996, when the poll was conducted, President Bill Clinton, Senate Majority Leader Robert (Bob) Dole, and House Speaker

Newt Gingrich were arguably the three most powerful elected officials in the United States. Yet neither one is rated by as many as 10 percent of respondents as having done an excellent job. The highest excellent rating is for Gingrich at 7.1 percent. Dole's excellent rating is 5.2 percent. Additionally, none of the three has a combined rating (excellent plus good) of more than 40 percent; the highest is for Dole at just 36.5 percent, with Gingrich at 27.4 percent. Gingrich also has the highest poor rating, with 36.4 percent ranking him in the lowest possible category, with Dole at 22.6 percent.

We find the same result when we change the focus from individuals to institutions. When we asked people to evaluate the job the U.S. Congress was doing, it had a lower rating than the president (19.5 percent, or 14.7 percent lower than Clinton's evaluations). Consequently, it is possible that not only are presidents held to a higher standard than past presidents, but that expectations for other top governmental incumbents and institutions also may be excessive and unrealistic. This raises the possibility that there is a larger concern about trust in America's government and its leaders. If so, then the expectations gap may be a symptom of a larger problem for American democracy, an issue we will return to later in this book.

We also note that even though Bob Dole, the eventual Republican candidate for president in the 1996 election, has a higher approval rating than Clinton, it is only by a narrow 2.3 percent. Yet, when asked who they planned on voting for in the fall election (between Clinton and Dole), Clinton led Dole by a healthy 8.6 percentage points. In fact, 54.3 percent of those people who responded to the question of who they intended to vote for said they would likely vote for Bill Clinton in November 1996. Hence, while our respondents ranked Clinton's performance low in comparison to past presidents, they simultaneously expressed the opinion that they intended to vote for him. In this regard, our respondent's perceptions were contradictory.

Perhaps the most interesting evidence from our survey relates to evaluations of George H. W. Bush. While the first President Bush was often a popular president, at one point securing the support of 89 percent of the American people in a Gallup poll, his approval ratings actually fell into the

TABLE 3.3. The Incumbent Bill Clinton versus the Approval Ratings of His Contemporary Officeholders, Jan/Feb 1996 Survey

Contemporary Leader	Excellent	Good	Fair	Poor
President Bill Clinton	6.4%	27.8%	37.6%	28.2%
Senate Majority Leader Bob Dole	5.2%	31.3%	40.9%	22.6%
Speaker of the House Newt Gingrich	7.1%	20.3%	36.2%	36.4%
U.S. Congress	2.0%	17.5%	44.7%	35.8%

30 percent range during the 1992 reelection year. He received less than 40 percent of the popular vote in a three-way presidential election contest, losing to Bill Clinton by 5 percentage points. Despite his electoral defeat, just over three years before our survey was conducted, his approval ratings rank with those of Ronald Reagan, John Kennedy, and Dwight Eisenhower. Considering that Bush lost New Mexico, as well as the presidency, this is a particularly interesting result. It suggests that our respondents had a far different perception of George H. W. Bush after he left the White House than they did a mere 39 months before. The retrospective evaluations of George H. W. Bush's performance may be the most convincing evidence we can present in support of the hypothesis that the public holds incumbents to a different and higher standard than they do their past presidents.

George W. Bush and His Predecessors

In 2007 we conducted a national survey and evaluated the performance of President George W. Bush. We also asked our respondents to evaluate the performance of the forty-third president's four immediate predecessors in office, Bill Clinton, George H. W. Bush, Ronald Reagan, and Jimmy Carter. We present the survey results in table 3.4.

Remember that Bill Clinton was rated excellent by only 6.4 percent of the respondents to the 1996 survey, that 28.2 percent ranked his performance as poor, and that his overall excellent and good rating was a mere 34.2 percent. By 2007, with Clinton out of office, his evaluations are much more positive: 21.2 percent ranked his performance as excellent, 57.9 percent as either excellent or good, and 18.6 as poor. Even if we consider that the first survey was of New Mexicans only, and the second a national survey, it is unlikely that the differences that we see are merely the result of the different samples employed in the two surveys. Clinton's excellent/good combined

TABLE 3.4. Retroactive Evaluations of Past Presidents Compared to the Incumbent George W. Bush's Evaluations, 2007 Survey

	Excellent	Good	Fair	Poor	Ranking (Exc. + Good)
Clinton	21.2%	36.7%	23.5%	18.6%	2
GHW Bush	7.4%	44.9%	36.6%	11.2%	3
Reagan	32.2%	41.0%	20.5%	6.3%	1
Carter	8.3%	37.1%	31.1%	23.5%	4
GW Bush	6.6%	24.5%	25.2%	43.7%	5

rating progressed from 34.2 percent in 1996, when he was overwhelmingly reelected, to 57.9 percent in 2007, an increase of more than 23 points.

No longer the direct predecessor compared to the incumbent, George H. W. Bush does not fare as well in 2007 as he did in 1996. Only 7.4 percent rate his performance as excellent and 11.2 percent poor. Bush 41's excellent and good combined rating is 52.3 percent, a decrease of about 7 points. On the other hand, Reagan has become far more popular in retrospect. His excellent evaluations increased from 16 percent to 32.2 percent, his poor ratings were but 6.3 percent, and his combined excellent/good rating went from 54.5 percent to 73.2 percent (an increase of almost 20 points). Finally, Carter's ratings improved marginally, with 8.3 percent versus 6.8 percent ranking his performance as excellent, 23.5 percent as poor, and an excellent/good rating of 45.4 percent in 2007 versus 37.7 percent in 1996.

Although questions of generalizability may make it difficult to compare results of a state and a national survey across time, we can examine the evaluations of the incumbent George W. Bush directly to his immediate predecessors. We should note that our results comport well with many other national surveys taken at the same time. Simply stated, the then incumbent president's evaluations were dreadful. Only 6.6 percent ranked his performance as excellent, the lowest of the five presidents we asked our respondents to evaluate. As for W's poor rating, it was a whopping 43.7 percent (Carter is second with 23.5 percent). When we bifurcated George W. Bush's ratings he receives 31.1 percent excellent/good and 68.9 percent fair/poor ratings.

Consistent with our hypothesis, and with our findings regarding George H. W. Bush from our 1996 survey, in 2007 former president Bill Clinton's ratings compare quite favorably to the incumbent George W. Bush, while Bush trails his predecessor's evaluations. At least indirectly, then, an evaluation of retrospective evaluations from two surveys provides evidence that incumbent presidents do not fare well in comparison to their predecessors, a finding that is consistent with the logic that incumbent presidents face uniquely high and unrealistic expectations once they arrive in office. Once they leave office, and the burdens of the presidency are lifted, they can be seen in a more positive light.

Conclusions

When we examine retrospective evaluations of presidential performance and compare them to various measures of the expectations gap, we find a rich source of insight about how expectations impact the presidency. First, we found that Clinton's approval ratings, while he was in office, were closer to the presidents of the Vietnam-Watergate era than they were to those of the presidents who served before and after that era. Since the Vietnam-Watergate era presidents had the lowest evaluations of our sample of eight presidents, and since there were issues of trust in leadership associated with each of their presidencies, this was not good news for the then incumbent president. On the other hand, at the very same time a majority of those who responded favored Clinton for reelection. Thus, while our respondents awarded Clinton with poor approval ratings overall, they also intended to vote for him. These findings support the idea that the public has contradictory and even unreasonable expectations of presidential performance.

In our 2007 national survey, the incumbent, George W. Bush, had more negative evaluations than any of his four immediate predecessors. Furthermore, Clinton, no longer the incumbent, had excellent/good ratings above 50 percent. Combined, these results provide the first indication that an expectations gap may exert a deleterious impact on public perceptions of incumbent presidents. We note, however, that we have examined retrospective evaluations for only two incumbent presidents. The pattern we observe in this chapter may not hold for other presidents. For example, in a number of national surveys conducted between 2009 and 2012 various respondents blamed George W. Bush for the nation's bad economy rather than the incumbent, Barack Obama. This may be the result of the extraordinary events that occurred in the fall of 2008, when the economy nearly collapsed, or it may be a reflection of George W. Bush's historically low evaluations.[1] These counter-results suggest that we should be modest in our claims. They also suggest that we need a more direct and rigorous test of the expectations gap thesis, one that is theoretically driven. We turn to that task in the next chapter.

CHAPTER 4

Analyzing Public Expectations

The people of the United States . . . are looking to you for guidance and intelligent leadership. They have a right to expect from you a constructive program of action in which they as individuals, and collectively as communities and organizations, may participate. It should be a challenge to you to respond to these expectations.

President Franklin Roosevelt, conference on crime,
December 10, 1934

Thus far we have examined public expectations from a historical perspective and indirectly by comparing retrospective evaluations of past presidents with two incumbent president's approval ratings. In this chapter we shift the focus to a more direct test of the expectations gap thesis. A direct test is important because, while some scholarly work suggests that an expectations gap exists, research methods to date generally have employed surrogate measures to test the gap thesis. We therefore use the literature on expectations to operationalize and test the gap thesis for two presidents, Bill Clinton and George W. Bush. Before we do so, however, we first review how scholars conceptualize the expectations gap.

Defining the Expectations Gap

How does one define and operationalize the expectations gap? To answer this question we turn first to an examination of the presidential literature. Even though the expectations gap is a central thesis in the presidential literature, little empirical work has been conducted to determine its validity or generalizability. And surprisingly, while the concept is often cited, scholars seldom define it. Most studies either mention an expectations gap without discussing its specific parameters or, when there is an attempt to measure the concept, proxy measures are used. For example, in an early empirical work on the gap, Seligman and Baer (1969) measured the concept by asking party activists whether they believed presidents should choose a moral course rather than an expedient one when they make decisions. They found that activists in the late 1960s favored a moral course. As we shall discuss in this chapter, other studies analyzed results from existing public opinion polls or polling data. Still, as Simon (2009, 135) notes, "there are no long-standing and well-agreed upon measures of public expectations."

Despite Simon's warning, fortunately we do not have to start from scratch. An analysis of the presidential literature provides several useful ways of conceptualizing the gap:

1. The gap is represented by a pattern of declining presidential approval ratings over time, with ratings declining as each president fails to satisfy excessive and unrealistic public expectations.
2. The gap is the idea that the public compares an incumbent president to an ideal prototype (often referred to in the presidential literature as a comparison to an ideal image of Franklin Roosevelt), resulting in increased dissonance between expectations and reality.
3. The gap is related to perceptions of presidential performance; that is, whether the president is living up to expectations on key issues of peace and prosperity.

We examine the first two of these definitional approaches in this chapter. Later, in chapters 6 and 8, we directly test the performance-based assumptions of the expectations gap thesis.

Approval Ratings

We start with a simple question. Do all presidents face a pattern of declining approval ratings? Since scientific polling commenced only with Franklin Roosevelt's presidency: we must limit our analysis to the so-called modern presidents. Of these, complete data exist for Presidents Truman through George W. Bush. Advocates of the declining approval rating gap thesis posit that newly elected presidents are generally popular during their first months in office, with the recently elected candidate's approval ratings increasing substantially between their November election and Inauguration Day

(Wood 2009). With a few notable exceptions (e.g., Ford or Clinton), the weeks and months following the actual inaugural represent a time of good-will, often referred to as the "honeymoon period," a time when the public, the media, and even the president's staunchest political opponents are optimistic or at least restrained in their criticism of the new president. Praise of the new president is common, reflecting the high expectations generated by the arrival of the latest incumbent. The first several months of a new president's term generally exhibit relatively high levels of public approval. This is the period when presidential scholar James Pfiffner (1988) recommends that presidents should "hit the ground running" to take advantage of high public approval and a muted opposition. Yet, Paul Light (1983) contends that even though this is the period when presidents have the greatest available political resources, they are still learning how to do the job and have not yet developed the necessary political skill sets needed to accomplish their most cherished policy objectives. Hence, due to their political inexperience, most presidents are incapable of fully exploiting the political advantages provided by the honeymoon period. By the time they are wiser and more adept and have a more amenable advisory team in place, their poll ratings have declined and with them many of the political resources they need to be successful presidents (e.g., leverage over Congress).

But why do presidential ratings decline? As Mueller (1973) notes, over time presidents face a series of unpopular decisions. Each president creates new sources of political opposition as they make decisions on a series of controversial issues. Over time this provides the basis for a wide and growing series of opposition movements, some of which coalesce, thus representing a tangible threat to the incumbent's leadership and reelection prospects. As FDR's adviser Louis Brownlow (1969, 35) wrote, "As the President exercises the duties of his high office he will be compelled to make choices, and every choice he makes, whether in respect of measures or of men, will displease or disillusion those who do not agree with him."

Scholars therefore argue that this reoccurring governing cycle results in a general pattern of declining presidential approval ratings over time. Lowi (1985, 17) postulates that "presidential performance ratings will tend downward and continue downward unless interrupted by an international event associated with the president." Yet even international events generally alter public opinion only in the short term, as did the killing of Osama bin Laden during the Obama presidency. This is followed by a renewed decline in the president's approval ratings, that is, until the next presidential election cycle or the next event interrupts the normal downward trend in the president's ratings.

What evidence exists with regard to the declining presidential approval thesis? Of the twelve presidents from Harry Truman through Barack Obama most exhibited a decline in their approval ratings over time. The main exceptions are Ronald Reagan and Bill Clinton. Their approval ratings actually increased over time, particularly during their second terms in office. The pattern of declining approval ratings is strikingly apparent for six of the eleven presidents. Truman, Johnson, Nixon, Carter, G. H. W. Bush, and G. W. Bush experienced substantial and long-lasting declines in their approval ratings while in office. Of these presidents, Truman decided not to run for reelection in 1952 (though he had served nearly two full terms already), Johnson decided not to seek reelection in 1968, Nixon resigned from office in 1974, and Carter and G. H. W. Bush were defeated in their reelection bids. Of these six presidents only George W. Bush was reelected and by a fairly narrow margin in both the popular and electoral vote counts. Ford, an unelected president, also experienced a decline in his approval ratings, though his evaluations improved after he was defeated in the 1976 election. While Eisenhower's ratings declined over time, he still remained remarkably popular throughout his two terms in office. As for Kennedy, his approval ratings were declining at the time of his assassination as the nation turned its attention to the battle over civil rights.

Although Barack Obama was reelected, the 2012 election was a highly competitive one, as well. After a relatively healthy start, there was a steady decline in Obama's approval ratings throughout his second and third years in office. Although his ratings rose in many polls to the 50 percent range by the spring of 2012, he was reelected with a smaller percentage of the vote than in 2008. Consequently, of the twelve presidents following Franklin Roosevelt there is an observable pattern of declining approval ratings over time for ten presidents.

Various scholars have examined this trend in presidential approval ratings. In a classic article, Stimson (1976) found a pattern of declining approval over time within each individual presidency. He later attributed this phenomenon specifically to the expectations gap (Stimson 1976–77). Raichur and Waterman (1993) later compiled approval data from a series of Gallup polls. Their analysis demonstrates a pattern similar to the one identified by Stimson. While these studies attributed their findings to an expectations gap, they did not produce an actual measure of the gap. Rather, they interpreted the pattern of declining Gallup approval ratings as evidence that a gap exists and that it exerts a negative impact on the modern presidents. But there are a number of other possible explanations for the observed pattern of declining approval ratings, such as Tufte's (1978) economic theory of the presidency or Riker's (1984) theory of minimum-winning coalitions. Therefore, while the evidence of a pattern is compelling, it alone does not confirm that all presidents face a persistent expectations gap. Rather, it may only represent a symptom of the gap.

Ideal Prototype

The presidential literature also provides a second means of conceptualizing the gap. The gap is presented as the difference between perceptions of an ideal, hypothetical president or an ideal prototype of a past president and actual evaluations of a real flesh and blood incumbent. This method of conceptualizing the gap is derived from the initial tendency of presidential scholars to compare all presidents to the Olympian ideal of Franklin Roosevelt (see Neustadt 1980 [1960]; Burns 1965, 1984; and Schlesinger 1957, 1958, 1960). In the decades following his death, Franklin Roosevelt saw his standing elevated by many historians, but not all (see Corwin 1984), to the status of an ideal president whose leadership style should be replicated by each of his successors. As a result, FDR's successors were compared to this great man's indefatigable and frankly unrealistic image. Most presidents did not fare well in this comparison, especially since none has been able to match FDR's astonishing record of accomplishment during his first 100 days in office. What both means of defining the gap can agree on is that the modern presidents are in serious trouble and that they face the constant specter of failure, lower approval ratings, and rejection at the polls.

A Presidency under Siege

One focus of the expectations gap literature is an attempt to explain the perceived failure of the modern presidents, particularly since Lyndon Johnson ascended to the executive office. Of the nine presidents from Johnson through G. W. Bush, three (Ford, Carter, and GHW Bush) failed to secure reelection (or in Ford's case, technically speaking, election, since he was never elected in the first place). Lyndon Johnson dropped out of the 1968 presidential race when it became apparent that he would have a difficult time securing his own party's nomination. Of the twentieth-century presidents before Johnson, only William Howard Taft and Herbert Hoover failed to win reelection. Rose (1997) notes this electoral trend is evidence of a presidency under siege.

Elections are not the only perceived evidence of an expectations gap. Scholars also note that the modern presidents have faced an unprecedented series of crises and scandals. The competence and veracity of Presidents Johnson and Nixon were challenged by the prolonged nature of the Vietnam War. Nixon was forced to resign as a result of the many related Watergate scandals. Ford lost credibility when he pardoned Nixon. Carter appeared incompetent in response to the Iranian hostage crisis and the nation's economic malaise. Questions about Reagan's competence arose during the Iran-contra scandal. There were also allegations of improprieties in the same scandal involving his vice president and Reagan's successor, George Herbert Walker Bush. The Clinton presidency was rocked by scandal after scandal including allegations of shady dealings in the Whitewater real estate development deal, campaign finance abuse (with wealthy contributors allowed to spend a night in the Lincoln bedroom), and the Monica Lewinsky case, which led to the president's impeachment. George Walker Bush's presidency also was consumed with questions about whether he cherry-picked intelligence and misled the public over the extent of Saddam Hussein's weapons of mass destruction and his ties to Osama Bin Laden: key reasons for the preemptive war against Iraq. Bush also was questioned on the legality of his wiretapping program and his competence was questioned after what was generally perceived as the federal government's tepid response, and the president's own seeming indifference, to Hurricane Katrina. Obama was likewise questioned about his competence in dealing with the BP oil spill in the Gulf of Mexico. In a theme we will return to later in this book when we examine how Clinton survived impeachment, the prevalence of scandals in recent decades is perceived as a major symptom of the expectations gap (e.g., Rose 1997).

As a result of these scandals most modern presidents have found their political fortunes decline. Reagan's approval ratings declined by 20 percent virtually overnight with the initial revelations of the Iran-contra scandal and George W. Bush's approval ratings plummeted during his second term to unprecedentedly low levels, bottoming out in some polls just above 20 percent. His approval ratings were also below both 40 percent and 30 percent for a longer continuous period than any other president since scientific polling was first conducted.

Again, while the evidence from the polling data is intriguing, it does not directly demonstrate that a gap exists. Rather, the increased propensity toward scandal may be another manifestation of the gap, or it might be explained by increasing partisanship and polarization and a more hostile Washington press corps. It should be noted that not all presidential scholars even believe that an expectations gap exists. Renowned presidential scholar Richard Pious argues that expectations "gap theorists have the problem the wrong way around: by the 1990s Presidents Bush and Clinton entered office without popular mandates or great expectations that they could accomplish much at all" (1996, 7). Pious therefore believes that "popular expectations had little impact on their actual performance." Pious believes the public had become so cynical by this time that it no longer mattered who was elected to the presidency.

There is some evidence in the polling data to support Pious's alternative perspective. Not all presidents seem to have been equally affected by the scandals that have become common occurrences during the era of the modern presidency. Reagan's approval ratings rebounded following the initial revelations in the Iran-contra scandal. In January 1998, when allegations first surfaced that President Bill Clinton had an affair with a twentythree-year-old White House intern and then lied to cover it up, his poll numbers actually increased. An astonishing 68 percent of the respondents to a February 1998 *CBS News/New York Times* poll said they approved of Bill Clinton's job performance (Bennet and Elder 1998, A1). At the same time, 59 percent of the poll's respondents said they were "inclined to believe that President Clinton had an affair with Monica S. Lewinsky." Fifty-nine percent also said they "would understand if Clinton were not telling the truth about his sexual conduct." Concomitantly, however, 55 percent said the president had "a responsibility to be completely truthful when questioned in public about his sex life." As political pundits routinely predicted the demise of the Clinton presidency, only 21 percent of the *CBS News/New York Times* poll respondents believed the president should "resign," and only 12 percent favored impeachment. Forty-six percent felt an apology would be sufficient, while 16 percent believed the whole matter should be dropped. In the end, Clinton left office with the highest approval ratings of any departing president since modern polling began. If the public had inflated expectations of presidential performance, wouldn't the poll results have indicated greater dissatisfaction with Clinton's presidency?

Beyond Clinton's behavior, the same *CBS News/New York Times* poll found 84 percent of respondents agreed that "someone can be a good President even if they do things in their personal life that you disapprove of." Furthermore, in a November 1992 Gallup poll, while most people expected the newly elected Bill Clinton to be an "outstanding" or "above average" president, over 70 percent "did not expect him to keep his campaign promise not to raise taxes, and clear majorities did not expect him to reduce the deficit or control federal spending" (Edwards and Wayne 1997, 100). Given these poll results, it is possible that the public may not have excessive expectations of presidential performance. In other words, there may be no expectations gap!

We therefore believe that a direct empirical test of the gap thesis is necessary to determine whether expectations of presidential performance indeed are related to lower presidential approval ratings, an increased likelihood of reelection defeat, and to presidential scandals. In this chapter we examine the first two of these three possible effects. We turn to the third issue in chapter 7.

Measuring the Expectations Gap

To test the gap thesis we first need to develop a measure of public expectations. One approach to operationalizing the concept is to use a method first developed by David Kimball and Samuel Patterson (1997, 722). They examined expectations of congressional performance and found that "[c]itizens appear to make comparisons between what they expect their elected representatives in Congress to be like, and what they perceive these representatives actually are like." They concluded, "Public attitudes toward Congress hinge very much upon public expectations, citizen's perceptions of congressional performance, and presumably, the actual performance of the institution."

To examine what they called the "expectations-perception differential," the authors conducted a survey of Ohio citizens' attitudes about Congress. Their methodology employed the logic of the prototype literature, which derives from social psychology and examines how people use ideal images of a group to establish expectations of the group's members (see Bem and McConnell 1970). Kinder and Fiske (1986) argue that individuals who employ ideal images of the presidency, such as those derived from a textbook interpretation of the presidency taught in most grade schools, will later compare these ideal images with the less attractive reality of the performance of individual presidents. In this process dissonance is created between the ideal prototype and the performance of individual presidents, contributing to the establishment of an expectations gap.

Where do ideal images come from? Some presidential scholars argue that they come from a comparison of incumbent presidents to a Franklin Rooseveltian ideal. As Hess (1976, 43) writes, "The Rooseveltian legacy was to expand the reach of the presidency and to change the people's expectations of what government could do and should do. Whether the growth of government would far outstrip a President's ability to oversee its activities was a conundrum that Roosevelt left to his successors." The idea, then, is that all presidents have been compared unfavorably to an ideal image of Franklin Roosevelt.

A second explanation involves the larger than life manner in which presidents often are portrayed in textbooks on American government. According to Cronin (1980, 80), "To the teenager or young adult, textbook discussions of the extensive resources available to the president cannot help but convey the impression that a president must have just about all the inside information and good advice anyone could want, especially when they point out the vast array of experts, strategic support staffs, and intelligence systems." Why is this important? "The significance of the textbook presidency is that . . . [it] presents a cumulative presidential image, a legacy of past glories and impressive performances . . . which endows the White House with a singular mystique and almost magical qualities." As a result, "the office of the presidency seems to clothe its occupants in strength and dignity, in might and right, and only men of the caliber of Lincoln, of the Roosevelts, or of Wilson can seize the chalice of opportunity, create the vision, and rally the American public around that vision." In other words, the textbook president provides yet another powerful ideal image. It is possible, then, that citizens introduced to this exalted image may then be disappointed with the performance of real incumbent presidents.

In this case there is a difference between an ideal image and reality. On this point, Erikson, MacKuen, and Stimson (2002) examined presidential images and found that images related to increased presidential competence are associated with increased presidential approval ratings. These findings are consistent with Waterman, Wright, and St. Clair's (1999) contention that presidents can use image making as a resource to ameliorate the expectations gap. These various studies then suggest that one means of testing the expectations gap thesis is to compare perceptions of incumbent presidents with those of an ideal, hypothetical, excellent president. In the pages that follow, we do so for two incumbent presidents: Bill Clinton (in two surveys of citizens of New Mexico, conducted in January and February 1996 and October and November 1996, as well as two national surveys conducted in 1998 and 1999), and a nationwide survey conducted of George W. Bush's performance in the fall of 2007. The specific details on how and when all of our surveys were conducted are presented in appendix A.

These five surveys allow us to examine an ideal and an incumbent president at the beginning and end of a reelection year (1996), as well as in a midterm election year (1998), and during the seventh year (1999, 2007) in office of two presidents of different political parties. We therefore examine the potential effects of the expectations gap during election and nonelection years and during two different types of election years. We also do so over time for two different presidents facing radically different domestic and foreign policy agendas. Finally, we evaluate both a Democratic and a Republican incumbent president in relation to the expectations gap.

Comparing an Ideal and an Incumbent President

In the most comprehensive empirical study of the expectations gap to date, George Edwards (1983, 189–91) examined a variety of national polls and found that the public expects "successful policies from the White House" and for "their presidents to be extraordinary individuals." The public not only had "high expectations for the president's official performance, but also had lofty expectations for his private behavior." Edwards cited an impressive array of survey data demonstrating, for example, that 81 percent of respondents (to a 1979 Gallup poll) believed that "sound judgment in a crisis" was an important presidential attribute. Another 66 percent of the respondents to the same poll also believed that "high ethical standards" were important. Among the other findings, 74 percent believed competence and an ability to get things done were important; 50 percent believed the president should have a sense of humor; 42 percent identified imagination; and 33 percent identified personal charm, style, and charisma. Regarding the president's personal behavior 70 percent said they would strongly object "if the president smoked marijuana occasionally; 43 percent believed it was inappropriate for the president to tell an ethnic or racial joke, even in private; 38 percent were concerned if the president was not a church member; 36 percent reacted negatively to the president using an occasional tranquillizer; 33 percent if he used profane language; 30 percent if he spoke to a psychiatrist; 21 percent if he wore blue jeans in the Oval Office; 17 percent if he were divorced; and 14 percent if he had a cocktail before dinner at night." Edwards also concluded that the public expects more of its presidents than it did in the past. In the fall 1979 Gallup poll, 73 percent of the respondents believed that the "public's expectations of the president are higher than in the past"; 77 percent believed "the problems presidents must solve are more difficult" than they were in the past; and 75 percent believed "Congress is more difficult to deal with" than it was in the past.

Using Edwards's work as a starting point, we examine four leadership qualities that relate to perceptions of the president's job skills and personal qualifications. They are (1) sound judgment in a crisis, (2) experience in foreign affairs, (3) high ethical standards, and (4) an ability to work well with

Congress. Sound judgment in a crisis and high ethical standards relate to the personal characteristics of a president, while experience in foreign affairs and an ability to work well with Congress relate to the president's job tasks and skills. High ethical standards is a direct measure of what Simon (2009, 136) calls "image-based expectations of the presidency," while sound judgment in a crisis, experience in foreign affairs, and an ability to work well with Congress measure what he calls "performance-based expectations." These four measures, then, encapsulate distinctive dimensions of the expectations gap.

We then combined Edwards' measures with the logic of the presidential prototype literature and its emphasis on a comparison of an ideal and incumbent president. We therefore asked the following question:

Excellent presidents have certain qualities. Thinking about the kind of person you believe would be an excellent president, how important are the following four qualities? On a scale from 0 to 10, where 0 means not at all important and 10 means extremely important, and you can choose any number from 0 to 10, how important are the following qualities?

We then asked our respondents to separately evaluate an excellent president on each of the four leadership qualities. Each time the survey was administered we rotated the leadership questions so that they were not asked in the same order. For the January-February 1996 survey we also asked our respondents to rank order the four leadership questions by their level of perceived importance. Respondents were specifically asked what is the most important, what is the second most important, and what is the third most important leadership characteristic. We present the results in table 4.1.

The order of the rankings is as follows: 36.8 percent rated high ethical standards as the most important quality; 34.8 percent an ability to work well with Congress; 22.6 percent sound judgment in a crisis; and only 5.8 percent experience in foreign affairs. If we sum the first and second most important qualities, an ability to work well with Congress is first at 63.26 percent, high ethical standards is second at 56.72 percent, sound judgment in a crisis is

TABLE 4.1.   Ranking the Four Leadership Qualities for Bill Clinton, Jan/Feb 1996 Survey

	Quality 1	Quality 2	Quality 3
Sound judgment in a crisis	22.6%	31.12%	24.10%
Experience in foreign affairs	5.8%	20.49%	33.72%
High ethical standards	36.8%	19.92%	21.07%
An ability to work well with Congress	34.8%	28.46%	20.11%

third at 53.72 percent, and experience in foreign affairs is fourth at just 26.29 percent. The most apparent result from this analysis is that our respondents ranked experience in foreign affairs lower than the other three criteria. If we take the total percentage of those who answered the quality one and quality two questions (1,059) and then take the sum of the experience in foreign affairs responses to both questions (139), the result is even less impressive, with only 13.13 percent placing experience in foreign affairs in one of the top two categories. This result may stem from the fact that during the Clinton years the focus was mainly on the economy. The Cold War was over and the American public had not yet become alerted to the threat of international terrorism. With the nation, relatively speaking, at peace, our respondents likely considered this dimension as much less important than the others.

In table 4.2 we examine the leadership qualities from a second perspective. Here we use the scale from 0 to 10 with zero being not at all important and 10 being the most important to evaluate our respondent's perceptions of how important the four leadership dimensions are for an ideal or excellent president. Our respondents expect a great deal from an ideal or excellent president. On a scale from 0 to 10, the mean expectation for an ideal "excellent" president on sound judgment in a crisis is 9.08 in the January-February poll and 9.22 in the October-November 1996 poll. High ethical standards rank second in both polls at 8.48 and 8.58 respectively. An ability to work well with Congress is third with respective means of 8.17 and 8.45, while experience in foreign affairs ranks last with means of 7.49 and 7.82 out of 10. On none of the four dimensions, then, did our respondents evaluate the expected performance of an ideal "excellent" president with a mean of less than 7.49. But we again see, in both surveys, that experience in foreign affairs is considered to be the least important of the four leadership qualities.

To place these findings in a broader temporal context, and with national

TABLE 4.2. Mean and Standard Deviations for Each of the Four Excellent President Questions, for Clinton and Bush

	Jan/Feb 1996 Survey	Oct/Nov 1996 Survey	1998 Survey	1999 Survey	2007 Survey
Sound judgment	9.08	9.22	9.58	9.26	9.45
	(1.76)	(1.63)	(1.02)	(1.48)	(1.27)
Foreign affairs	7.49	7.82	8.52	7.94	8.22
	(2.16)	(2.12)	(1.75)	(1.84)	(1.67)
High ethical standards	8.48	8.58	8.69	8.79	9.20
	(2.10)	(1.99)	(2.00)	(1.81)	(1.41)
Work with Congress	8.17	8.45	8.74	8.36	8.41
	(2.03)	(1.68)	(1.58)	(1.74)	(1.63)

survey results, we compare these results to the fall 1998 and 1999 surveys. In the fall of 1998, sound judgment in a crisis was again the most important quality of excellent presidents with a mean of 9.58. Ability to work well with Congress was next with a mean of 8.75, statistically tied with high ethical standards at 8.69. The mean rating for experience in foreign affairs came in last at 8.52. The figures for 1999 are comparable with a mean rating of 9.26 for an ideal or "excellent" president's sound judgment in a crisis and 8.79 for high ethical standards. The importance given to working well with Congress declines modestly to 8.36 and experience in foreign affairs again comes in last at 7.94. With the exception of the decline in importance of working well with Congress in 1999, the order of the four "excellent" president questions is similar across the two years.

The results of our 2007 survey again show similar results. Sound judgment in a crisis has a mean of 9.45, high ethical standards has a mean of 9.20, an ability to work well with Congress is 8.41, and experience in foreign affairs has a mean of 8.22. Consequently, over five surveys spanning more than a decade, we find consistency in terms of expectations of an ideal/excellent president and in terms of the rankings of the four leadership qualities. Clearly, then, at least in the abstract our respondents expect a great deal from their presidents. What do they expect of an incumbent president?

Expectations of Incumbent Presidents

Next we measured the performance of an incumbent president on each of these same four leadership qualities. We asked, "Now thinking specifically about President Clinton, how well do you think President Clinton rates on these four qualities?" In this case a 0 represented "extremely poor" performance while a 10 represented "extremely good" performance. Based on the assumptions of the expectations gap and presidential prototype literatures, we expected Clinton's ratings to be lower than those of the "excellent" or ideal president.

With reference to table 4.3, for the first 1996 survey, Bill Clinton ranks lowest on his perceived ability to work well with Congress. This survey was conducted just after the second governmental shutdown in January 1996, a period when Republicans in Congress played a game of budgetary chicken with the Clinton administration, believing that if they shut down the government the president would be forced to accept draconian cuts in many domestic programs. The strategy backfired, however. As historian Taylor Branch (2009, 313) notes, "Clinton said he thought [House Speaker] Gingrich and his caucus were fooled by their own propaganda about the moral force of their proclaimed crusade. In the past week of shock and shutdown, as the president's approval ratings skyrocketed while those of Congress plummeted, they clung to hopes that the adverse reaction was temporary panic." Although Clinton's overall ratings may have been positively affected by the shutdown, our survey indicates that evaluations of his ability to work well with Congress were negatively affected. By the October-November survey, however, with the shutdown a distant memory, Clinton ranked much higher on this question—almost as high as he did on the sound judgment in a crisis question in the January-February survey. Hence, perceptions of Clinton's performance on this issue were much more favorable as the election approached.

With regard to experience in foreign affairs we also see a slight increase in Clinton's ratings from the beginning to the end of 1996. His early rating was 5.35 compared to 5.78 nearing election time. The difference between the means of the ideal and incumbent presidents is 2.14 in January-February and 2.04 in October-November. Finally, with regard to high ethical standards, Clinton's rating actually declined a bit from the beginning of 1996—from 4.97 to 4.74. Consequently, on three of the four leadership dimensions we see Clinton's ratings improve as the fall presidential election neared, both in relationship to his own prior ratings and to an ideal president rating. The only dimension upon which we see a decline is the high ethical standards dimension. We should note the obvious, that Clinton was reelected in 1996, this despite the fact that his ethical lapses had been well publicized as early as the 1992 presidential campaign.

A difference of means tests between the two surveys indicates that there is no statistical difference on two dimensions (foreign affairs and ethics) between Clinton's gap as measured in the January-February and October-November surveys. There is a statistical difference over time between Clin-

TABLE 4.3.   Mean and Standard Deviations for the Four Clinton and Bush Leadership Questions

	Jan/Feb 1996 Survey	Oct/Nov 1996 Survey	1998 Survey	1999 Survey	2007 Survey
Sound judgment	6.01	6.58	6.70	6.24	5.09
	(2.63)	(2.46)	(2.90)	(2.72)	(3.34)
Foreign affairs	5.35	5.78	6.59	6.15	4.68
	(2.50)	(2.53)	(2.70)	(2.55)	(3.01)
Ethical standards	4.97	4.74	3.59	3.22	5.72
	(2.92)	(3.14)	(3.16)	(2.98)	(3.42)
Work with Congress	4.47	5.85	6.17	5.75	4.40
	(2.71)	(2.46)	(2.52)	(2.44)	(2.82)

ton's gap on sound judgment in a crisis, as well as his ability to work well with Congress. As noted before, this latter finding is indicative that the president had improved relations with Congress or that he was seen as more effective in dealing with Congress.

We also have national data for the 1998 and 1999 surveys. We note that the 1998 survey was conducted at the height of the Clinton impeachment fever, while the 1999 survey was conducted after the president had been impeached and after the Senate voted not to remove him from office. These two surveys therefore allow us to compare expectations of Clinton both during and after the impeachment affair, one of the most prominent scandals to rock the White House in recent decades. Despite the impeachment debate, the order of Clinton's ratings remains the same across the two years. The highest mean is for sound judgment in a crisis at 6.70 in 1998 and 6.24 in 1999. Experience in foreign affairs is second in both years, with a mean of 6.59 in 1998 and a mean of 6.15 in 1999. An ability to work well with Congress is next with respective means of 6.17 and 5.75. Finally, and not unexpectedly, Clinton performs worst on the high ethical standards dimension, with respective means of 3.59 and 3.22.

Are these findings generalizable to other presidents? To address this question, we examine a second incumbent with a 2007 survey. We note that the 2007 results for the "excellent" president leadership questions were comparable to those from the four Clinton surveys, thus providing one measure of validity. On the other hand, while Clinton's Gallup approval ratings were in the 60 percent range in 1998 and 1999, it is an understatement to say that George W. Bush was not a popular president in 2007. The war in Iraq, the failed response to Hurricane Katrina, an economy that was classified in December 2007 as having fallen into recession, and other factors including scandals at the Justice Department, did not work to Bush's political advantage. Therefore, our fall 2007 survey of George W. Bush did not occur during his halcyon days, when his approval ratings hovered in the 60 percent and 70 percent range, or even at the height of his approval ratings, 90 percent in a Gallup poll taken after the tragedies of September 11, 2001. We therefore need to remember that at the time of our survey Bush was in the seventh year of his presidency. Fortunately, we have comparable data for Clinton during his seventh year as president. By comparing two consecutive presidents of different political parties at the same time in office, we can better assess public attitudes and expectations regarding the four leadership qualities.

In the final column of table 4.3 we present the expectations statistics for Bush in 2007. We see that Clinton rates higher than Bush on three out of four leadership qualities. On sound judgment in a crisis the comparison is a mean of 6.24 for Clinton, versus a mean of 5.09 for Bush. On experience in foreign affairs, supposedly a major strength of the Bush presidency, Clinton's mean is 6.15, while Bush's is 4.68. For an ability to work well with Congress, Bush has a mean of 4.40, while Clinton, who was tried by the Senate that very year, has a mean of 5.75. Only on the issue of high ethical standards does Bush rate higher than Clinton: by a substantial 5.72 to 3.22. What is most interesting is that both incumbent presidents were evaluated more critically (that is, they received lower scores) than the "excellent" or ideal presidents.

Weighted Incumbent Gap Measures

We next used the evaluations of "excellent" and incumbent presidents to develop a weighted gap measure for each of the four leadership qualities and an overall average weighted gap. We began by calculating the difference between Clinton's evaluations (on all four questions) and the corresponding ideal president questions. We first calculated the difference between the highest rating Clinton could have received from any individual on any particular question (a 10) and the actual rating Clinton received from each respondent on each of the four leadership questions. Gaps or differences were calculated in this manner for each of the four leadership questions for each respondent. We then multiplied these ratings with the results of the "excellent" president questions to provide a weight related to how important each respondent considered each leadership criterion to be. Thus, we hypothesize that respondents with higher expectations on the excellent president questions (e.g., someone who rates sound judgment in a crisis as a 10) should hold President Clinton to a higher standard than those who have lower expectations of presidential performance on this dimension (e.g., those who rate sound judgment as a 5 for an excellent president). The result produces a scale running from 0 to 100 for each of the four leadership dimensions, with 0 representing no gap whatsoever and 100 the largest possible gap.

   In table 4.4 we present these gap ratings for each of the four leadership dimensions. For the January-February survey Clinton's largest gap is 45.30 (out of a possible high of 100) for an ability to work well with Congress. His gap for high ethical standards is next with a mean of 43.16. Sound judgment in a crisis ranks third at 36.06 and experience in foreign affairs last at 34.37. For the October-November poll the average gap measures are 31.61 for sound judgment in a crisis, 33.15 for experience in foreign affairs, 46.10 for high ethical standards, and 35.06 for an ability to work well with Congress. For three of the four measures we then see a decline in Clinton's gap from the beginning to the end of the 1996 election year. The largest decrease is on the ability to work well with Congress. The only increase is with the high ethical standards issue.

To develop a third overall measure of the president's average expectations gap we then combined these four measures by using the following formula:

[(10 – Evaluations of Clinton's performance on each leadership criteria) * (Weight for each leadership criteria)]/4 = Clinton's weighted expectations gap

This measure provides an overall scale ranging from 0 to 100, with zero again equaling no gap and 100 the largest possible gap in perceptions of Clinton's performance. By using this method, we incorporated both the respondents' individual evaluation of Clinton's performance and their relative weighting of the importance of each of the four leadership criteria. We therefore call this the "weighted Clinton gap" measure. For the January-February poll Clinton's weighted gap was 39.82 with a standard deviation of 21.90. By the time of the election his gap had declined slightly to 36.59 with a standard deviation of 22.18. The standard deviations indicate that there is considerable variation around the mean. This means that there is considerable variation across individual perceptions of the gap measure.

With regard to the other two surveys, Clinton has an expectations gap of 31.58 for sound judgment in a crisis for 1998 and 34.72 for 1999. For experience in foreign affairs his mean gaps are 28.55 in 1998 and 29.76 in 1999. For high ethical standards his mean gaps are 57.14 in 1998 and 61.23 in 1999. Finally, for an ability to work well with the same Congress that impeached him he has gap ratings of 32.97 in 1998 and 35.17 in 1999. The apparent trend

TABLE 4.4. Mean and Standard Deviations for the Four Weighted Clinton and Bush Gaps

	Jan/Feb 1996	Oct/Nov 1996	1998 Survey	1999 Survey	2007 Survey
Sound judgment	36.06 (25.60)	31.61 (24.04)	28.55 (23.47)	34.72 (26.25)	46.02 (23.47)
Foreign affairs	34.37 (21.77)	33.15 (22.97)	31.59 (24.55)	29.76 (21.25)	43.86 (24.55)
Ethical standards	43.16 (29.06)	46.10 (31.92)	57.14 (28.47)	61.23 (31.54)	38.60 (29.47)
Work with Congress	45.30 (26.27)	35.06 (22.64)	32.97 (33.47)	35.17 (21.97)	47.45 (33.47)

is that Clinton's gap measures increased in all four leadership categories from 1998 to 1999, suggesting that either his lame duck status or the impeachment case had a deleterious impact on his expectation gap ratings. We find more evidence for this point when we examine Clinton's overall weighted expectations gap, which was 37.63 for 1998 and 40.43 for 1999.

Comparing the gaps over time (see figure 4.1), Clinton's evaluations on sound judgment in a crisis remained relatively stable over the four surveys. There was a consistent and statistically significant decline in his gap measure for experience in foreign affairs, perhaps because Clinton, as is common for presidents in second terms, concentrated more attention on foreign policy. As for high ethical standards, given Clinton's problems in the Monica Lewinsky scandal, it is not surprising that his expectations gap measure increased substantially, statistically, and consistently over time, from a low of 43.16 to a high of 61.23. Finally, his gap measure on an ability to work well with Congress declined by about 10 percentage points from the first survey in 1996 (at the time of the government shutdown) to the second one, then remained fairly stable thereafter, even with his impeachment in 1998 by the U.S. House of Representatives. As for Clinton's overall weighted expectations gap, it decreased prior to the 1996 election, then increased again afterward. His ratings from the first to last survey, however, did not vary much: from 39.82 to 40.43. The larger gap in the fall of 1999 is largely due to the magnitude of his high ethical standards gap.

Finally, to provide a comparison, we calculated the weighted gap measures for each leadership quality for George W. Bush. The 2007 survey reveals that Bush's gaps are 46.02 for sound judgment, 43.86 for experience in foreign affairs, 38.60 for high ethical standards, and a mean of 47.45 for an ability to work well with Congress. Clinton's seventh year comparable scores are 34.72, 29.76, 61.23, and 35.17. Clinton therefore has much lower gap ratings on three of four dimensions than does Bush. The final overall weighted gap measures (which combine the four leadership qualities) for both presidents are closer, but largely because Clinton fares so poorly on the ethics dimension. George W. Bush's gap is 43.97, while Clinton's is 40.43.

Although we compare these two incumbent presidents at only one point in time, the data suggest that, other than on ethical grounds, George W. Bush does not fare well in a comparison with his immediate predecessor. If we remember that Clinton's national Gallup approval ratings in 1999 were in the 60 percent range, while Bush's approval ratings had fallen to the 30 percent and even in some polls the 20 percent range, the results are more understandable.

What are we to make of these various evaluations? Obviously, it would be

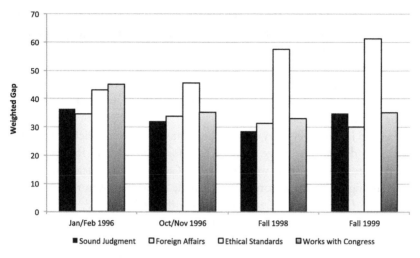

Fig. 4.1. Comparing Clinton's Weighted Gap Measures

useful to have comparative measures that would allow us to contrast presidential expectations to some other benchmark. Fortunately, we have another benchmark: Bill Clinton's challenger for the 1996 presidential election, former senator Robert "Bob" Dole. For Dole in both 1996 surveys we asked respondents the same questions and therefore can develop a comparable measure of what we call the challenger gap.

The Challenger Gap

According to Richard Reeves, "In the darkest days of William Jefferson Clinton's roller-coaster ride through history, the days after the Republicans took over Congress, when he seemed to have blown it all, he used to tell the people around him that he couldn't wait until the 1996 election. Why? 'Because,' he answered, 'I'll be compared with someone else, rather than being compared to some perfect ideal'" (Reeves 2000, A14).

As this quote suggests, during an election year the president is compared not only to "some perfect ideal" but also to a real red-blooded alternative candidate. In other words, in a reelection year presidents are compared to an actual challenger and not merely an ideal image. Hence, when we speak of an expectations gap in a presidential reelection year, we also need to consider public expectations of the president's main challenger. For this reason we developed two measures of the challenger gap. First, we asked our respondents to rate Bob Dole on the same four leadership qualities (sound judgment in a crisis, an ability to work well with Congress, high ethical standards, and experience in foreign affairs) that we used to evaluate Bill Clinton and an ideal president. As is apparent in table 4.5, Senator Dole's evaluations on each of the four leadership dimensions are actually more favorable than the ratings of the incumbent, President Clinton.

For the January-February survey, the means for Dole on each of the four leadership dimensions range between 6.14 for experience in foreign affairs and 6.76 for an ability to work well with Congress. The mean values for Dole are higher than Clinton on every single dimension. On the Congress dimension Dole's mean is 2.29 points higher than Clinton. We see the same pattern for the October-November survey. Dole's means fall between a low of 6.61 for experience in foreign affairs to 7.26 for high ethical standards.

In the third and fourth columns of table 4.5 we present a second measure, Dole's weighted gap measures for each leadership dimension. We used the same method to calculate the weighted challenger gap measure as we did to create the Clinton and Bush weighted gap measures, only we substitute Dole's evaluations in place of the president and then compare them to the ideal/excellent president. Remember that smaller numbers signify a narrower gap between evaluations of Dole and the ideal "excellent" president. Dole's gap measures in the early 1996 survey range from a low of 26.41 for an ability to work well with Congress to a high of 33.17 for sound judgment in a crisis. For the late 1996 survey Dole's gap measures are all in the 20 percent range, with two of them below 25 percent. Again, on every single dimension for both surveys, Senator Dole has lower expectations gap measures than

TABLE 4.5. Mean and Standard Deviations for the Dole Challenger Gaps

	Jan/Feb 1996 Survey	Oct/Nov 1996 Survey	Jan/Feb 1996 Survey	Oct/Nov 1996 Survey
	Dole Leadership Questions	Dole Leadership Questions	Dole Weighted Gaps	Dole Weighted Gaps
Sound judgment	6.31	6.78	33.17	29.36
	(2.33)	(2.16)	(22.48)	(20.59)
Foreign affairs	6.14	6.61	28.48	25.56
	(2.15)	(2.04)	(18.48)	(16.69)
Ethical standards	6.45	7.26	29.41	22.16
	(2.40)	(2.35)	(21.90)	(19.87)
Work with Congress	6.76	7.23	26.41	22.87
	(2.27)	(2.12)	(20.93)	(18.77)

the incumbent president. And yet, while the incumbent president received consistently lower evaluations on all four leadership questions over both surveys, when asked about a hypothetical race between Dole and Clinton (Dole was not yet the Republican nominee in January and February), 54.3 percent said they intended to vote for Clinton. Clinton's margin over Dole was 8.6 percentage points. Clinton then easily won the state of New Mexico in the November election and in the October-November survey a majority of our respondents said they would or had already voted for Clinton over Dole.

What are we to make of these findings? One implication is that the incumbent president again appears to be held to a higher standard even in comparison to his electoral challenger. When our respondents evaluated the incumbent president's performance they consistently rated him more harshly than his Republican opponent. This is consistent with our comparisons of an incumbent to retrospective evaluations of past presidents and a comparison to an excellent/ideal president.

In the end, however, the incumbent was reelected. This may suggest that when voters make their final decision, other criteria than the four leadership qualities that we measure, such as likeability, party identification, or who runs the best campaign are more important criteria. But our results can at least be interpreted as evidence of the high standard to which the public holds our incumbent presidents. To fare so comparatively poorly on all four dimensions for both surveys in comparison to both an ideal president and a challenger is evidence that our respondents were critical of the performance of an incumbent president.

Conclusions

We have developed measures for two incumbent presidents and one challenger. The comparisons between two incumbents and an excellent president, as well as the comparison between Clinton and his main challenger, Bob Dole, suggest that incumbent presidents indeed are held to a high standard. On all four leadership dimensions over five surveys both incumbents had much lower evaluations than the excellent presidents. In two different surveys Dole consistently outranked Clinton, this despite the fact that clear majorities intended to and did vote for Clinton.

The comparison of Bill Clinton and George W. Bush also allows us to compare two incumbents at the same time period in their presidencies (the end of their seventh year). Other than the high-ethical-standards dimension, in which Clinton understandably did not fare well, Clinton had much lower gap ratings than Bush. These results show interesting variations between our two incumbent presidents.

With regard to the expectations gap itself, our results suggest that in the aggregate it is much more stable over time than are a president's public approval ratings. While an incumbent's poll ratings vary considerably, with George W. Bush's moving from the 90s to the 20s in a six-year period, our measures of excellent presidents, the individual evaluations of incumbent presidents on four leadership dimensions, the challenger gap, and our over-all weighted expectations gap all suggest that while there are some mod-est variations in public perceptions of the gap over time, they do not vary widely. On the other hand, the gap—as we measure it—does vary from in-dividual to individual. Hence, variation does exist. Not in the aggregate over time, but rather individually, from person to person. In the next chapter we will use each individual's expectations gap measures to directly examine whether the expectations gap exerts a deleterious impact on presidential ap-proval ratings and reelection success, as long hypothesized by presidential scholars. We will also examine whether it has an impact on vote choices in midterm elections.

CHAPTER 5

Testing the Expectations Gap Thesis

The Presidency of Bill Clinton

Large funding increases are likely to be wasteful and often merely contribute to overly optimistic expectations.

President Gerald Ford, Special Message to
Congress on Energy, January 7, 1977

An essential attribute of the expectations gap thesis is the idea there is a gap between what we expect our presidents to do and what presidents actually are capable of doing. As we have noted, presidential scholars have hypothesized that this gap is systemic, thus affecting all modern presidents. It is further posited that the expectations gap induces lower approval ratings and a decreased likelihood of reelection success. We also will examine whether the gap has a deleterious impact on the fate of the president's congressional party in midterm elections. The evidence provided therefore represents a direct test of two basic assumptions of the gap thesis.

As we have operationalized it, the expectations gap is not a constant for all individuals. Just as all people do not have the same opinion of the performance of an incumbent president, there are variations among individuals in terms of how much one expects from an excellent president or from an incumbent president. Our measures therefore allow for variation in perceptions of the gap's magnitude and influence, from one respondent to another. An individual focus on the expectations gap still incorporates the other more commonly expressed attributes about a gap (e.g., it still is hypothesized to exert a deleterious impact on presidential ratings and election outcomes). We now, however, extend the thesis and argue that for those individuals who either have low expectations of "excellent" presidential performance, in general, or who believe that the incumbent's performance is satisfying their expectations, the gap will engender a less harmful impact than for those individuals who have higher expectations of "excellent" presidential performance or a lower assessment of the incumbent's job performance, or both. It is these types of variations, from individual to individual, that allow us to employ survey research techniques to measure and test the impact of the expectations gap on an incumbent president. Using data from both statewide New Mexico and national surveys, we examine Clinton at the beginning and the end of the 1996 presidential election, at midterm in 1998, and in a nonelection year, 1999.

Bill Clinton and the Expectations Gap: 1996

To test our measures of the expectations gap we examine whether our respondents identified themselves as approving of Bill Clinton's performance and whether they intended to vote for him. As mentioned, we derived a measure of Bill Clinton's approval rating by asking the following question: "Using a scale of (1) excellent, (2) good, (3) fair or (4) poor, how would you rate the job Bill Clinton is doing as President of the United States?" At the beginning of the presidential election year Clinton's performance was ranked as follows: 6.4 percent of our respondents rated Clinton's performance as "excellent," 27.8 percent as "good," 37.6 percent as "fair," and 28.2 percent as "poor." At the end of the campaign, his performance was ranked as follows: 7.5 percent as "excellent," 31.4 percent as "good," 36 percent as "fair," and 25.1 percent as "poor."

    With regard to vote preference, for the January-February survey we asked the following question: "If the presidential election were held today and your only choices were Bill Clinton and Bob Dole, who would you vote for?" Of our respondents, 54.3 percent said they would vote for Bill Clinton, while 45.7 percent said they would vote for Bob Dole. The October-November survey commenced prior to the presidential election. If the interview was conducted prior to the election, we asked, "If the presidential election were held today, who would you vote for?" If the interview was conducted after the election, we asked, "The presidential election was held November 5th. From among the following candidates, who did you vote for?" The results of the October-November survey are as follows: 49.7 percent said they had voted for or would vote for Bill Clinton (49.1 percent before the election and 50.8 percent after), While 37.4 percent said they would vote or had voted for Dole. Another 7.8 percent said they would vote for or had voted for Ross Perot. The responses, both before and after the election, are similar. Additionally, the figures are close to the final election results, both in New Mexico and in the United States as a whole.

We use these two variables (Clinton's approval rating ranging from 1 = excellent to 4 = poor and vote choice with Clinton = 1 and Dole and all others = 0) as the two dependent variables for our analysis. We also control for a variety of other independent variables in our models. To control for specific demographic characteristics we include measures of each respondent's age, education, race/ethnicity, and gender (for an explanation of how we operationalized our independent variables, see appendix B). We hypothesize that the older the respondent is the more likely they are to favor Clinton, largely because he made protection of Social Security a centerpiece of his campaign. Women, the more highly educated, African Americans, and Latinos are also more likely to approve of Clinton's job performance and to vote for Clinton rather than Dole. We included a variable measuring each respondent's income. Though the variable was significant in some models, we have dropped it from the models we present here because (as is often the case in telephone surveys) a number of individuals did not respond to this particular question. As a result, including income greatly reduces our overall number of observations, while the overall results of the model do not change once income is eliminated.

We also included a number of measures to control for our respondent's political inclinations such as the party identification and political ideology of our respondents. Party identification is measured as a dummy variable with Democrats coded one and all others coded zero. We hypothesize that Democrats are more likely to favor Clinton over Dole. We also include a seven-point self-identified ideological scale that ranges from 1 = very liberal to 7 = very conservative. The more liberal a respondent is the more likely she is to support Bill Clinton. We also include a proxy variable for how active our respondents are in the political process by using a dummy variable that is coded one if the respondent identified herself as registered to vote and zero otherwise. For the January-February survey only, we also control for whether the respondent watched the State of the Union address (1 = yes, 0 = no), their expressed level of interest in the campaign, and who they blame for the two government shutdowns that occurred in late 1995 and early 1996 (1 = blame the president, 2 = blame both the president and Congress equally, and 3 = blame Congress). We also control for the primary source of news for our respondents. "TV news" is coded as one if a respondent gets their news primarily from television and zero otherwise. Finally, since 1996 was a year in which divided government prevailed, we also asked our respondents to evaluate the job performance of the U.S. Congress. For the January-February survey 1.96 percent rated Congress's performance as "excellent," 17.47 percent as "good," 44.74 percent as "fair," and 35.83 percent as "poor." The comparable percentages for the October-November survey were 2.8 percent, 28.4 percent, 49.1 percent, and 19.7 percent. Since the Republicans were the majority party in Congress we hypothesize that the more favorably one evaluates the performance of Congress, the less likely one is to favor Bill Clinton over Bob Dole, or to approve of the president's job performance.

One limitation of the 1996 surveys, one that we address in the 1998, 1999, and 2007 surveys, is that we only have a rough proxy measure for respondent's perceptions of the state of the economy. For the 1996 surveys we asked our respondents what they considered to be the most important issue facing the nation. Respondents were then given a list, of which "jobs" was one of the alternatives. Those who chose "jobs" as the most important issue were coded as a one and all others as zero.

Our Results

One of our dependent variables, Clinton's approval rating, consists of four categories (excellent, good, fair, and poor). For this reason we analyzed the data using an ordered logit model with the president's approval rating as the dependent variable. For the January-February survey we also employ a measure of whether our respondent intended to vote for Clinton (coded as one) or Bob Dole (coded zero). For the October-November survey we asked whether our respondents intended to vote or actually did vote for Clinton (coded as one) or Dole, Perot, or someone else (coded as zero). Since the vote choice models involve a dichotomous dependent variable we employed logit models for these analyses.

In column 1 of table 5.1 we present a model that includes all four of Bill Clinton's weighted gap measures: sound judgment in a crisis, experience in foreign affairs, high ethical standards, and an ability to work well with Congress. Since the dependent variable is measured as excellent = 1, good = 2, fair = 3, and poor = 4, positive values of these gap measures would indicate that as the size of Clinton's gap increases, his job approval evaluations should decrease, which is the hypothesized effect.

We begin with the January-February surveys. We include all four of the gap measures in the model. We note that we found no evidence of multicollinearity among the four leadership qualities. Additionally, all four of the Clinton gap measures are positive and three of them achieve the two-tailed standard for statistical significance. This means that for our respondents, the broader Clinton's gap for sound judgment in a crisis, experience in foreign affairs, and high ethical standards the lower his approval ratings are. While the ability to work well with Congress gap measure is not significant, the measure of congressional approval is, but it signifies that the more one approves of the performance of Congress, the more likely one is to approve of the incumbent president's performance. The government shutdown coefficient is negative and significant meaning that the more one blamed the president for the shutdown the less likely one was to approve of Clinton's job performance.[1] Finally, we hypothesize that those individuals who get their news primarily from television had higher evaluations of Clinton, as did those who had higher levels of education.

In column 2 of table 5.1 we substitute the weighted Clinton gap measure (which ranges from 0 to 100) for the four leadership qualities. There are a few differences between the two models. Among the demographic variables education is no longer significant, but gender is, with men less likely to approve of the president's performance. With regard to political factors, TV news, the government shutdown, and evaluations of Congress are all still significant and their effects are in the same direction. The key finding from the table, however, is that the weighted Clinton gap measure is related as hypothesized to the president's approval rating. The results from the first two columns of table 5.1 therefore provide substantial evidence that the expectation gap is related to lower approval ratings.

Is there evidence that the gap is also related to expected vote choice? Since the dependent variable is 1 = Clinton, 0 = Dole, a negative coefficient for the expectations gap measures reflects less support for the president. The case here is not as strong. In column 3 of table 5.1 none of the four gap measures is related to vote choice, though presidential approval is, as are party identification and evaluations of Congress. On the other hand, in column 4 of table 5.1 the weighted Clinton gap measure is significantly related to vote choice, with larger gap measures related to less support for Clinton. Again, the effect is in the hypothesized direction. Though the overall weighted gap measure is significant, the vote choice models provide less consistent evidence supporting a main hypothesis of the expectations gap thesis.

In column 1 of table 5.2 we examine the four leadership gap measures generated, this time, by asking respondent's questions about their assessment of Senator Bob Dole's qualifications. None of the four Dole leadership gap measures is related to Clinton's overall approval rating, though Latinos and African Americans are more likely to express a vote preference for Clinton. Likewise, Democrats favor Clinton's performance, while those who

TABLE 5.1. Clinton Approval and Vote Choice Models, Jan/Feb 1996 Survey

	Presidential Approval	Presidential Approval	Vote Choice	Vote Choice
	Gap Measures			
Clinton: Sound judgment	.02***	—	.001	—
	(.01)		(.008)	
Clinton: Experience in foreign affairs	.02*	—	-.001	—
	(.01)		(.008)	
Clinton: High ethical standards	.03***	—	.004	—
	(.01)		(.007)	
Clinton: An ability to work well with Congress	.005	—	-.01	—
	(.006)		(.006)	
Clinton: Weighted expectations gap	—	.08***	—	-.02*
		(.01)		(.008)
Presidential approval	—	—	-.91***	-.87***
			(.19)	(.19)
	Demographic Variables			
Age	-.003	-.002	.0008	.001
	(.10)	(.007)	(.008)	(.008)
Education	-.23*	-.19	.15	.15
	(.10)	(.10)	(.12)	(.12)
Latino	-.47	-.44	.36	.39
	(.25)	(.25)	(.27)	(.27)
African American	-.49	-.45	.39	.41
	(.25)	(.25)	(.28)	(.27)
Gender	.41	.43*	.21	.20
	(.22)	(.21)	(.24)	(.24)
	Political Variables			
Democrats	-.41	.44	.79**	.79**
	(.25)	(.25)	(.28)	(.28)
Ideology	-.05	.03	-.16	-.15
	(.07)	(.08)	(.09)	(.08)
TV news	-.58*	-.59**	-.03	-.03
	(.23)	(.28)	(.26)	(.26)
State of the Union	-.37	-.40	-.13	-.15
	(.25)	(.25)	(.28)	(.28)
Registered to vote	-.31	-.21	-.43	-.40
	(.27)	(.27)	(.31)	(.31)
Attention to campaign	.02	.01	-.13	-.13
	(.14)	(.14)	(.16)	(.16)
Government shutdown	-1.65***	-.70***	.43	.43
	(.28)	(.27)	(.31)	(.31)
Jobs	-13	-.11	.36	.34
	(.24)	(.23)	(.27)	(.27)

TABLE 5.1.—*Continued*

	Presidential Approval	Presidential Approval	Vote Choice	Vote Choice
Evaluation of Congress	.40***	.39**	.70***	.69***
	(.15)	(.14)	(.18)	(.17)
N	432	432	419	419
Chi-square	352.1	342.57	206.44	204.89
Pseudo R^2	.33	.32	.28	.28

* significant at .05; ** significant at .01; ***significant at .001.

blame the president for the shutdown are less inclined to approve of his performance. In column 2 of table 5.2 we substitute the weighted Dole gap measure (0 = 100) for the four leadership qualities. Again, Dole's gap is not significantly related to Clinton's approval rating.

We get a different story when we examine the vote choice model. Two of Dole's leadership gap measures (sound judgment and high ethical standards) are related to an increased propensity to vote for Dole and when we substitute the weighted gap measure in column 4 it is again significant. What these results suggest then is that there is a different dynamic in the way the various gap measures affect the approval and vote choice calculus of our respondents to the January-February survey. The president's expectations gap is more consistently associated with his approval ratings than with expected vote choice. Conversely, the evaluations of the likely Republican nominee, Bob Dole, while not related to Clinton's approval ratings, are related to vote choice.

To dig deeper into this possibility in table 5.3 we use a different measure of the challenger gap. This one is measured as the difference between Dole's and Clinton's evaluations. Here a positive value indicates that Dole's gap is larger than Clinton's and a negative value indicates the opposite, with zero indicating that there is no difference between the two candidates' gap measures. When we examined expectations in this manner the challenger gap is significant and negative in all four models, both for approval and vote choice. It is related to lower presidential approval ratings, even when we control for Clinton's weighted gap measure, which is also significant. Of greater interest, the challenger gap measure is significant in terms of vote choice, but the Clinton weighted gap is not. Again, this is convincing evidence that Clinton's gap has less of an affect on vote choice decisions than does a comparison to his likely challenger for the nomination.

TABLE 5.2. Dole Expectation Gap Models for Jan/Feb 1996 Survey with President Clinton's Approval Rating and Vote Choice as Dependent Variable

	Presidential Approval	Presidential Approval	Vote Choice	Vote Choice
Gap Measures				
Dole: Sound judgment	−.07	—	.02**	—
	(.05)		(.008)	
Dole: Experience in	.04	—	−.004	—
foreign affairs	(.04)		(.009)	
Dole: High ethical	.06	—	.02**	—
standards	(.05)		(.008)	
Dole: An ability to work	−.04	—	.004	—
well with Congress	(.04)		(.008)	
Dole: Weighted expectations	—	−.007	—	.04***
gap		(.007)		(.009)
Presidential approval	—	—	−.90***	−.91***
			(.18)	(.18)
Demographic Variables				
Age	−.003	−.004	.004	.004
	(.007)	(.007)	(.009)	(.009)
Education	−.11	−.12	.19	.19
	(.10)	(.10)	(.13)	(.13)
Latino	−.72**	−.72**	.59*	.57
	(.24)	(.24)	(.29)	(.30)
African American	−.73**	−.73**	.61*	.59*
	(.24)	(.24)	(.30)	(.30)
Gender	.26	.24	.27	.25
	(.21)	(.21)	(.26)	(.26)
Political Variables				
Democrats	−1.13***	−1.13***	1.00**	.98***
	(.24)	(.24)	(.29)	(.28)
Ideology	.21**	.22**	−.18*	−.18*
	(.07)	(.07)	(.09)	(.09)
TV news	−.54*	−.53*	.09	.03
	(.22)	(.22)	(.28)	(.28)
State of the Union	−.04−	.05	−.37	−.39
	(.25)	(.25)	(.31)	(.30)
Registered to vote	.09	.11	−.69*	−.64
	(.27)	(.27)	(.33)	(.33)
Attention to campaign	−.01	−.23	−.06	−.05
	(.14)	(.14)	(.17)	(.17)
Government shutdown	−2.38***	−2.33***	.43	.50
	(.28)	(.27)	(.33)	(.32)
Jobs	−.16	.13	.20	.24
	(.23)	(.23)	(.29)	(.29)

TABLE 5.2.—*Continued*

	Presidential Approval	Presidential Approval	Vote Choice	Vote Choice
Evaluation of Congress	.42**	.43**	.48*	.55**
	(.15)	(.14)	(.19)	(.19)
N	399	399	391	391
Chi-square	203.17	200.22	226.91	219.36
Pseudo R^2	.21	.20	.33	.32

* significant at .05; ** significant at .01; ***significant at .001.

In columns 5 and 6 of table 5.3 we measure the challenger gap in yet a third way: we include both Bob Dole's and Bill Clinton's weighted gap measures together in the same model. Again, we find similar results to those from the first four columns of table 5.3. With presidential approval as the dependent variable both gap measures are significant and in the expected direction (column 1). But when we move to vote choice (column 2) only Dole's weighted gap is significant.

These combined results from the tables provide only some support for the gap thesis. Yet while the incumbent's gap measures are related to his approval ratings, as hypothesized, the various challenger gap measures exert a stronger impact when the calculus turns to vote choice. Still the results presented in tables 5.1 through 5.3 only examine attitudes at the beginning of an election year. What happens as we move closer to Election Day? We address that question first in table 5.4.

For the October-November 1996 survey, two of Clinton's leadership qualities are related to his approval ratings: sound judgment in a crisis and high ethical standards. Experience in foreign affairs, which was related to his performance evaluations in the earlier survey, is not significant here. We also see that the partisanship and ideology measures are strongly significant (they were not significant in the January-February survey) with Democrats approving of Clinton. The more conservative one is the less likely one is to approve of Clinton's job performance. Evaluations of Congress are still significant with higher approval for Congress related to higher levels of approval for Clinton. The level of education is also significant in the four leadership quality gap models.

The results from column 2 of table 5.4 also demonstrate that Clinton's weighted gap measure is related to his approval rating (the larger his gap, the less likely one is to approve of his performance). Therefore, with the exception of experience in foreign affairs, the results from the two 1996 surveys

TABLE 5.3. Challenger and Clinton Gaps with Clinton's Approval Rating and Vote Choice as the Dependent Variables, Jan/Feb 1996 Survey

	Presidential Approval Clinton versus Dole	Presidential Approval Clinton versus Dole	Vote Choice Clinton versus Dole	Vote Choice Clinton versus Dole	Presidential Approval Weighted Gap	Vote Choice Weighted Gap
Dole: Challenger gap	-.42*** (.05)	-.18** (.06)	.40*** (.06)	.42*** (.08)	-.02** (.01)	.05*** (.009)
Clinton: Weighted expectations gap	—	.06*** (.01)	—	.018 (.01)	.07*** (.011)	.02 (.011)
Presidential approval	—	—	—	-.60** (.21)	—	.61** (.21)
Demographic Variables						
Age	-.01 (.007)	-.008 (.008)	.003 (.009)	.004 (.01)	-.007 (.008)	.002 (.009)
Education	-.17 (.10)	-.22* (.11)	.25 (.13)	.23 (.13)	-.24* (.13)	.24 (.13)
Latino	-.67** (.25)	-.62* (.26)	.63* (.28)	.53 (.29)	-.61* (.26)	.51 (.29)
African American	-.69** (.25)	-.64* (.26)	.66* (.28)	.55 (.30)	-.63* (.26)	.54 (.30)
Gender	.15 (.22)	.33 (.23)	.15 (.26)	.29 (.27)	.34 (.23)	.26 (.27)
Political Variables						
Democrats	-.48 (.26)	-.25 (.27)	.64* (.29)	.70* (.30)	-.29 (.27)	.78** (.30)
Ideology	.06 (.08)	-.01 (.08)	-.10 (.09)	-.11 (.09)	-.02 (.08)	-.11 (.09)
TV news	-.56* (.23)	-.65** (.24)	.09 (.27)	.08 (.28)	-.67** (.24)	.09 (.28)
State of the Union	-.05 (.26)	-.17 (.26)	-.33 (.30)	-.36 (.31)	-.17 (.26)	-.37 (.31)
Registered to vote	-.06 (.27)	-.29 (.28)	-.41 (.32)	-.53 (.34)	.30 (.28)	.52 (.34)
Attention to campaign	-.12 (.14)	-.08 (.15)	-.05 (.17)	-.07 (.17)	-.10 (.15)	-.04 (.17)
Government shutdown	-1.75*** (.29)	-1.62*** (.29)	.57 (.30)	.32 (.33)	-1.64*** (.29)	.35 (.33)
Jobs	.05 (.24)	.001 (.24)	.24 (.28)	.19 (.29)	-.01 (.24)	.19 (.29)
Evaluation of Congress	.65*** (.15)	.48** (.16)	.50** (.18)	.57** (.19)	.48** (.16)	.56** (.19)
N	397	397	390	389	397	389
Chi-square	280.65	327.18	213.24	227.47	326.25	226.47
Pseudo R^2	.28	.33	.31	.34	.33	.33

* significant at .05; ** significant at .01; *** significant at .001.

TABLE 5.4.   Clinton Approval and Vote Choice as the Dependent Variables, Oct/Nov 1996 Survey

	Presidential Approval	Presidential Approval	Vote Choice	Vote Choice
Gap Measures				
Clinton: Sound judgment	.03***	—	–.01	—
	(.008)		(.01)	
Clinton: Experience in foreign affairs	.001	—	–.01	—
	(.007)		(.01)	
Clinton: High ethical standards	.04***	—	–.03***	—
	(.005)		(.008)	
Clinton: An ability to work well with Congress	.01	—	–.019	—
	(.007)		(.01)	
Clinton: Weighted expectations gap	—	.09***	—	–.07***
		(.007)		(.01)
Presidential approval	—	—	–1.06***	–1.14***
			(.25)	(.25)
Demographic Variables				
Age	–.01	–.008	.007	.006
	(.006)	(.006)	(.009)	(.009)
Education	–.21*	–.18	.25	.22
	(.09)	(.09)	(.15)	(.14)
Latino	–.29	–.32	.87*	.83*
	(.25)	(.25)	(.38)	(.37)
African American	–.02	–.04	1.30**	1.32**
	(.32)	(.32)	(.49)	(.48)
Gender	.02	.03	–.22	–.24
	(.19)	(.19)	(.30)	(.29)
Political Variables				
Democrats	–.85***	–.90***	1.02***	1.01***
	(.24)	(.23)	(.30)	(.30)
Ideology	.23***	.27***	–.19	–.197
	(.07)	(.07)	(.10)	(.101)
TV news	–.28	–.20	.10	.01
	(.19)	(.19)	(.30)	(.29)
Registered to vote	–.34	–.25	.155**	1.48**
	(.36)	(.35)	(.51)	(.51)
Jobs	–.17	–.09	–.55	–.55
	(.22)	(.22)	(.34)	(.33)
Evaluation of Congress	.27*	.28*	.31	.28
	(.14)	(.13)	(.22)	(.21)
N	505	505	498	498
Chi-square	462	439.36	367.13	363.39
Pseudo R^2	.36	.35	.53	.53

* significant at .05; ** significant at .01; *** significant at .001.

are consistent. We do not find the same pattern, however, with regard to the vote choice models.

At the beginning of 1996 none of Clinton's leadership gap measures were related to expected vote choice. As the fall election approaches, one measure is significant: the broader Clinton's gap on the high ethical standards quality is, the less likely one is to vote for Clinton (column 3 of table 5.4). Since Clinton's personal behavior was one of Bob Dole's few campaign assets (with a growing economy and peace abroad he had to focus on Clinton's personal qualities), this finding is not particularly surprising. Consistent with the January-February survey (table 5.1), the broader Clinton's weighted gap is, the less likely one is to vote for the incumbent. What of the challenger gap models?

In column 1 of table 5.5 we again examine Bob Dole's evaluations on the four leadership qualities. Whereas none were related to Clinton's approval ratings in the January-February survey, sound judgment in a crisis and experience in foreign affairs are significant. The larger Dole's gap is, the more likely one is to approve of the president's performance. On the other hand, in column 2 of the same table we see that Dole's overall weighted gap measure is now significant (it was not in table 5.2). The broader Dole's weighted gap is, the more likely one is to approve of the president's job performance. Although we do not have the full array of control variables that we had for the January-February survey, the results between the various models are quite similar. What changes from the beginning to the end of the election year then is a stronger association between the challenger gap measures and the president's approval ratings. As the election nears, it appears that individuals are more attentive to the challenger's characteristics when they evaluate the incumbent's performance.

With regard to vote choice (column 3 of table 5.5), Dole's measure of sound judgment in a crisis is significant, as it was in the early 1996 survey results, but high ethical standards is no longer significant. The Dole challenger gap measure (column 4) also is still significant and the effect is in the hypothesized direction. As with the early 1996 survey, then, attitudes toward the challenger are related to our respondents' vote choice. And contributing to the validity of our findings, there is a remarkable similarity in the models for the two periods in 1996, with the most interesting difference being that evaluations of Congress were no longer significantly related to the vote choice in the fall 1996 models.

In table 5.6 we again consider the difference between Dole's and Clinton's gap measures to determine whether this challenger gap measure is related in the expected direction to Clinton's job performance evaluations and vote

TABLE 5.5. Clinton's Approval and Vote Choice as Dependent Variables, Oct/Nov 1996 Survey

	Presidential Approval	Presidential Approval	Vote Choice	Vote Choice
Gap Measures				
Dole: Sound judgment	-.02**	—	.03**	—
	(.007)		(.10)	
Dole: Experience in foreign affairs	-.01*	—	-.007	—
	(.007)		(.01)	
Dole: High ethical standards	.002	—	-.008	—
	(.006)		(.01)	
Dole: An ability to work well with Congress	-.002	—	.006	—
	(.006)		(.01)	
Dole: Weighted expectations gap	—	-.03***	—	.02*
		(.007)		(.01)
Presidential approval	—	—	-1.79***	-1.77***
			(.23)	(.22)
Demographic Variables				
Age	.005	.004	.005	.003
	(.006)	(.006)	(.009)	(.009)
Education	-.13	-.14	.09	.10
	(.09)	(.09)	(.14)	(.14)
Latino	-.33	-.27	.85*	.74*
	(.24)	(.24)	(.37)	(.36)
African American	-.24	-.26	1.54**	1.51**
	(.30)	(.30)	(.52)	(.50)
Gender	.13	.41	-.20	-.28
	(.18)	(.18)	(.29)	(.29)
Political Variables				
Democrats	-1.78***	-1.75***	1.33***	1.31***
	(.22)	(.22)	(.30)	(.29)
Ideology	.39***	.39***	-.21*	-.21*
	(.06)	(.06)	(.10)	(.10)
TV news	-.42*	-.44*	.41	.42
	(.18)	(.18)	(.29)	(.28)
Registered to vote	.51	.45	1.13*	1.26**
	(.33)	(.33)	(.51)	(.50)
Jobs	-.009	-.01	-.62	-.61
	(.21)	(.20)	(.32)	(.32)
Evaluation of Congress	.32**	.32**	.07	.15
	(.13)	(.13)	(.21)	(.20)
N	489	489	483	483
Chi-square	255.38	250.66	330.65	325.51
Pseudo R^2	.21	.20	.50	.49

* significant at .05; ** significant at .01; *** significant at .001.

TABLE 5.6. Challenger and Clinton Gaps with Approval Rating and Vote Choice as Dependent Variables, Oct/Nov 1996 Survey

	Presidential Approval	Presidential Approval	Vote Choice	Vote Choice	Presidential Approval	Vote Choice
Gap Measures						
Dole: Challenger gap	−.59***	−.33***	.78***	.41***	−.04***	.05***
	(.05)	(.06)	(.09)	(.12)	(.007)	(.01)
Clinton: Weighted expectations gap	—	.06***	—	−.04**	.09***	−.09***
		(.01)		(.02)	(.007)	(.01)
Presidential approval	—	—	—	−.95***	—	−.94***
				(.26)		(.26)
Demographic Variables						
Age	−.008	−.01	.016	.01	−.008	0.16
	(.006)	(.01)	(.009)	(.01)	(.006)	(.01)
Education	−.21*	−.21*	.29*	.22	−.20*	.22
	(.09)	(.10)	(.14)	(.15)	(.10)	(.15)
Latino	−.06	−.16	.66	.72	−.20	.79*
	(.25)	(.25)	(.38)	(.40)	(.25)	(.40)
African American	−.26	−.21	1.95	1.67**	−.22	1.66**
	(.33)	(.34)	(.52)	(.54)	(.34)	(.54)
Gender	−.14	−.12	.05	−.02	.09	.04
	(.19)	(.20)	(.29)	(.31)	(.20)	(.31)
Political Variables						
Democrats	−.95***	−.76**	1.09***	.87**	−.75**	.87**
	(.24)	(.24)	(.30)	(.32)	(.24)	(.32)
Ideology	.21**	.20**	−.12	−.08	.21**	−.07
	(.07)	(.07)	(.10)	(.11)	(.07)	(.11)
TV news	−.27	.21	.41	.34	−.25	.35
	(.19)	(.20)	(.30)	(.31)	(.20)	(.32)
Registered to vote	−.12	−.36	1.98***	1.93***	−.36	1.90***
	(.36)	(.37)	(.54)	(.55)	(.37)	(.54)
Jobs	−.17	−.17	−.56	−.62	−.17	.12
	(.22)	(.22)	(.34)	(.36)	(.23)	(.24)
Evaluation of Congress	.47***	.39**	−.07	.15	.38**	−.08
	(.13)	(.14)	(.22)	(.24)	(.14)	(.22)
N	491	488	486	482	482	482
Chi-square	422.91	456.24	354.35	377.12	378.04	378.04
Pseudo R^2	.34	.37	.53	.57	.57	.57

* significant at .05; ** significant at .01; *** significant at .001.

choice. In the models presented in table 5.3 the challenger gap was related to Clinton's approval rating and to vote choice. On the other hand, while the Clinton gap was related to his approval ratings, it was not related to vote choice once we controlled for the challenger gap. The results in table 5.6 paint a different picture. Clinton's weighted expectations gap is related to both his own approval ratings and to vote choice. At the beginning of 1996 the Clinton weighted gap measure was related to presidential approval, but not to vote choice. Yet, by election time both the Dole and Clinton gap measures are related to vote choice in the expected direction (columns 5 and 6 of table 5.6). This is consistent with our earlier findings (Waterman, Jenkins-Smith, and Silva 1999, 962), which employed different models and somewhat different measures. There we found that "the difference between the two gap measures [the Clinton and challenger gaps] narrowed considerably over time." Additionally, we find here that the relationship between the president's gap measures appears to be even more relevant as we move closer to a presidential election.

In sum, the results from the two 1996 surveys provide compelling evidence that the expectations gap exerts a deleterious impact on presidential approval ratings and vote choice, which is consistent with hypotheses derived from the expectations gap thesis. But we also find that the nature of the gap's effect changes over time, from the beginning of an election year to the end of it. At the beginning of 1996 Clinton's evaluations were related to the incumbent's approval ratings, while his challenger's evaluations were not. Contrarily, the various Dole gap measures were more strongly related to vote choice and the Clinton measures had less effect once we controlled for the Dole expectations gaps. By the fall of 1996 the picture changed considerably. The Clinton gap measures were now related to approval ratings and to vote choice, even when we controlled for the Dole gap. Conversely, the Dole gap measures were more strongly associated with Clinton's approval ratings. What does this finding suggest?

At the beginning of the election year, without an official opponent to run against, the president's evaluations were not related to vote choice. Once Dole was nominated and the fall election commenced, however, respondents were more inclined to consider the qualifications of both candidates in making their vote selection. Likewise, with the energy of a presidential campaign, respondents also were more willing to apply their evaluations of Bob Dole when they evaluated Bill Clinton's job performance. Therefore, as the election approached, the expectations gap, in multiple forms, had a greater and more consistent impact than it had at the beginning of the year.

This finding suggests that in conceptualizing the expectations gap in election years we should examine evaluations of the president in concert with those of his or her challenger. While the presidential expectations gap is therefore important, as presidential scholars long have contended, the challenger gap in an election year is also an important determinant of how the public evaluates its incumbent presidents.

Bill Clinton and the Expectations Gap: 1998 and 1999

As we noted, two limitations of the 1996 surveys are their generalizability and the proxy used to measure the state of the economy. The 1998 and 1999 surveys are derived from national samples and allow us to examine the impact of the gap in a midterm election year and in a nonelection year. Both surveys also introduce two new economic measures: our respondents' perceptions of the state of the U.S. economy and their own personal finances, more generally called "sociotropic" and "pocketbook" attitudes, respectively. Sociotropic attitudes exist when "political judgments are shaped by evaluations of the nation's economic health, and not by" an individual's perceptions of their "own" economic situation. Pocketbook attitudes result when one's perceptions of one's personal financial well-being are related to support for the incumbent (Markus 1988, 138). To measure sociotropic attitudes we asked the following question: "Using a scale of one to seven, where one means very poor and seven means very good, how would you rate the current performance of the U.S. economy?" To test the pocketbook thesis we then asked, "Would you say that your family is financially better off, worse off, or about the same as you were a year ago?" We then coded the variable as 1 = worse off, 2 = about the same, and 3 = better off. We discuss the results of these questions in further detail in the next chapter. Since the survey was conducted during the impeachment crisis, we also control for attitudes toward impeachment. Those who favored impeachment were coded as a one and those opposed as zero. Again, we present more detail on our respondents' views of impeachment in chapter 7.

For 1998 we have two dependent variables. Our first is the job performance or approval rating of incumbent President Bill Clinton: 16.6 percent of our respondents rated Clinton's performance as "excellent," 38.6 percent as "good," 22.1 percent as "fair," and 22.6 percent as "poor." Our second dependent variable is whether respondents said that they intended to vote Democratic in the upcoming midterm elections. Of those who responded to this question, 406 said they would vote Democratic (coded as a one) and 562 said they would vote Republican (coded as a zero). For the 1999 survey, which was not an election year, we have but one dependent variable—Clinton's job approval rating. Of the respondents, 11 percent rated the incumbent president's performance as "excellent," 33.6 percent as "good," 29.4 percent as "fair," and 26 percent as "poor." Because the approval dependent variable employs an ordinal scale we use an ordered logit analysis for these models. Because our measure of vote choice is dichotomous, we used a logit model for the midterm model. We present the results for the 1998 survey in table 5.7 and the 1999 survey in table 5.8.

In table 5.7 we once again find convincing evidence that the expectations gap is related to both the president's approval rating and vote choice, even in a midterm election when the president is not on the ballot. All four of the leadership qualities are significantly related to Clinton's approval rating and each is in the hypothesized direction; the broader gaps on each leadership quality are related to lower approval ratings for the incumbent president. In column 2 of table 5.8, we substitute the weighted gap measure for the four leadership quality gaps. Again, a larger expectations gap is related to lower approval ratings. Note that we control for support for impeachment, which is positive and significant, indicating that those who favor impeachment were less likely to approve of the president's performance. Whereas the measure of pocketbook attitudes is not related to Clinton's evaluations in either model, the sociotropic perceptions of the U.S. economy are significant in both models. The relationship is negative, indicating that those who have a more favorable impression of the nation's economy are more likely to approve of Clinton's job performance (which is coded 1 = excellent to 4 = poor).

In the last two columns of table 5.7 we include a measure of those who intend to vote Democratic in the midterm elections. Only one of the four leadership qualities, sound judgment in a crisis, is related to vote choice. On the other hand, in the model presented in column 4, Clinton's weighted gap measure is related to vote choice, while the presidential approval variable is not significant. Again, this supports the hypothesis that the gap exerts a deleterious and direct impact on election outcomes. Although the president is not on the ticket in midterm elections, it is generally believed that these elections represent a referendum on the incumbent president (Erikson 1988). Our findings provide evidence in support of the presidential referendum thesis.

The year 1999 represents a nonelection year and the seventh year of the Clinton presidency. In this sense it is the first time we have examined the gap in a nonelection year. This is of interest because we do not know if the gap operates in the same manner in less overtly partisan times. The results

TABLE 5.7. Clinton Approval and Midterm Vote as Dependent Variables, 1998 Survey

	Presidential Approval	Presidential Approval	Vote Democrat in Midterm Election	Vote Democrat in Midterm Election
Expectations Gap				
Sound judgment	.03***	—	-.02*	—
	(.005)		(.01)	
Experience in foreign affairs	.01*	—	-.003	—
	(.005)		(.008)	
High ethical standards	.02***	—	-.009	—
	(.003)		(.005)	
Ability to work well with Congress	.01**	—	.004	—
	(.005)		(.008)	
Clinton's weighted expectations gap	—	.08***	—	-.03***
		(.005)		(.009)
Presidential approval	—	—	-.21	-.22
			(.18)	(.18)
Demographic Variables				
Age	-.003	-.003	-.01	-.01
	(.005)	(.005)	(.008)	(.008)
Education	.05	.05	.27*	.27*
	(.07)	(.07)	(.11)	(.11)
Latino	.06	.09	.35	.28
	(.34)	(.34)	(.52)	(.52)
African American	-.69*	-.71*	.08	.04
	(.32)	(.32)	(.51)	(.50)
Gender	-.02	-.005	-.24	-.23
	(.15)	(.15)	(.24)	(.24)
Political Variables				
Democrats	-.34*	-.36*	3.39***	3.39***
	(.16)	(.16)	(.25)	(.25)
Ideology	.03	.02	-.22*	-.21*
	(.06)	(.05)	(.09)	(.09)
TV news	-.01	-.01	.04*	.04*
	(.01)	(.01)	(.02)	(.02)
Registered to vote	-.09	-.04	.40	.33
	(.26)	(.26)	(.39)	(.39)
Impeach the president	1.46***	1.52***	-1.47***	-1.50***
	(.21)	(.21)	(.37)	(.37)
U.S. economy	-.26***	-.26***	.16	.16
	(.07)	(.07)	(.11)	(.11)
Pocketbook	-.10	-.09	-.05	-.07
	(.13)	(.12)	(.20)	(.20)

TABLE 5.7.—*Continued*

	Presidential Approval	Presidential Approval	Vote Democrat in Midterm Election	Vote Democrat in Midterm Election
Evaluations of Congress	.20*	.19*	−.04	−.01
	(.09)	(.09)	(.15)	(.15)
N	879	879	825	825
Chi-square	878.06	868.07	620.07	615.42
Pseudo *R*²	.37	.36	.55	.54

* significant at .05; ** significant at .01; *** significant at .001.

presented in table 5.8 indicate that it does. Three of the four leadership gap measures (sound judgment in a crisis, high ethical standards, and an ability to work well with Congress) are related to Clinton's approval ratings with increases in each gap measure contributing to lower incumbent approval ratings. Likewise, when we substitute in the weighted gap measure, it too is significant, with the same deleterious consequences. Consequently, in election or nonelection years, the expectations gap has a consistent affect on presidential approval ratings. This is an important finding, because in a nonelection year the political rhetoric is at least somewhat muted, meaning that the gap is not merely a manifestation of electoral campaigns.

Conclusions

In this chapter we provided a direct empirical test of the expectations gap thesis using multiple measures of the gap. Although there are some variations in the impact of the gap over time, the overall conclusion to be drawn from the various analyses of the four leadership gap measures, the incumbent's weighted expectations gap, and various measures of the challenger gap is that public expectations do promote both lower presidential approval ratings and, to a somewhat lesser extent, a diminished likelihood of electoral success. Interestingly, we find that this latter effect increases as we move closer to a presidential election and that it exists even in a midterm election year. The gap therefore is important to consider in both types of elections. Given that midterms are often described as a referendum on the sitting president, this latter finding makes sense.

While we have used multiple measures of the expectations gap in this chapter, there are yet other ways of conceptualizing the expectations gap. As

TABLE 5.8. Clinton Approval as the Dependent Variable, 1999 Survey

	Presidential Approval	Presidential Approval
	Expectations Gap	
Sound judgment	.30***	—
	(.007)	
Experience in foreign affairs	.01	—
	(.007)	
High ethical standards	.02***	—
	(.005)	
Ability to work well with Congress	.02**	—
	(.006)	
Clinton's weighted expectations gap	—	.08***
		(.007)
	Demographic Variables	
Age	−.009	−.009
	(.006)	(.006)
Education	.02	.02
	(.02)	(.02)
Latino	1.08	1.04
	(.62)	(.62)
African American	−.28	−.33
	(.40)	(.40)
Gender	.41*	.43*
	(.20)	(.28)
	Political Variables	
Democrats	−1.37***	−1.38***
	(.26)	(.07)
Ideology	.09	.10
	(.07)	(.07)
TV news	−.03	−.004
	(.19)	(.34)
Registered to vote	.34	.33
	(.35)	(.34)
U.S. economy	−.25**	−.25***
	(.09)	(.09)
Pocketbook	.009	.01
	(.15)	(.13)
Evaluations of Congress	.15	.14
	(.13)	(.13)
N	510	510
Chi-square	441.14	438.16
Pseudo R^2	.32	.32

* significant at .05; ** significant at .01; *** significant at .001.

many presidential scholars note, the public has high expectations for presidential performance, particularly when it comes to issues of peace and prosperity. In this chapter we provided some evidence that the economy matters. In the next chapter we turn to a more direct test of the performance-based expectations gap thesis in relation to the competing partisan thesis identified by Wood (2009). In particular, we concentrate on the impact of the state of the U.S. economy on the perceptions of Democrats and Republicans toward the incumbent, William Jefferson Clinton.

CHAPTER 6

The Economy, Ethical Standards, and Partisanship

All our efforts as Republicans are guided by the fixed star of this single principle: that freedom always exceeds our highest expectations. This is the greatest task before the Republican Party: to raise the bar of American expectations. Of the potential of our economy. Of the order and civility of our culture. Of what a president can be, and what the presidency must be again.

The 1996 Republican Party Platform

In the previous chapters we examined the expectations gap from a historical perspective, by comparing evaluations of two incumbents with retrospective evaluations of their immediate predecessors, and by using the presidential prototype approach to compare an ideal/excellent president with an incumbent president. In this chapter we approach the expectations gap from yet another direction that is identified in the presidential literature: we test a performance-based model of presidential expectations.

Another key assumption of the expectations gap paradigm is the idea that the public expects successful performance from its presidents. Although we do not have a dichotomous measure of the success or failure of various presidencies, and while available historical rankings of the presidents are too subjective to provide one, we can examine key aspects of the president's job performance on such issues as the economy.

Louis Brownlow (1969, 35), a main architect of the Executive Office of the President, argues that the public expects the chief executive to be "a skilled engineer of the economy of the nation." Failure to lead on this dimension represents an inability to satisfy a key public expectation of presidential performance. According to Brownlow's formulation, the entire public should expect the president to preside over a healthy economy. There is no distinction in this formulation between the president's political supporters and opponents. All Americans expect a healthy economy and should, at least in theory, respond favorably to successful presidential performance. This means the president should have higher approval ratings among all Americans during good economic times. As Brownlow (1969, 4) adds, "Couched in the crudest form of political expression, the dictum runs that if the country is prosperous the President gets the credit, if it is not prosperous the President gets the blame."

Yet there are reasons to believe that all partisans do not give an incumbent equal credit for a good economy. In 2000, several electoral models based largely on the nation's economic performance predicted a comfortable victory for Vice President Al Gore. Given the eventual closeness of that race, Michael Lewis-Beck later admitted the eventual outcome "totally" undermined his theory. John Green added, "The relationship between income and politics has changed—it's not as dramatic" (both are quoted in Solomon 2000, 3870). Is it possible that as American politics has become more polarized, presidents are not equally likely to get credit for good economic performance from their political supporters and opponents? Is it possible that party effects mediate public expectations, a finding that would be more consistent with B. Dan Wood's (2009) partisanship thesis?

In this chapter we ask whether Democrats, independents, and Republicans were equally predisposed to reward Bill Clinton with higher approval ratings in response to the positive performance of the U.S. economy in the late 1990s. If so, this would be evidence supporting the broad performance-based assumptions of the expectations gap thesis as enunciated by Louis Brownlow, that is, the idea that all Americans should give the president credit for good economic performance. An alternative explanation is that the public is divided in its sentiments along partisan lines, with Democrats more likely to approve of the president's performance and Republicans less likely to do so. Partisan divisions in assessments of the president would have to exist if both Democrats and Republicans had the same perceptions of the state of the economy and their personal finances. If there is no real variation in these perceptions of the economy, then differences in perceptions of the president's performance would suggest that public expectations are mediated by partisan considerations. In other words, good performance would not be sufficient to satisfy the public expectations of all Americans! This finding would have important implications for how we conceptualize one key aspect of the expectations gap paradigm. It would indicate that expectations are not a constant, but rather that they vary across existing partisan divides.

The economy's performance is one important direct measure of policy-based performance. Yet presidential scholars (see Edwards 1983) also discuss another expectation related to presidential performance: a character-based expectation. In recent decades media and public scrutiny of the president's personal life and ethical behavior has intensified. We therefore examine a measure of the president's ethical behavior to examine if public perceptions of a non-policy-oriented expectation are driven by broad-based agreement or narrow partisan divides. By comparing a policy and a nonpolicy expectation, our goal is to derive a clearer theoretical picture of the nature and scope of public expectations of presidential performance in relation to the prevalent role of partisan politics. To address these questions we examine incumbent President Bill Clinton using two national surveys (1998 and 1999).

Performance-Based Expectations

According to Brownlow's conceptualization of the expectations gap, presidents are expected to preside over a robust economy. When they do so, they are given "credit," that is they are rewarded with higher approval ratings and a greater chance of reelection. The central idea of this policy-based expectation is that the entire public has similar expectations of the presidency and therefore is equally likely to reward presidents for good performance. Partisanship is not a key construct in this theoretical formulation of the gap thesis. The gap exists for all Americans regardless of party. We note that the gap thesis as it is presently formulated provides no means of differentiating between the gap for followers of the president and the gap for the president's political opponents. But is this one-gap-size-fits-all model realistic? It is not if, as Wood (2009) contends, partisanship serves as a mediating force in public perceptions of presidential performance.

A key concept then in this formulation of the gap thesis is that all Americans expect a high level of performance. But what do we mean by performance? According to Erikson, MacKuen, and Stimson (2002, 14), "Competence and control are universal goods. Let us call the combination 'performance' for short." To measure performance, Erikson, MacKuen, and Stimson employ survey respondent assessments of the state of the U.S. economy. That, too, will be our measure.

There are specific reasons to believe that public expectations of presidential economic performance are important. Presidents use their rhetoric to influence public perceptions of the economy (see Druckman and Holmes 2004; Wood, Owens, and Durham 2005; Wood 2007). Likewise,

once MacKuen, Erikson, and Stimson (1992) control for public expectations of the economy they do not find that any other concrete measure of
the economic performance (e.g., unemployment, inflation) is significant.
Durr (1993) also concludes that "expectations of a healthy (or improving)
economy contribute to the willingness within the American public to un-
derwrite a liberal policy agenda."

There already is a copious literature demonstrating that a relationship
exists between presidential approval ratings and the economy. For instance,
Brace and Hinckley (1992, 165) note that as a determinant of a president's
approval ratings "[e]conomic circumstances . . . can be powerful condition-
ing factors" (see also Brody 1991, 91, and Kernell 1978, 510, as well as Kramer
1971; Mueller 1973; Bloom and Price 1975; Tufte 1978; Weatherford 1978;
Hibbs 1987; MacKuen, Erikson, and Stimson 1992; Cohen 1997; Garand
and Campbell 2000). Yet while scholars agree that the economy is an important determinant of presidential approval ratings, they often do not agree
on precisely how the economy exerts its impact. For example, Hibbs (1982)
argues that unemployment and real income growth have a small impact on
presidential approval, unless the economic effects are sustained for two years
or longer. MacKuen (1983) finds that inflation's impact is of a longer duration than unemployment, while Ostrom and Simon (1985, 351) argue that
"high levels" of unemployment and inflation "and a substantial degree of
public concern with economic problems are required" to influence presidential approval ratings. In an analysis of presidential voting behavior Erikson
(1989) concludes the change in per capita income is the best economic indicator. There also is disagreement over how the public evaluates the economy.
MacKuen, Erikson, and Stimson (1992) argue that the public acts prospec-
tively, looking forward to future economic expectations, while Norpoth
(1996) concludes they are "retrospective," looking back at past economic
conditions. Whether the public uses prospective or retrospective evaluations
also is related to whom its takes its cues from regarding the state of the
economy. Brody (1991) contends there is a cycle of economic news reporting.
MacKuen, Erikson, and Stimson (1992) argue that the public learns about
the state of the economy from media stories of "professional economic forecasts." Nadeau et al. (1999) find that media reporting of "elite retrospections"
influences how the public perceives the state of the economy.

We do not seek to replicate this vast literature here. Rather, our primary
contribution is to extend this literature and provide a theoretical test of the
central performance-based assumption of the expectations gap thesis in an
important policymaking venue. One subject, however, that is relevant to
our analysis is the debate over the relative importance of sociotropic versus

pocketbook attitudes. Scholars generally conclude that the public is more likely to be influenced by sociotropic than pocketbook attitudes. Feldman (1982) argues that the public considers these attitudes to be more relevant to the governmental realm because the state of the national economy depends on decisions by government officials, while pocketbook voting depends on idiosyncratic factors related to each individual. In Feldman's formulation, then, sociotropic attitudes would reflect broader performance-based perceptions of the economy than pocketbook attitudes. Likewise, Abramowitz, Lanoue, and Remesh (1988, 859) conclude that the reason why sociotropic attitudes are more resonant is because pocketbook voting "depends upon the ability of citizens to connect changes in their personal financial situation to broader economic trends and government policies" (see also Kinder and Kiewiet 1979, 1981; Kinder, Adams, and Gronke 1989). Meanwhile, Markus (1988, 1992) finds support for both types of attitudes, though he concludes that sociotropic attitudes have the greatest impact. Frolich and Oppenheimer (1978) and Weatherford (1983) also find support for pocketbook voting, while Lewis-Beck (1985) argues that evidence of pocketbook voting is not an artifact of question placement in surveys.

Although there are disagreements regarding how the precise economic mechanisms influence public perceptions, scholars do agree that the economy has an impact on presidential approval ratings. Yet, as both scholars and pundits acknowledge, as our political system is becoming more politically polarized (see McCarty, Poole, and Rosenthal 2003; Brady and Volden 2005) is it possible that perceptions of the economy are more likely to be mediated by the partisan predispositions of the electorate? For example, it is possible that Republicans may be less willing than Democrats to give a Democratic incumbent president credit for a good economy.

To test this possibility, we examine the perceptions of Republicans and Democrats to determine how they are related to evaluations of Clinton's job approval ratings. There is precedent for this research approach. A few studies examine subsets of the American electorate in relationship to presidential approval ratings. Kinder and Kiewiet (1979) find no difference between union workers and other occupational groups in their perceptions of the economy. Fiorina (1981) finds no difference among various socioeconomic groups and Sigelman (1991) finds that Jews are no more likely to engage in pocketbook voting than are members of other religions. While Welsh and Hibbing (1992) identify differences between men and women with regard to pocketbook voting, they find no such differences with regard to sociotropic voting.

While these studies find no or limited differences between various demographic groups, other studies conclude that differences do matter. In a time-series analysis, Hibbs (1982, 327) concludes that among "occupational/ labor force groups, blue-collar workers exhibit relatively greater sensitivity to movements in unemployment and real income growth and relatively less sensitivity to the inflation rate than white-collar workers or retirees." Hibbs also finds that "[t]he political approval indices for Democrats and Independents are far more responsive to movements in unemployment and the real income growth rate, and less responsive to movements in the inflation rate, than is the approval index of Republican partisans" (328). Research by Weatherford (1978, 1983) and Rivers (1988) also suggests that differences may exist between subsets of the electorate, as does Krause (1997, 1171) who addresses the question: "What factors significantly shape voters' egocentric [or pocketbook] and sociotropic economic expectations?" He finds that expectations of the economy vary according to the level of education (a proxy for information) members of the public attain. He does not, however, examine whether these differential perceptions affect evaluations of the presidency.

Regarding the role of partisanship, Coleman (1997) concludes that House Republicans are more likely than Democrats to get credit for the state of the economy in midterm elections, while Bartels (2000) finds that the impact of partisanship on voting behavior has increased in recent presidential elections. In combination, these studies suggest the value of examining the effect of partisanship. Before we do so, however, we first discuss a second non-policy performance-based dimension relevant to the expectations gap thesis.

High Ethical Standards

To provide a comparative analysis of the impact of performance, we also examine a non-policy-based expectation of presidential performance. In addition to its assumptions regarding the economy, the expectations gap thesis posits that the public as a whole expects appropriate presidential comportment. In his seminal analysis of public expectations of the presidency, Edwards (1983, 189–91) cites a 1979 Gallup poll in which 66 percent of respondents believed that "high ethical standards" were important to the presidency. Other research also shows that presidential character is important. A study by Goren (2002) identifies a relationship between the strength of attachment to an incumbent president, perceptions of the candidate's character, and candidate evaluations. Thus, there is evidence that a substantial majority of Americans consider high ethical standards to be an important expectation of presidential performance and it was particularly relevant to the Clinton presidency.

Once again we ask: Do all partisans have the same expectations regarding a president's personal private behavior? There are reasons to believe they do not. With regard to Bill Clinton there were ethical concerns from the very beginning of his presidential quest. In 1992 allegations of marital improprieties were raised during the New Hampshire primary campaign. During his presidency, several investigations (Whitewater, Travelgate, Filegate) raised additional ethical concerns. During his second term the revelation that the president had a consensual sexual relationship with a White House intern became the subject of a prolonged investigation by an independent counsel (Kenneth Starr) and ultimately led to the president's impeachment by the House of Representatives. Although the Senate did not convict Clinton, he became only the second president in U.S. history to be impeached. Therefore, the issue of Clinton's character, and the numerous and often partisan investigations of it, suggests that ethical concerns, a non-policy-making area, may be driven by partisan considerations.

We therefore use a policy and a non-policy-making criterion to examine the impact of partisan attitudes on presidential performance. In so doing, we follow Hibbs's (1982, 313) recommendation with regard to the economy:

> If economic performance is as important to the electorate as survey data indicate, cleavages among voters concerning economic priorities should be clearly revealed by analysis of data on partisan groups. Moreover, dividing the electorate along party identification is probably the dimension most relevant to the thinking of elected officials, and elected officials determine macroeconomic policy.

We also follow Krause's (1997, 1171) lead by casting aside the assumption of "voter homogeneity" or "the treatment of the electorate as a singular entity or aggregate." Duch, Palmer, and Anderson (2000) and Duch (2001) also examine the importance of heterogeneity in perceptions of the national economy. We test the following two hypotheses:

HI: One assumption of the expectations gap thesis is that all individuals expect the president to preside over a sound and healthy economy. Consequently, all partisans should give the president credit for a good economy. We hypothesize that the more positive a respondent's evaluations of the economy are, or the more positive their personal finances/pocketbooks are, the more positive their evaluations of the president's approval ratings should be.

H2: The expectations gap thesis also posits that all individuals expect the president to live up to high ethical standards. Thus, we hypothesize that the more positive the evaluation of President Clinton's ethical standards, the more positively evaluations of his presidential approval ratings will be for all individuals.

Before we test these hypotheses, we describe our data and measures.

Data and Measures

To test the possibility that economic attitudes and perceptions of the president's character are politicized, we analyzed individual-level data from two national surveys. In so doing, we follow the methodology employed by Weatherford (1983), Kiewiet (1981), and Feldman (1982), with one important difference: we examine presidential approval ratings in a midterm election (1998) and a nonelection year (1999). This allows us to determine whether expectations and partisan attitudes are driven by electoral stimuli or if they exist in both election and nonelection years. More compelling evidence for the expectations and partisan theses would therefore reflect partisan cleavages in both election and nonelection years.

Because we are interested in partisan differences we provide separate models to capture the effects for each year. We present all Republicans in one model and Democrats and others (independents and nonparty identifiers) in the other. Our dependent variable is the job performance or approval rating of incumbent president Bill Clinton. Again, for 1998 16.6 percent rated Clinton's performance an "excellent," 38.6 percent as "good," 22.1 percent as "fair," and 22.6 percent as "poor." For 1999, 11 percent rated his performance as "excellent," 33.6 percent as "good," 29.4 percent as "fair," and 26 percent as "poor." Because the dependent variable employs an ordinal scale we use an ordered logit analysis. For interpretative purposes it is important to remember that our approval scale runs from 1 = excellent to 4 = poor.

Since we are interested in the relationship between presidential approval ratings and the economy, our primary independent variables are our respondents' sociotropic and pocketbook attitudes. Most of our respondents perceived the U.S. economy as performing well in both 1998 and 1999. On a seven-point scale ranging from "very poor" to "very good," 10.7 percent gave the economy the highest ranking in 1998 compared to just 1.2 percent who gave it the lowest ranking. The modal category was 5.76 percent ranked the economy as a five or higher. For 1999, 12.7 percent ranked the economy as "very good" with again only 1.2 percent ranking it as "very poor." The modal category again was five. 78.7 percent ranked the economy as a five or better on the seven-point scale.

As for pocketbook concerns, for 1998, 32.2 percent perceived themselves as being "better off," 57.9 percent were "about the same," and only 9.9 percent were "worse off." The figures for 1999 provide evidence of even greater optimism about one's personal finances. 40.1 percent identified themselves as being "better off," 51.6 percent as "about the same," and only 8.3 percent as being "worse off." Clearly, then, according to the expectations gap thesis, these positive economic conditions should have worked to the benefit of the incumbent president in both years—that is, unless perceptions of the economy were mediated by partisan attitudes. To address this point, we examine the difference of means for sociotropic and pocketbook attitudes. We find that while Republicans tended to perceive the economy as slightly less robust than Democrats in 1998, the difference is modest and it disappears by 1999.

What about the responses to questions about Clinton's character? Unlike the perceptions of the economy, attitudes about Clinton's ethics should have been negative for both years. We measure Clinton's ethics by taking Clinton's ranking, subtracting it from 10 (his highest possible rating), and then multiplying it by the weight given to "high ethical standards" for an "excellent president" question.

(10 − Clinton Rating) * Weight of Ethical Standards for an
Excellent President

A scale from 0 (no gap whatsoever) to 100 (Clinton's largest possible gap) was created. For 1998 Clinton's mean ethics mean gap was 57.14 with a standard deviation of 33.47. For 1999 the mean was 61.23 with a standard deviation of 31.54. Gaps were therefore broad for both years. While Clinton's ethics were not highly rated, there is considerable variation in evaluations within each sample, and perceptions related to the president's personal ethics gap were consistently larger for Republicans.

The economy and presidential character/ethics are not the only factors that potentially influence perceptions of an incumbent president. We also control for potential political support for the president. With regard to political support, the idea is that certain groups are more or less likely to support President Bill Clinton or approve of his job performance. For instance, the "gender gap" suggests that women are more likely than men to support Democratic presidential candidates. Likewise, because Bill Clinton specifically appealed to the elderly on the issue of saving Social Security (as well as support for Medicare), we posit that the elderly are more likely to approve of his job performance. African Americans and Latinos were two of Bill Clinton's most loyal constituencies and thus should be more likely to approve of his job performance. Alternatively, we posit that individuals with higher incomes are more likely to vote Republican and less likely to favor Clinton. We also include a rough indicator to measure the level of political information by examining whether the respondent identified TV news as the primary source of information about politics. We also examine whether Republicans have different levels of support than Democrats and others (e.g., independents) on economic and ethical issues.

Expectations and Partisanship

According to the expectations gap thesis all individuals should expect the president to preside over a robust economy. The data indicate that during both 1998 and 1999 most Americans believed that the economy was performing quite well. Although there are statistically significant differences between how Republicans and Democrats evaluated the performance of the economy and their own personal finances, substantively speaking these differences are quite modest: for example, for the entire population the mean for Democrats is 5.15 while it is 4.99 for Republicans (on the seven-point scale for sociotropic attitudes). These minor substantive differences do not suggest that Democrats and Republicans perceived the performance of the nation's economy in fundamentally different ways. We also note that both Democrats and Republicans had positive views of their own finances. This is an important finding. If we find partisan differences in perceptions of the presidency, we cannot attribute them to differential views of the performance of the U.S. economy or one's own finances. Finally, the analysis of independents are similar.

In table 6.1 we present the results of a test of the performance-based thesis for both the policy- and non-policy-based expectations. The first column presents the results for Republicans only in 1998, while the second column represents Democrats and independents (what we will call "all others") in 1998. As can be seen the coefficients for Republicans and Democrats and all others in 1998 are significant and negative. Since our approval rating measure runs from 1 = excellent to 4 = poor, this means that both groups gave Clinton credit for the good economy, a finding that is consistent with Brownlow's expectations gap thesis and for our first hypothesis. All individuals expect a good economy and the results indicate that they give the president credit for it. Interestingly, we also find that Democrats and independents also give the president credit for their own finances (pocketbook attitudes), while Republicans do not. Clearly, Republicans are willing to give the president credit, but only so far.

For 1999, we find similar results. Again, both Republicans (column 3 of table 6.1) and Democrats and all others (column 4) give the president credit for a sound economy. The only difference relates to pocketbook effects. The coefficients for these effects are not significant in either model. Still, the results from table 6.1 provide support for our first hypothesis.

What happens when we turn our focus to a non-policy-making expectation of presidential performance? In all four models, for Republicans and Democrats and all others, for 1998 and 1999, the coefficient is significant and positive, indicating that perceptions of Clinton's ethics in general led to lower approval ratings. Considering the nature of Clinton's ethical standing

TABLE 6.1. Analysis of President Clinton's Approval Rating in 1998–99

	Republicans 1998	Democrats & Others 1998	Republicans 1999	Democrats & Others 1999
Sociotropic attitudes	-.47***	-.27***	-.27**	-.37***
	(.12)	(.08)	(.13)	(.09)
Pocketbook attitudes	-.10	-.30*	-.27	-.04
	(.20)	(.15)	(.23)	(.17)
Clinton's ethics gap	.06***	.05***	.05***	.04***
	(.005)	(.004)	(.006)	(.004)
Gender	.60***	.27	.57**	.35*
	(.23)	(.18)	(.27)	(.20)
Age	-.003	-.009	.006	-.004
	(.008)	(.006)	(.009)	(.007)
African American	.22	-1.01***	.62	-.58*
	(.97)	(.35)	(1.67)	(.34)
Latino	-1.25	.33	.31	.34
	(.73)	(.36)	(1.25)	(.57)
Income	-.008	-.001	-.03	.02
	(.04)	(.03)	(.05)	(.04)
TV news	-.001	-.02	.17	-.03
	(.02)	(.02)	(.27)	(.20)
N	325	516	249	397
Pseudo R^2	.24	.21	.16	.14

Note: "Republicans" = "Strong Republican," "Republican," and "Lean Republican"; "Democrats & Others" = "Strong Democrat," "Democrat," "Lean Democrat," "Other Party," and "No Party."

***significant at .01; ** significant at .05; * significant at .10.

and the impeachment case against him, this is not a particularly surprising finding. The results provide consistent support for our second hypothesis.

Conclusions

The expectations gap thesis long has been a mainstay of presidential literature. Presidential scholars argue that a gap exists between what the public expects and what presidents actually can do. They also assert that the public expects presidents to preside over a sound, healthy, and robust economy. When presidents do so the theory postulates that they are rewarded with higher approval ratings. The theory also postulates that this is a broadly held expectation. In sum, all Americans expect a sound economy. Hence, even the president's political opposition should both expect sound presidential performance on the economy and reward the president for good economic times.

The results of our analysis are consistent with Brownlow's view that everyone expects the president to lead on economic policy, as well as on a personal measure of the president's performance, Clinton's ethical behavior. Where does this leave us in terms of our analysis of the expectations gap thesis? In earlier chapters we found evidence in retrospective evaluations that two incumbent presidents are compared quite unfavorably to their predecessors and in particular to their immediate predecessor. In addition, once Bill Clinton left office his retrospective evaluations were far more favorable than his incumbent ratings. We then conducted an analysis of expectations as they relate to Bill Clinton during four different points in time, from the beginning of a reelection year to its end, a midterm election, and a nonnational election year. We found that various measures of Clinton's gap measures were quite similar over time and that his weighted gap measure was related to his approval ratings. Although the evidence with regard to electoral outcomes was mixed, we found that the president's weighted gap measure is related to both presidential and midterm election outcomes. Most of the evidence therefore supports the idea that there is an expectations gap effect. The findings in this chapter are consistent with our prior findings.

These results therefore indicate that it is important not merely to study the effects of the expectations gap, but also to examine its basic determinants, a subject we will turn to later in this book. Before we do so, however, given our findings with regard to Clinton's ethics in this chapter, we turn to another aspect of the expectations gap thesis: the idea that modern presidents face a greater number of scandals than in the past. We focus on one such scandal and ask, why did President Clinton survive the impeachment process?

CHAPTER 7

Presidential Scandal and the Expectations Gap

Why Did Clinton Survive the Impeachment Crisis?

Ours has become—as it continues to be, and should remain—a
society of large expectations. Government helped to generate these
expectations. It undertook to meet them. Yet, increasingly, it proved
unable to do so.

President Richard Nixon, State of the Union, January 22, 1970

This is a book on the presidential expectations gap. So why examine the
Clinton impeachment case? The primary reason is that another component
of the expectations gap thesis is the idea that because the public focuses increased demands on the White House, presidents are forced to push the let-
ter of the law to get things accomplished. This dynamic has resulted in an increasing propensity for congressional investigations of presidential scandal,
as well as an increase in congressional investigations of presidential performance and even presidential behavior. These scandals range from concerns
about Lyndon Johnson's prevarications regarding the Vietnam War (which
contributed to a so-called generation gap), to Richard Nixon's Watergate
scandals, to Reagan's Iran-contra scandal. Of all the scandals in recent years
few eclipse Bill Clinton's impeachment for its dramatic impact. Yet, while
the media questioned Clinton's ethics on a series of issues, he survived impeachment, eventually leaving office with the highest approval ratings of
any departing president. This result seems to run counter to the idea of an
expectations gap, both in terms of the high level of Clinton's approval ratings
and his ability to survive the scandal.

The obvious question then is why did Clinton survive? The answer to this question will tell us not only about the nature of the impeachment case against Bill Clinton but also whether performance-based criteria, such as Clinton's leadership on the economy, served to mitigate the negative effects of a presidential scandal. If so, this would be powerful evidence that the performance-based assumptions of the expectations gap thesis worked to Clinton's advantage.

There are reasons to believe that the healthy state of the U.S. economy preserved the Clinton presidency. On the eve of the Senate impeachment trial of President William Jefferson Clinton, the political analyst for the *Chicago Tribune,* William Neikirk, wrote, "at this moment, one overpowering fact has emerged: President Clinton's popularity appears to be speaking louder than the evidence." (Neikirk 1999). Despite the December 1998 House vote to impeach him, and polls showing that the public was deeply concerned with his personal ethics (further confirmed by our findings in the last chapter), Clinton's Gallup job approval rating remained in the 60 percent range. In explaining this apparently contradictory phenomenon, many political pundits pointed to the performance of the U.S. economy. For example, Kenneth T. Walsh of *U.S. News and World Report* (February 22, 1999, 29) wrote, "Most of the disparity between voters' judgment of his character and his job performance is due, quite simply, to the booming economy." A poll by the same magazine found that "73 percent of voters feel that because the economy is in such good shape, people will look the other way [on impeachment] as long as Clinton is reprimanded" (29). There may be another explanation why Clinton survived: he may have survived because of partisan considerations, again, a finding that would be more consistent with Wood's (2009) partisanship thesis.

Using data from a 1998 national survey, we test whether the economy, perceptions of Clinton's job performance (along several dimensions), and perceptions of his principal investigators, Judge Starr and the U.S. Congress, are related to public support for four possible methods of punishing the president: impeachment, resignation, congressional hearings on impeachment, and censure of the president.

The Politics of Impeachment

One aspect of the expectations gap thesis is the idea that the modern presidency has been racked by a series of continuing scandals. In particular, scholars such as Richard Rose (1997) argue that scandals are one piece of evidence that the presidency currently is under siege. Since the 1960s, Presidents

Johnson and Nixon faced skepticism and strong opposition to their Vietnam War policies; Nixon was engulfed in the various Watergate scandals; Ford was pilloried for pardoning Nixon; Carter's approval ratings plunged during the Bert Lance controversy; Reagan faced congressional investigations regarding the Iran-contra scandal, with Vice President George H. W. Bush, the next president, also involved in the same scandal; Clinton faced a variety of investigations culminating in the Monica Lewinsky scandal and his impeachment by the House of Representatives; and George W. Bush faced questions about whether he had cherry-picked evidence or perhaps outright lied to the American people about the possible presence of weapons of mass destruction (WMD) as a justification for the preemptive attack on Iraq in the spring of 2003. Scandals, therefore, have become a mainstay of the modern presidency. Our 1998 survey data allow us to directly examine one of these scandals: the impeachment of William Jefferson Clinton.

Impeachment

Article II, Section 4, of the Constitution prescribes, "The President, Vice President, and all civil Officers of the United States shall be removed from Office on Impeachment for, and Conviction of, Treason, Bribery, or other high Crimes and Misdemeanors." Partly because this provision is so seldom employed, particularly with regard to presidents, the impeachment process is a broadly misunderstood constitutional mechanism. It is not a criminal process, but rather a political one. As Walter Ehrlich (1974, 39) writes, impeachment "is a political decision (a vote) made by a political institution (the elected members of Congress) to remove a political official (the President, Vice-President, or other civil officers of the United States)." Ehrlich continues, "impeachment as understood by the Framers of the Constitution was not a criminal litigation. It was a political procedure used to remove officials who committed either a *criminal* or a *non-criminal* wrong" (italics in the original).

Likewise, in *Federalist Paper* #65, Alexander Hamilton notes, "The subjects of its [impeachment's] jurisdiction are those offences which proceed from the misconduct of public men, or, in other words, from the abuse or violation of some public trust. They are of a nature which may with particular propriety be denominated POLITICAL, as they relate chiefly to injuries done immediately to the society itself." Hamilton was remarkably prescient in describing the nature of this political process. He continues, "The prosecution of" impeachment cases "will seldom fail to agitate the passions of the whole community, and to divide it into parties more or less friendly or inimical to the accused. In many cases, it will connect with the preexisting factions, and will enlist all their animosities, partialities, influence, and interest on one side or on the other; and in such cases there will always be the greatest danger that the decision will be regulated more by the comparative strength of parties, than by the real demonstrations of innocence or guilt."

Hamilton deduced that impeachment involves not only the various constitutional actors (the House, the Senate, the chief justice of the Supreme Court, and the president), but also the two great evils the Founders feared most—party/faction and the unregulated passions of the people. What Hamilton forecast in March 1788 is to a remarkable degree a description of the political dynamics of the impeachment of President Clinton. The two articles of impeachment enacted on December 19, 1998, passed the House of Representatives mainly along partisan lines, with only five Democrats voting with the Republican majority. Likewise, the Senate vote on conviction broke down largely along party lines, with all Democrats voting for acquittal. While the House and the Senate voted, politicians and pundits alike kept a watchful eye on another key manifestation of American politics: public opinion polls.

Performance versus Personal Assessments of Clinton

Polls conducted as early as January and February 1998 indicated that while the public was concerned with the president's personal behavior, it also continued to approve of his performance as president. A *CBS News/New York Times* poll registered the president's approval rating at an astonishing 68 percent, even though 59 percent of the respondents from the same poll "were inclined to believe the president had an affair." Still, only 21 percent favored resignation and just 12 percent impeachment (*New York Times,* February 24, 1998, A1). Public opinion scholar John Zaller (1998, 182) notes that Clinton actually received a bounce in the polls "in the initial 10 days of the Lewinsky imbroglio," an approximate 10 percent increase. While the bounce was temporary, Clinton's approval ratings continued to hold steady at about 60 percent in most national polls throughout 1998, despite continuing evidence that a majority of Americans thought him guilty of both adultery and perjury.

As the debate over impeachment grew more heated, we sought data that would permit us to evaluate a range of arguments about the public's assessments of Clinton, his investigators, and the factors that may have had a bearing on preferences regarding the impeachment process. In our fall 1998 survey (which was conducted just prior to the House vote to impeach the president), 16.6 percent of our respondents rated President Clinton's job performance as "excellent," 38.6 percent as "good," 22.2 percent as "fair," and 22.6 percent as "poor." Not surprisingly, given these evaluations, support for impeachment of the president was limited: 68.6 percent opposed impeachment, while only 31.2 percent supported it. Similarly, support for the president's resignation was only 36.2 percent, while 63.8 percent opposed it. There was somewhat greater backing for the idea that Congress should hold hearings to investigate whether the allegations merited impeachment: 44.4 percent favored hearings while 55.6 percent were opposed to them. Public support was broadest for censure, with 65 percent of our respondents favoring this option and 35 percent opposing it. While the severity of the four options varies, each one has something in common; each method was a means of punishing the president for his actions.

Thus, as various polls (including our own) indicate, the president's job approval ratings were high and large majorities opposed both impeachment and resignation. At the same time, some form of punishment (continuing the impeachment process through hearings or censuring the president) had greater support. Given this dynamic, one possible explanation for Clinton's survival may be that the public saw the events leading up to the impeachment crisis as a largely personal and not a public matter. If so, then perceptions of Clinton's personal ethics also would be relevant. Asked to rate Clinton's personal ethics, 31 percent of our respondents gave Clinton the lowest possible rating. Slightly more than 70 percent rated his ethics as a five (the scale midpoint) or less. Consequently, while Clinton received broad support for his job performance, the public was far less enamored with his personal ethics. We therefore conjecture that two distinct kinds of evaluations of President Clinton were operating to affect preferences in the impeachment crisis: those who believed he was doing a good job would be more likely to oppose punishment, but those who had reservations about his ethics would be more likely to support punishing the president.

Clinton received higher ratings on the other three leadership dimensions that were included in our survey. While the mean value for high ethical standards was only 3.59 on the zero-to-ten scale, the mean for his ability to work well with Congress, even during the midst of an impeachment crisis, was 6.17. With regard to experience in foreign affairs the mean value was 6.59 and for sound judgment in a crisis it was 6.70. Since the White House had clear incentives to focus the public's attention on the president's other leadership attributes, rather than perceptions of his personal ethics, we also include these measures in our analysis. We do not use the weighted gap measures here, because we are more interested in direct measures of Clinton's performance as tests of the performance-based model of the expectations gap. The scale for these four leadership qualities ranges from 0, the lowest possible rating, to 10.

We then asked our respondents the following question: "Would you say that President Clinton's moral behavior has been a lot worse, slightly worse, about the same, slightly better, or a lot better than the moral behavior of other political leaders in Washington?" Slightly less than one-fifth, or 24.06 percent, responded "a lot worse," while 24.91 responded "slightly worse," meaning that almost half of our respondents viewed Clinton's morals as worse than other political leaders in Washington. On the other hand, the modal category was "about the same" with 43.65 percent in this response category. Only 5.32 percent thought Clinton had slightly better morals than other political leaders, with 2.06 percent believing that Clinton's morals were "a lot better." Slightly more than half of our respondents to this question, then, did not perceive Clinton's moral behavior as egregious in comparison to other political leaders.

So there is somewhat mixed evidence that our respondents disapproved of Clinton's personal ethics. And even for those who did not approve of Clinton's morality, some may have based their judgment about impeachment on their evaluations of his overall job performance on other leadership dimensions. The president and his advisers did much to encourage the public to think in this manner. The president was portrayed by White House officials as actively working on the business of government. The clear message from the White House was that the president had the nation's best interests in mind, while congressional Republicans were playing politics with a personal matter (Blumenthal 2003). Thus political pundit William Schneider (1998, 3042) was able to write, "Most Americans say they want Clinton to remain in office because they think he's doing a good job. They [therefore] set his personal values aside." But did they? That is the empirical question we will address.

It's the Economy, Stupid!

A second alternative explanation for Clinton's survival, one that is consistent with the performance-based assumptions of the expectations gap thesis, is that because the nation's economy was robust and individuals were financially better off, the public approved of the president's overall job performance, and therefore opposed removing him from office. They may have favored other lesser punishments than impeachment or resignation, such as censure or a congressional investigation, but they would be less likely to favor removing a president who had met their performance-based expectations with regard to the economy.

There is much support for this alternative in the scholarly literature, as well as from political pundits. Writing in early 1998, Zaller (1998, 186) speculated about the president's approval ratings and the impeachment crisis. He wrote, "My personal hunch . . . is that public support for Clinton will be more affected by future performance of the economy than by the clarity of the evidence concerning the charges against him." If so, then in the famous words of Democratic political consultant James Carville from the 1992 election, the reason that Clinton survived may have been, "It's the economy, stupid!"

As Clinton reminded the nation in his 1998 State of the Union address, and would remind them consistently thereafter, the nation's economy was in very good shape. In 1998 the unemployment rate was the lowest (during peacetime) since 1957. The inflation rate was the lowest in 30 years. Added to these results, the stock market had hit record levels and the budget had been balanced for the first time in decades. As a result, as we demonstrated in the last chapter, most Americans said they were pleased with the performance of the economy.

With a number of public opinion polls showing high levels of support for Clinton's management of the economy, was it the extraordinary performance of the U.S. economy that encouraged the public to oppose impeachment? There is ample support for this possibility in the scholarly literature. Academics long have argued that the economy is an important determinant of presidential approval ratings and electoral outcomes (see Tufte 1978; Kinder and Kiewiet 1979, 1981; Feldman 1982; MacKuen 1983; Ostrom and Simon 1985; Markus 1988, 1992; Kinder, Adams, and Gronke 1989; Erikson 1989; Brody 1991; Brace and Hinckley 1992). If the economy affects approval ratings and election results, then it also may have driven perceptions of the impeachment crisis.

The President's Investigators

There is a third possible explanation for Clinton's political survival. While the public broadly approved of Bill Clinton's job performance, support for those who sought to remove him from office was lukewarm at best. This is particularly evident with regard to Clinton's primary investigator, Independent Counsel Kenneth Starr. Starr quickly developed a negative image in the minds of many Americans. On the nightly news, he held impromptu meetings with the press while taking his garbage to the curb outside his house. The image created was not flattering: Kenneth Starr was only interested in digging up dirt on the president. The White House was delighted with this symbolic turn of events (Blumenthal 2003). It allowed them to build an image of Bill Clinton as presidential, while Kenneth Starr was portrayed as vengeful, politically motivated, and interested only in pursuing higher office (purportedly a Supreme Court appointment). The Clinton image machine thus portrayed Starr as far from an impartial investigator. As Edwards (2009, 67) writes:

> The White House fought back, accusing Starr of engaging in an intrusive political investigation motivated by a political vendetta against the president. The basic White House defense was that the president made a mistake (personal failing) in his private behavior, apologized for it, and was ready to move on to continue to do the people's business of governing the nation. Impeachment, the president's defenders said, was grossly disproportionate to the president's offense. The public found the White House argument compelling and strongly opposed the president's impeachment.

Ironically, Starr's personal behavior also raised questions about his fitness. The media reported that Starr surrounded himself with partisans in the Independent Counsel's office and that he often fell to his knees and prayed while jogging. The latter allegation suggested that he might even be part of what then First Lady Hillary Rodham Clinton famously characterized as "a vast right-wing conspiracy" (see Toobin 1999).

Given the critical attention that Starr received from the White House and many media outlets, it is not surprising that his job approval rating trailed far behind that of the president. When asked how they evaluated Independent Counsel Kenneth Starr's job performance, only 35.8 percent of our respondents rated it as either "excellent" or "good." Negative feelings toward the independent counsel were particularly strong, with 42.1 percent rating his performance as "poor," the lowest possible rating on our scale. Clinton's rating, by comparison, was 55.2 percent "excellent" or "good," and only 22.6 percent "poor." While the criteria for evaluating an independent counsel are surely quite different from those for a sitting president, the difference in the two men's overall approval ratings is striking.

While Starr received much of the attention from the media, the Office of the Independent Counsel was not the only one investigating the president's behavior. As Starr investigated possible criminal charges against the president, the Republican-controlled Congress considered impeachment. As it did with Kenneth Starr, the White House public relations operation also portrayed Republicans in Congress as politically motivated. Like the independent counsel, Congress had lower job approval ratings than the president. On our four-point scale, which ranged from "excellent" to "poor," only 35.3 percent rated Congress' performance as either "excellent" or "good," while 19 percent rated its performance as "poor." Even though a smaller percentage rated Congress's performance as "poor" compared to the president, overall its approval ratings lagged far behind the president's.

We also asked the following question regarding the constitutional impeachment crisis. "In your view, has the current situation involving the President, Ken Starr, and Congress damaged the United States?" Of the 841 respondents to this question, 25.09 percent answered "no," 11.7 percent said "slightly," 37.34 percent "somewhat," and 25.80 percent "a great deal." Approximately three-fourths of our respondents therefore considered the impeachment case as damaging to the nation. Who then did they blame?

For those respondents who believed the "current situation" damaged the nation (n = 608), we then asked, "Which of the following do you hold responsible for the damage to the United States?" A majority, 57.4 percent, answered "the President and the White House," 32.24 said "the leadership in Congress," and just 10.36 percent said "both equally." In terms of perceived damage to the United States, our respondents were more likely to blame the president.

Although most of our respondents blamed the president, we were interested in whether the Clinton impeachment had an impact on Congress. We asked the respondents a series of questions about the possible effect of impeachment on the upcoming congressional elections. We asked, "Congressional elections will be held this coming November. Will the current situation in Washington make it more likely that you will vote in November, less likely that you will vote, or will have no affect on whether you will cast a vote?" More than two-thirds, or 67.53, said it would "have no affect" and 30.11 percent said it would make them "more likely" to vote. Only 2.36 percent said they would be "less likely" to vote. The impeachment case therefore did not have a major impact on turnout.

For those who answered "more likely" (n = 400) we then asked, "Suppose that your U.S. representative to Congress supports efforts to impeach and remove President Clinton from office. Would such efforts make you more or less willing to vote for your U.S. representative in the upcoming elections?" Slightly more than half, or 50.35 percent, said they would be "less willing" to support their House member, while 49.65 percent said they would be "more likely" to support their House member. These questions reveal a deeply divided electorate with regard to impeachment. They also suggest that while our respondents did not blame Congress for the damage to the nation, they did intend to consider the impeachment case when they voted.

Hypotheses

With these data in mind, we test three explanations about why Clinton survived the impeachment ordeal. First, the White House strategy of portraying Clinton as presidential, combined with his own high approval ratings, may have helped him to survive. On the other hand, his personal ethics may have promoted support for punishment of some sort. Second, consistent with the performance-based assumptions of the expectations gap thesis, the state of the nation's economy and the fact that many Americans considered themselves to be better off financially may have led them to doubt the wisdom of rocking the boat during good economic times. Third, the low public support for the independent counsel and the Republican-controlled Congress may have worked to the president's advantage. Of these three explanations, which ones best explain why Clinton survived in office?

To answer this question we first need to create an appropriate dependent variable. Examining preferences for impeachment separately raises a serious methodological concern related to endogeneity. We conjecture that higher approval for the independent counsel would result in greater support for impeachment. At the same time, however, greater support for impeachment might lead to greater support for Starr because Starr was seen as the agent charged with establishing the case for impeachment. Unfortunately, given the cross-sectional nature of our data, there is no straightforward way for us to determine which way this effect occurs. We therefore need a modeling strategy that allows us to address the endogeneity issue.

Our strategy consists of three elements. First, we constructed an aggregated dependent variable so that impeachment is but one part of the overall "punishment" construct. We did this by creating a scale that combines the four possible punishment options. The scale runs from 0 (no punishment at all) to 1 (support for all four punishment options) (see figures 7.1 and 7.2). The scale passes the basic threshold test with a Cronbach's alpha value of .71. For those who preferred to employ only one punishment option, support

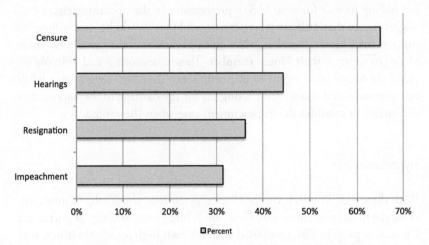

Fig. 7.1. Preferred Punishments by Percentage of Sample

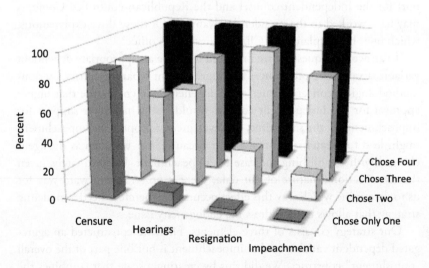

Fig. 7.2. Combinations of Punishments

was chiefly for censure (88%). One might expect that censure is an alternative to impeachment or resignation, and that those who support censure might oppose the other two options. But this was not the case, as indicated by the positive (but very small) correlations among the measures of these options. So, when two punishment options were chosen, 56 percent of our respondents picked censure and hearings. For those respondents who chose three of the options, 51 percent picked resignation, impeachment, and hearings, omitting only the most lenient option (censure). Thus the combined punishment variable reflects an increasing severity of punishment, ranging from no action to modest punishment to a maximum "throw the book" level of punishment.

In estimating the link between Starr and punishment, we then stripped the respondents' evaluation of Starr of any covariation with evaluations of Clinton. This indicated that if the preference for punishment is indeed driving the measure of the evaluation of Starr, it is doing so in the absence of any effect of the level of approval or opprobrium for Clinton. That assumption seems to us to be implausible. Indeed, in a simple OLS model using Starr's approval to predict preferences for punishing Clinton, inclusion of measures of Clinton's approval rating and the evaluation of Clinton's ethics as controls reduced the magnitude of the estimated coefficient of Starr's approval by nearly two-thirds—from -0.71 to -0.26. Third, we ran the model with and without the evaluation of Starr, and found that the estimated coefficients to be remarkably stable. These results are shown in table 7.1, column 3. As is evident, none of the estimated coefficients changed signs, none lost or gained statistical significance, and the proportion of variance explained in the punishment variable dropped only slightly (from a pseudo R^2 of 0.24 to 0.23). And fourth, we remain modest in what we can conclude from the analysis. Should the relationship between approval for Starr and preference for punishment prove to be substantively and statistically significant, the result will be consistent with the hypothesis that dislike for Clinton's enemies reduces the preference for punishing Clinton—but it cannot be taken as definitive evidence. More convincing evidence is provided, however, if we consider the results related to all three of our hypotheses.

We therefore use all three explanations for Clinton's survival with the punishment scale as our dependent variable to test six hypotheses. With regard to the president's leadership we posit the following:

H1: Among respondents, the higher the president's personal job approval rating the less likely one will be to support punishing the president, which is represented by lower values on the five-point punishment scale.

H2: Likewise, the more positively one evaluates Clinton's personal ethics, the less likely one should be to support punishment (represented by lower values on the punishment scale).

H3: The higher one rates Clinton's performance on other presidential leadership tasks (foreign policy, the ability to work well with Congress, and his overall sound judgment in crisis situations) the less likely one should be to support punishment.

With regard to the economy we hypothesize:

H4: The more positive one's assessment of the performance of the economy is, the less likely one will be to support punishment.

H5: Likewise, the better the respondent's own financial circumstances, the less likely one will be to support punishment.

Finally, with regard to the president's political investigators we posit:

H6: The lower of the approval rating of the independent counsel, Kenneth Starr, and the lower the approval rating of the U.S. Congress, the less support there will be for punishing the president.

We also control for an array of demographic and political factors. Regarding demographics, Bill Clinton received strong support in the 1992 and 1996 elections from women, the elderly, African Americans, and Latinos. Hence, for each of these groups we expect lower levels of support for any form of punishing the president. On the other hand, we conjecture that the higher one's income, the more likely one should be to support punishment. We also control for the respondent's level of education though we offer no directional hypothesis for it.

With regard to political factors, knowledge of the details of the allegations that would form the basis of the impeachment case should be important. "The Starr Report" was transmitted to the House Judiciary Committee along with much media fanfare. It identified in often rather salacious detail the independent counsel's charges against the president. Since the report's transmittal occurred prior to our survey, we asked how much respondents had read or heard about Ken Starr's report. Only 3.3 percent said they had read or heard nothing at all about the report, while 78.5 percent said they had read or heard "a great deal" or "a moderate amount" about it. Since the report was highly critical of the president, we hypothesize that the more one heard about it the more likely one would be to favor punishment.

Other political factors also may have had an affect on the impeachment crisis. The more conservative one is ideologically the more likely one should be to support punishment, while Democrats should be less likely than Republicans and independents to do so.

Given the array of independent variables included, it is necessary to consider whether multicollinearity may mask or distort the relationships estimated in the model. To address this potential problem, we calculated the tolerance of each of the independent variables. Tolerance indicates the fraction of the variance in each of the independent variables that is not "explained by" the other independent variables. Tolerance ranges from zero (all of the variance for a given variable is accounted for by the other independent variables—or perfect multicollinearity) to one (none of the variance is accounted for). Low tolerances generally lead to unstable and inefficient estimates. The lowest tolerance was, not surprisingly, for Clinton's approval rating. The other independent variables accounted for 34 percent of the variation in this measure, resulting in a tolerance of 0.66. Tolerances for the presidential performance measures were also moderately affected, with scores ranging from .73 for sound judgment in a crisis to .81 for ability to work well with Congress. Tolerances of these magnitudes generally do not pose serious multicollinearity problems for models using large data sets, as is the case here. However, given that the measure of approval for Clinton had the lowest tolerance, we include in the analysis a comparison model that excludes this explanatory variable from the model (see the second column of table 7.1).

Our Results

Since our dependent variable is ordinal, we employ an ordered logit model. The results are presented in table 7.1. We also estimated the magnitudes of the effects of each of the variables that proved to be statistically significant by calculating the average number of punishment types (0 through 4) that would be preferred by a respondent at the extreme ends of the scales for that variable. For example, we calculated that respondents who rated Clinton's ethics as "extremely good," but had average scores for all other independent variables, would prefer (on average) to impose 0.73 of the punishment categories. But respondents who rated Clinton's ethics as "extremely poor" would impose (average) 1.88 punishments—making a difference of 1.15 for this variable. The estimates were derived by first calculating the logit for each of the levels of punishment scale, setting all independent variables at

TABLE 7.1. Logit Analysis of Punishment Scale

	Punishment Scale (Clinton approval included)	Punishment Scale (Clinton approval excluded)	Punishment Scale (Starr approval removed)
Clinton Variables			
Clinton's approval rating	-.77***	—	.79***
	(.11)		(.11)
Clinton's ethics	-.30***	-.35***	-.32***
	(.04)	(.04)	(.04)
Sound judgment in a crisis	-.04	-.11**	-.06
	(.04)	(.04)	(.04)
Experience in foreign affairs	.05	.03	.07
	(.04)	(.04)	(.04)
Work well with Congress	-.05	-.08*	-.07
	(.04)	(.04)	(.04)
Economic Variables			
Sociotropic attitudes	.15**	.09	.12*
	(.07)	(.07)	(.07)
Pocketbook attitudes	-.00	-.00	.01
	(.12)	(.12)	(.12)
Impeachment Investigators			
Starr's approval rating	.29**	.38***	—
	(.09)	(.09)	
U.S. Congress approval rating	-.16*	-.11	-.25**
	(.09)	(.09)	(.09)
Demographic Factors			
Education	.08	.07	.07
	(.07)	(.07)	(.07)
Age	-.001	-.001	-.001
	(.004)	(.005)	(.005)
Gender	.04	.04	.01
	(.14)	(.14)	(.14)
Income	-.02	-.02	-.01
	(.03)	(.03)	(.03)
African American	-.58*	-.67*	-.58*
	(.37)	(.35)	(.35)
Latino	-.17	-.16	-.13
	(.35)	(.35)	(.35)
Political Factors			
Read or heard of the Starr report	.05	.03	.06
	(.09)	(.09)	(.09)
Ideology	.07	.07	.09*
	(.05)	(.05)	(.05)
Democrats	-.33**	-.38**	-.42**
	(.16)	(.16)	(.16)
N	763	764	774
Pseudo R^2	.24	.21	.23

*** significant at the .01 level; ** significant at the .05 level; * significant at the .10 level.

TABLE 7.2. Estimated Magnitudes of Effects of Independent Variables, Holding All Else Constant at Mean Values

Explanatory Variable	Average Number of Punishments at Lowest Scale Value	Average Number of Punishments at Highest Scale Value	Magnitude of Effect
Clinton's approval (1 = poor 4 = excellent)	2.41	0.82	1.59
Clinton's ethics (0 = extremely poor 10 = extremely good)	1.88	0.73	1.15
Starr's approval (1 = excellent 4 = poor)	1.99	0.94	1.05
Congress's approval (1 = excellent 4 = poor)	1.68	1.03	0.65
U.S. economy (1 = very poor 7 = very good)	0.94	1.39	0.45

their means except for the variable that was the focus of interest. We then converted the logit values into probabilities for each respondent. Finally we calculated the sum of the products of the probability for each level of punishments (0 through 4) for each respondent. This permitted us to calculate the average number of punishments preferred across each of the independent variables. These estimates are presented in table 7.2.

One of the primary explanations provided for Clinton's survival of the impeachment crisis relates to the president's personal popularity. We find that the higher one rated Clinton's job approval, the less likely one was to support punishing the president. This is consistent with conventional wisdom on the subject, as well as our own first hypothesis (H1). More important, this relationship accounted for a change from a preference for an average of 2.41 punishments for those rating Clinton's performance as "poor" to 0.82 for those who expressed a rating of "excellent." Consistent with hypothesis H2 we also find that the more positively one rated Clinton's ethics, the less likely one was to favor punishing the president. As we noted, unfortunately for the president, while he had high job approval ratings, far fewer respondents to our survey gave him favorable ratings on his personal ethics. Consequently, for many individuals more negative attitudes about his ethics translated into stronger support for punishing the president. To this extent, then, the two personal factors worked at cross-purposes.

On the other hand, White House attempts to shift the debate to other leadership dimensions appear to have failed. Our model provides little support for the idea that public perceptions of Clinton's performance in foreign affairs, his ability to work well with Congress, or his sound judgment in a crisis are independently related to support for punishment (H3). Considered as a whole, then, evaluations of Clinton's performance proved to be something of a double-edged sword, though his overall job approval had a greater impact than did assessments of his ethical behavior.

This assessment is confirmed by inspection of the results when Clinton's overall approval rating is removed from the model. The estimated effects of perceptions of Clinton's ethics remain strong and significant. The magnitudes of the coefficients for the other presidential leadership dimensions remain modest, though two of them increase in magnitude sufficiently to reach levels of statistical significance (judgment in a crisis and working well with Congress). The measure of experience in foreign affairs remains statistically not significant.

If the president's public standing had both positive and negative consequences, what effect did the perceptions of the economy have? As noted, most of the speculation was that the economy, which was strong, would work to the president's advantage. This finding also would be consistent with the performance-based assumptions of the expectations gap thesis. Our findings do not support this hypothesis (H4). Instead, as shown in table 7.2, we find that the more positively one evaluates the performance of the U.S. economy the more likely one is to favor punishment of the president. Although the magnitude of the effect is modest (shifting the average preferred number of punishments by only 0.45), it is nevertheless statistically significant and runs counter to the direction we had hypothesized.

We believe the reason for this counterintuitive finding is that our estimates control for presidential approval, which is affected by perceptions of the economy, thereby removing the indirect effect of the economy on punishment preferences. Once presidential approval is removed from the model, as shown in the second column of table 7.1, neither of the economy variables are significantly related to preferences for punishment. Simply put, once we control for presidential popularity, better perceptions of the economy increased the appetite for punishment. Furthermore, as for one's own finances, this variable is not directly related to the punishment scale at all (H5).

What accounts for our counterintuitive findings regarding the economy? We speculate that while the public considers economic performance to be an important determinant of how well a president is performing his or her job (see Zaller 1998), the impeachment debate was not about economics. It was about presidential ethics and popularity. As such, economic factors contributed to the president's survival indirectly by promoting higher approval ratings. It did not, however, directly diminish support for punishing the president.

If the president's popular support was a double-edged sword, and the robust economy actually led to higher levels of support for punishment, how did the president survive? The third explanation for Clinton's survival is that negative evaluations of his enemies (the independent counsel, Kenneth Starr, and the Republican-controlled U.S. Congress) diminished preferences for punishment. We find that higher ratings for Kenneth Starr's job performance are related to higher levels of support for punishing the president. As shown in table 7.2, those who rated Starr most positively preferred (on average) 1.99 punishments, compared to 0.94 for those who rated him most poorly. As we noted, however, the percentage of our respondents who rated Starr's performance as "poor" was quite high (over 40 percent). Thus, overall, Starr's low approval ratings appear to have dampened public support for punishing the president. But these results must be interpreted with caution: despite our use of the aggregated "punishment" variable, and our controls for Clinton's ethics and performance measures, we cannot reject the possibility that the effect is bidirectional. Moreover, there is considerable covariation between the Starr and Clinton ratings. Once the presidential approval measure is removed from the model, as shown in the second column of table 7.1, the estimated effect of Starr's approval increases modestly (from 0.29 to 0.38). This is as one would expect, but it also illustrates the overall stability of the model results.

Consistent with our sixth hypothesis (H6), as was the case with Starr, the coefficient for evaluations of Congress also is significant (though only at the one-tailed level), again suggesting that a higher approval rating for one of Clinton's primary investigators is positively related to increased support for punishing the president. Note that the effect is more muted than it was for Starr, resulting in a variation in preferred punishments of only 0.65, on average. Again, since Congress received lower approval evaluations than the president, this dynamic appears to have worked to President Clinton's advantage.

In addition to these results, only one of the basic demographic variables was related to the punishment scale. African Americans were less likely to support punishment but again the coefficient only meets a one-tailed test of significance. Finally, and not surprisingly, Democrats were less likely to favor punishment than were independents and Republicans.

Note that the model proved to be quite stable when the measure of presidential approval was omitted. None of the estimated coefficients changed signs, and the magnitudes of the changes were modest. The only changes of statistical note were the (modestly) increased magnitudes of several of the coefficients for the measures of Clinton's presidential leadership. In general, then, correlations among the independent variables employed do not alter the general conclusions of our analysis.

In summary, evaluations of the president proved to be something of a double-edged sword, with his approval ratings undercutting support for punishment, while negative evaluations of his ethics increased support for it. The more favorably one viewed the state of the economy (controlling for presidential approval) the more likely one was to favor increased punishment. Thus, while one can argue that the economy had indirect positive effects on Clinton's approval ratings, it is difficult to argue that the economy directly helped Clinton survive the impeachment crisis. Finally, with regard to the president's principal investigators, higher support for both Starr and Congress was related to increased support for punishment. Since both actors had relatively low approval ratings (especially in comparison to the president), this factor worked to the president's political advantage.

Conclusions

As Alexander Hamilton noted in *Federalist Paper* #65 the impeachment process is a decidedly political one. We have shown that evaluations of President Clinton represented a double-edged sword. While his (positive) job approval ratings were strongly related to lower levels of support for punishing the president, his (negative) personal ethics ratings promoted increased support for punishment. The economy did have an affect, but not in the expected direction. Indirectly, favorable economic views boosted Clinton's approval rating, which in turn reduced the desire for punishment. But the direct effect was negative: those with a more favorable view of the economy actually were more likely to favor punishing the president. Stated differently, once the effects of a robust economy on approval ratings are controlled for, those who benefited most from that economy were more inclined to want to punish the president.

This finding clearly is not consistent with the performance-based assumptions of the expectations gap thesis, for those who perceived a stronger economy were more likely to favor punishment. Attitudes toward Clinton's partisan opponents, both in Congress and in the Independent Counsel's Office, better explain the pattern of support and opposition to impeachment and the other related punishments.

In this regard, Clinton may well have been both lucky and smart in his choice of political enemies. Evaluations of the president's main political inquisitors, Independent Counsel Kenneth Starr and the Republican-controlled Congress, were related to the level of support for punishing the president (with higher evaluations related to greater support for punishing the president). Since Starr and Congress had much lower approval ratings than did the president, this factor appears to have worked to Bill Clinton's political advantage. The historical record demonstrates that the president and his advisers understood the importance of this political dynamic. They cultivated it throughout the crisis, continually polling the public to determine what it was thinking and repeatedly casting the independent counsel and his office in a negative partisan light. Meanwhile, the president's advisers created a public relations strategy that presented Bill Clinton as hard at work on the people's business (including maintaining a healthy economy), even when in private he was deeply concerned about his own personal fate. The president even delivered an upbeat State of the Union address in 1999 in the midst of his own impeachment trial, both to demonstrate that he was hard at work and to take advantage of a unique opportunity to directly influence public opinion (Blumenthal 2003). Clinton was rewarded for his political efforts. The public continued to support him, even though, as our data show, it had serious reservations about his personal ethics.

On a normative level, we believe our conclusions raise some serious and even disturbing concerns regarding future cases of impeachment. Since our results highlight the importance of the evaluations of the president and his principal investigator, they raise the specter of a future presidential investigation in which prosecutors use polling and public relations techniques to sell their case for (or against) impeachment to the public. This would almost certainly prove to be institutionally and politically corrosive, but given our findings it may be an inevitable result and legacy of the Clinton impeachment case, for as Hamilton reminds us, the impeachment process indeed is fundamentally political. We can therefore hope that impeachments take place only rarely and with the utmost need.

CHAPTER 8

George W. Bush

War and the Economy

[O]ne of our jobs is to pick and choose the time when we spend
capital, be judicious in how we approach these issues, to not create
false expectations, to be realistic about what's possible, and lead.

George W. Bush, interview with the *Wall Street Journal*, April 8, 2002

Unlike Bill Clinton's presidency, which was mostly identified with domestic
policy issues, particularly the economy and the budget deficit, the presidency
of George W. Bush was associated with the politics of war. Though Bush had
little foreign policy experience or expertise when he entered the presidential
office, and though he intended to focus his presidency on such domestic
issues as education and tax cuts, the events of September 11, 2001, utterly
transformed his presidency. From that date onward, the Bush presidency
was defined by the war on terror, the invasion of Afghanistan, and the second war in Iraq. Though Bush had domestic policy accomplishments (e.g.,
a prescription drug bill, the "No Child Left Behind" education bill), perceptions of his presidency also involve such controversial issues as whether there
was credible evidence of weapons of mass destruction in Iraq, whether the
search for Osama bin Laden at Tora Bora was thorough, and whether the use
of enhanced interrogation techniques such as water boarding promoted the
nation's security. All of these controversial issues share one common factor:
they all fall under the president's authority as commander in chief.

George W. Bush's presidency represents an interesting comparison case
to that of Bill Clinton. Foreign policy was at the forefront of the Bush presidency. In addition to this focus, the Bush presidency contrasts with the
Clinton presidency in other interesting ways. While the seventh year of the

Clinton presidency ushered in good economic times, the U.S. economy officially slid into recession late in 2007, a few months after our survey was conducted. And while Clinton's popularity was extremely high as his presidency came to an end, in 2007 there already was a sense of Bush fatigue, with George W. Bush's ratings falling consistently below 40 percent in national polls. Finally, both presidents dealt at this time in their presidency with divided government, though the party in control of Congress was different (Republicans for Clinton, Democrats for Bush). In this chapter we examine the impact of the expectations gap on a second incumbent president. In particular, we examine how both the economy and war affected the evaluations of President George W. Bush.

Expectations and War

One of the principal founders of the institutional presidency, Louis Brownlow (1969, 43), writes, "In the endowment of leadership by the Constitution and custom, there remains . . . the greatest expectation of all . . . the expectation that the President, with his unquestioned responsibility for maintaining the initiative in foreign affairs, shall keep us at peace; but if war does come, he shall as Commander-in-Chief lead us to victory." While expectations are broad, Brownlow notes that they may very well be unreasonable. "Here again we fail to give" the president the "authority commensurate with his responsibilities, but despite this failure to provide him with the means of accomplishing what we ask him to do, we still expect the President to give effect to the national purpose" (43).

While we think of the president's responsibility as commander in chief as one of the primary executive responsibilities, this was not always the case. Initially expectations were modest, except in time of war. As Hamilton wrote in *Federalist Paper* #69, as commander in chief the president was to be nothing more than the supreme commander of the military and naval forces, "as first General and Admiral of the confederacy." Since the enumerated war power rests with Congress, as well as the power to declare even limited wars (e.g., letters of marque and reprisal), one can narrowly interpret the commander in chief clause as representing a grant of power to the presidency only when the nation is at war or when war is imminent. Certainly, the founders were aware of the potential power that a war president could wield. They were particularly concerned with the power of standing armies and often cited the name of Oliver Cromwell to justify their fear of a renegade military under the control of a ruthless dictator. It is therefore unlikely that the Founders intended to give the presidency an unlimited grant of authority in foreign affairs. Given their concerns about dictatorship, and the few foreign policy powers they granted the executive in relation to the more specific powers delegated to the legislative branch, it is apparent that the founders wanted a commander in chief capable of defending the nation in wartime, but also one who would not be a threat during peacetime. In other words, they wanted the president to be accountable. In this regard it is also useful to remember that when George Washington served as commander in chief during the Revolutionary War, that position was subservient to the legislature. We also can listen to James Madison, who in his notes on the Constitutional Convention wrote, "A standing military force, with an overgrown Executive will not long be safe companions of liberty" (Farrand 1966, I:464–65).

One way to limit the power of the president was to limit the size of the standing army. At the Constitutional Convention there was an attempt to specify the size of the army. While this motion failed, early in the history of our republic the nation had few military resources. The army was small, the navy underequipped, and defense depended inordinately on the various state militias (Waterman 2010, chap. 2). The militia system, however, proved ineffectual during the War of 1812. And while war presidents such as Madison, James K. Polk, and Lincoln exerted considerable authority as commander in chief, during the nineteenth century issues of war and foreign policy were not the primary focus of most presidential administrations.

This dynamic changed irrevocably with the presidency of William McKinley and the Spanish-American War of 1898. The United States emerged from that war with its first imperial possessions and with them the continuing task of administering overseas properties. As the twentieth century dawned, with Theodore Roosevelt at the helm, American was poised to assume a major role on the world stage. As it did, the president's authority as commander in chief necessarily expanded to meet the nation's ever more active military role abroad. Hence, the president's power in this capacity expanded under Theodore Roosevelt and even more so during World War I under the leadership of Woodrow Wilson. By the end of World War II, America stood at center stage as a nuclear world power.

During the post–World War II years, as the nation's international role adjusted, so too did public expectations of presidential performance regarding foreign policy. Over time the American public came to expect that presidents would adopt a more active role as commander in chief. Why did expectations change? Why did an American public, ever fearful of the power of the U.S. government, and once fearful of standing armies, acquiesce in the birth of the national security state and the evolution of a powerful presidential role in foreign affairs? This development did not occur without controversy. Even during the midst of World War II, Franklin Roosevelt feared that once the war ended the nation would revert to its affinity for isolationism. Less than a decade after the war, the so-called Great Debate in Congress brought the issues of isolationism and internationalism directly to the political forefront. One of the primary reasons that Dwight Eisenhower felt compelled to run for the Republican nomination in 1952 was to stop Senator Robert Taft, an inveterate isolationist, from winning the nomination and the presidency. Eisenhower, a devout internationalist, believed that it was unsafe for America to retreat into a fantasy world of isolationism.

It therefore was not a fait accompli that the United States would seek to become a dominant player on the world stage once the Second World War came to an end. With a strong isolationist sentiment still brewing inside the country, during Harry S. Truman's presidency a new Department of Defense was established, along with the National Security Council (NSC) and the Central Intelligence Agency (CIA). Through the Marshall Plan the United States played a primary role in bringing order to a destabilized and war-ravished Europe. The United States also entered into a series of international agreements including the United Nations and the North Atlantic Treaty Organization. Most significant of all, when Truman believed international events impelled the United States to go to war in Korea, he did so, not by asking Congress for a declaration of war, as the Constitution prescribes, but by declaring unilaterally that America was joining a "police action" consistent with its various treaty obligations.

The Truman presidency represented an astonishing transformation in the president's war power, one that likely would have amazed even Franklin Roosevelt. And yet with a change of administration and the election of a Republican president, Dwight Eisenhower, in 1952, the nation continued on a path toward greater executive involvement in foreign affairs. Eisenhower used the newly formed CIA to overthrow unfriendly governments. He also used the NSC as a principal mechanism for the formulation of American foreign policy. Though he was wise enough to avoid an entanglement in Vietnam, Eisenhower, and then Kennedy, took incremental steps that allowed Lyndon Johnson to transform that conflict into a full-fledged war, again without seeking a formal congressional declaration of war. While the Vietnam War, like the Korean War, proved unpopular at home, America did not budge from its commitment to playing the dominant role on the world stage.

Again, this utter transformation in both elite and public expectations seems peculiar, given our nation's traditional fear of standing armies, big government, and what would later come to be known as the "imperial presidency." Yet expectations changed in response to a series of events. The end of World War II also ushered in the nuclear era and the Cold War. With the nuclear genie out of the bottle, isolationism suddenly seemed like a quaint nineteenth-century construct, rather than a viable foreign policy. Concomitant with the nuclear threat, the fear of international communism unsettled all reason, as Americans feared subversion at home as well as abroad. A nation enveloped in paroxysms of trepidation and outright panic viewed this external threat as far more compelling than the old idea that its own military would rise against its basic freedoms, though that idea reemerged in the fiction of *Seven Days in May*.

Rather than expecting the presidency to take a backseat in foreign affairs, the public looked to the White House for strong leadership and a firm continuing commitment to protect the nation. With the national security threat magnified, presidents were no longer occasional commanders in chief in wartime only. In a world in which one demented individual could place their finger directly on the nuclear button, both the public and elites embraced a more powerful role for the president in foreign affairs. While a former advocate of a strong presidency, Arthur Schlesinger Jr. (1973), noted the dangers of this developing trend in his work on the "imperial presidency," there was no ready alternative to a strong executive. In fact, the job of commander in chief became a twenty-four-hour-a-day, seven-day-a-week occupation. As the George W. Bush presidency demonstrates, even a president who planned on dedicating his administration to a domestic policy agenda could suddenly find his presidency focused on multiple foreign policy crises simultaneously.

Consequently, the presidency today exists in an entirely different realm of public and elite expectations than it did at the time of the founding. As the quote from Brownlow ably instructs, presidents have no greater calling than to preserve the peace. Their authority as commander in chief is now a permanent fixture of the presidential office. The public expects our presidents to provide leadership. No president can escape these expectations.

War and Presidential Approval

Although strong leadership in foreign affairs is now a basic expectation of the presidency, our own findings (delineated in chapter 4) demonstrate that the public ranks "experience in foreign affairs" lower than the other three leadership qualities we asked our respondents to rate. Four of the five surveys were taken during the Clinton years, when the nation was more concerned with domestic than foreign policy issues. Yet, even in the post-9/11 era, as represented by the results of our 2007 survey, the public continued to rate this leadership quality behind each of the others.

On the other hand, the president's ability to show "sound judgment in a crisis" consistently ranks as the number-one attribute. This finding suggests a bit of a disjuncture, for a well-informed public, concerned with sound judgment in a crisis, should be committed to finding presidents with vast experience in foreign affairs. That our respondents consistently did not do so suggests that they look for personal qualities of strong leadership, perhaps an image of strength, rather than a well-rounded resume of foreign policy accomplishments. One can interpret these results as somewhat contradictory, perhaps in itself yet another manifestation of unrealistic public expectations of presidential performance. It also likely reflects that fact that except at a moment of international crisis, the public generally is more concerned with domestic policy concerns and in particular the economy. Still, it is a bit odd that we find that the public values sound judgment much more than foreign policy experience. Our findings may help explain Barack Obama's successful 2008 campaign approach. His argument in that election came down to the idea that he alone had the best judgment in foreign policy—since he alone among the major contenders was the only one who had initially opposed the Iraq War. While Hillary Clinton and John McCain had far more practical foreign policy experience, Obama always brought the issue back to judgment. In this sense, then, our findings are consistent with the results of the 2008 presidential election.

Beyond the comparison of experience versus sound judgment, a venerable literature on public opinion demonstrates that war can exert contradictory affects on a president's stature over time. Mueller's (1973) classic work on the presidency and public opinion finds that while presidents benefit in the short term from foreign policy crises, over time this support evaporates and a war becomes a drag on the president's approval rating. Brace and Hinckley (1992) and Bartels and Zaller (2001) also demonstrate the deleterious effects of prolonged war over time. Based on their findings, since our survey of George W. Bush occurred during the fifth year of the war in Afghanistan and the fourth year of the war in Iraq, we anticipate that overall our respondents should reflect discontent with the president's policies and performance.

Another reason to so hypothesize is drawn from Schier's (2009, 10–11) conclusion, based on an event analysis, that the "turning point in the Bush presidency was clearly the Iraq war." Up to the war in Iraq the public perceived most of the events of the Bush presidency in positive terms. Schier continues: "The successful invasion was just about the last good international news that the Bush administration received. From 2003 through 2005, negative fallout from the war buffeted the administration: the Abu Ghraib prison abuse scandal in Iraq, the Valerie Plame CIA leak controversy, no weapons of mass destruction (WMD) found in Iraq, and no clear connection of Iraq with 9/11 revealed" (10–11).

As Patrick Dobel (2010) argues, the negativity of the press and public reaction was fueled by widespread and growing perceptions that the administration had mismanaged the war. As Dobel (2010, 70) writes, "George W. Bush's moral certainty and lack of doubt warred with his prudence from the very beginning." From the 9/11 attacks onward, Bush "framed his response . . . as a 'monumental struggle between good and evil'." Furthermore, rather than carefully analyzing all data, Bush's "decisions were largely generated from a small group of individuals governed by very rigid frames of the world."

Given the obvious centrality of war to the Bush presidency and its inherently controversial nature, we asked several specific questions related to George W. Bush's foreign policy performance. With regard to the response to 9/11 we asked, "Overall, do you think that President George W. Bush is doing an excellent, good, fair, or poor job in the broader War on Terror?" A modest 10.7 percent rated the president's performance as "excellent," 28.6 percent as "good," 27 percent as "fair," and 33.7 percent as "poor." Interestingly, given that the president often made September 11, 2001, a theme to justify the wars in Afghanistan and Iraq, the modal response to our question was "poor" and 60.7 percent rated the president's performance as either "fair" or "poor." This is an interesting finding because while the justification behind the invasion of Iraq was controversial and became even murkier and more contentious over time, there was a widespread sense that the war on terror was justified. After all, it was initiated after a surprise attack on U.S. soil that killed over 3,000 people and included attacks on New York City and Washington, D.C. Still, we find that over time the public grew weary of conflict, even the war on terror, and did not reward the president with higher ratings; this despite the fact that the Bush administration could and did boast that it had kept the nation safe from another attack.

The war on terror was not the most controversial aspect of George W. Bush's foreign policy. The war in Iraq starkly divided the nation even before the invasion commenced in March 2003. We therefore anticipate that that by 2007 our respondents would have a dim view of the war and the president's performance given the controversial nature of the invasion, the continued hullabaloo that followed Bush's bold—some would say arrogant—proclamation of "Mission Accomplished" (May 1, 2003) on the stage-crafted deck of the carrier USS *Abraham Lincoln,* the Abu Ghraib scandal, the failure to locate weapons of mass destruction, and an increased number of casualties from the war front. To measure opinion, we first asked, "In your view is the U.S. winning the war in Iraq?" Only 20 percent of our respondents answered "yes," 65.2 percent responded "no," and 14.8 percent answered either unsure or don't know. These findings are consistent with other national polls that demonstrated that the public did not believe the U.S. government was making steady progress in Iraq. Because these perceptions may be based on any number of criteria (including Iraq's domestic affairs, the intractability of the situation), we were particularly interested in determining how our respondents specifically rated the president's performance. We therefore asked, "Overall, do you think President George W. Bush is doing an excellent, good, fair, or poor job as Commander-in-Chief of the U.S. Armed forces in the War in Iraq?" In response, 7.9 percent rated Bush's performance as "excellent," 22 percent "good," 21.7 percent "fair," and 48.4 percent "poor." Just under a majority of our respondents then gave the president the lowest possible evaluation, while 70.1 percent rated his performance as either "fair" or "poor." These findings are consistent with the analysis of previous research suggesting that the longer the duration of a war the lower the president's approval ratings will be.

To get a better sense of how and why our respondents agreed or disagreed with the president we asked a follow-up question: "Regarding the War in Iraq, which of the following options do you most prefer? Should we a) send in additional troops the President recommends and stay the course as long as necessary; b) send the additional troops, but only in the short term; c) hold troop levels where they are now; d) begin to draw down U. S. forces in Iraq now, or should we e) immediately pull out U. S. troops from Iraq?" Of these the first option represented the surge proposal espoused by the White House, with each subsequent option a further step away from the president's stated position. About a quarter, or 22.4 percent, of our respondents agreed with the president that the United States should send in additional troops and stay the course. Furthermore, 16.3 percent agreed that additional troops should be sent to Iraq, with the caveat that they remain only for a short period of time, while 9.4 percent favored leaving the troops at their present level. If we broadly group these respondents as more favorable to the president's position, that is, they do not favor a troop reduction, we find that 48.1 percent opposed troop reductions. With regard to the clear anti-administration positions, 34.8 percent favored the option of beginning to withdraw troops while 17.2 percent favored an immediate withdrawal. These responses suggest a highly divided public, with about half of our respondent's either willing to consider the president's option or at least expressing opposition to troop reductions. Hence, on this specific policy proposal there is stronger support for the president's position than there was when we asked our respondents to evaluate George W. Bush's performance as commander in chief in the Iraq War. These results provide some evidence why there were major divisions within Congress over the issue of withdrawing troops, despite overwhelming opposition to the war itself. On tactics, nearly half our respondents were close to the president's policy preferences.

This finding is consistent with other evidence from a September 2007 Gallup poll. Gallup "asked whether respondents favored the plan of General David Petraeus and President Bush to withdraw about 40,000 troops from Iraq by the summer of 2009, but not to make a commitment to further withdrawals until that time. Gallup also asked whether respondents supported a plan introduced by Democratic senators that called for the withdrawal of most U.S. troops within nine months. The muddled results revealed that similar and large percentages of Americans favored each plan—and 45 percent favored both plans" (Edwards 2009, 94–95).

The president was not the only one to present a position on the war in Iraq. Under intense pressure, the president was forced to consider the options proposed by the Iraq Study Group. These options considered a short-term "surge" as an option, although the preponderance of the recommendations called for a radical new approach to the administration's war policy. In sum, the report could not be viewed as supportive of the Bush administration's conduct of the war. We wanted to know if our respondents paid attention to this report. We therefore asked, "Did you hear about the report written about options for ending the war in Iraq that was written by the Iraq Study Group, headed by James Baker and Lee Hamilton?" A solid 45 percent responded in the affirmative while 55 percent indicated that they had not heard about the report. Of those who responded yes to this question we then asked, "Did you read or hear about the specific recommendations made by the Iraq Study Group?" This allowed us to determine how attentive respondents were to the report's findings. Only 27.3 percent of those who answered yes to the previous question said that they heard or read about the specific recommendations, with 72.7 responding in the negative. Consequently, a report that was perceived by many pundits as critical of the president's policies and his administration of the war fell on "deaf ears," as George Edwards (2006) has observed, and almost three-fourths of those who heard about the report knew nothing of its specific recommendations. Certainly, these findings are not indicative of an activated public seeking information on the war.

Our findings help to explain the low level of accurate public knowledge regarding the war in Iraq. As Edwards (2009, 87–88) writes, after the commencement of the Iraq War "substantial percentages of the public believed that the United States had found clear evidence that Saddam Hussein was working closely with al Qaeda, that the United States had found weapons of mass destruction in Iraq, and that world opinion favored the United States going to war in Iraq. All of these beliefs were inaccurate, as even the White House admitted." Still, the White House often subtly, and sometimes not so delicately, inferred that each of these three points were factual (see Dobel 2010, 65). And when the public was presented with a meticulous study of the war by a variety of experts representing both political parties, it largely ignored the evidence.

The Economy

Although the Bush presidency can be characterized as a war presidency, George W. Bush also had responsibility for domestic affairs, and as such was expected to provide the nation with a sound economy. On this front the president faced several challenges. He entered office just as a fairly short and mild recession commenced. His prescription for stimulating the economy was a substantial tax cut. While the economy recovered from the twin shocks of recession and the 9/11 terrorist attacks, economic performance was not vibrant. Rather it was the weakest recovery on record since World War II. In addition, the tax cuts, two wars, and a significant prescription drug program inflated the federal budget deficit. The economy stalled again and technically entered recession by December 2007, shortly after our survey was conducted. The following year, the news of a possible second Great Depression startled the nation and doomed Republican candidate John Mc-Cain's chances of securing the White House. Given this panoply of bad economic news, it is not terribly surprising that a February 12, 2010, *New York Times/CBS News* poll as reported by *CNN* found, "More than a year after President George W. Bush left office, more Americans continue to blame his administration over any other entity for the nation's economic woes." Furthermore, "31 percent of Americans said the Bush administration is at fault for the current state of the economy while only 7 percent pointed their finger at President Obama and his team."[1] The finding from this poll contradicts our findings from chapter 3. In this case the public was willing to blame the predecessor rather than the incumbent. Whether this represents a clear change in public expectations, or just a harsh assessment of George W. Bush's historically unpopular presidency, is unclear. What we can say is that these survey results, combined with the Bush economic record, suggest that the president's stewardship of the economy was not particularly popular. What were the actual perceptions of the public during the critical period of 2007, just prior to the nation's entry into what would come to be described as the worst recession since the Great Depression of the 1930s?

To determine the public's perceptions of the economy we again asked our respondents the same sociotropic and pocketbook questions we asked in 1998 and 1999. Given the impending difficulties with the economy, it is a bit surprising that our respondents did not see the bottom falling out of the economy. Only 6.1 percent rated the economy as "very poor," and only one-fourth rated the economy's performance in the lowest three categories. A similar percentage ranked the economy as "very good," 6.5 percent, as ranked it "very poor." Still, slightly less than one half of our respondents rated the economy's performance in the top three categories, with another quarter ranking it at the midpoint. While these figures are not as positive as were the evaluations for Bill Clinton in 1998 or 1999, they are not as negative as one might anticipate given that the economy was on the cusp of an un-precedentedly deep recession. Our findings are interesting then in demon-strating that the public was not yet fully aware of the rising economic peril.

Further evidence is provided by the figures on a second question related to pocketbook concerns. A majority of our respondents, 52.6 percent, an-swered that they were better off than a year ago and 25 percent said that they were "about the same." Only 22.5 percent said they were "worse off." Again, while this latter figure is much larger than for Clinton in 1998 or 1999, it is not indicative of a public that believes it is headed into economic bad times. George W. Bush's evaluations on the economy were certainly respectable. As we did in chapter 6 for Bill Clinton, we will determine whether Bush received equal credit for the economy from all partisans. We also will be able to examine whether he received equal credit or blame regarding perceptions of the war in Iraq and the war on terror.

One reason that we may anticipate a partisan response to the Bush presi-dency is reflected in a quote from George Edwards (2009, 183). He writes, "In both his policies and his politics, Bush was a divider, not a uniter." Edwards (2009, 175) extrapolates: "[F]rom his first days in office, George W. Bush was a polarizing president, eventually the most polarizing in the history of public opinion polling. The first Gallup poll of his tenure found that he had the highest level of disapproval of any new president since polling began."

Edwards (2009, 175) provides evidence to back up his contention: "In the May 21–23, 2004, Gallup poll, the difference between his approval among Republicans (89 percent) and Democrats (12 percent) was an astounding 77 percentage points! That gap of 70 points or higher became common starting with Bush's fourth year in office." In the same Gallup poll "64 percent of Republicans said they strongly approved of the job Bush was doing as president, while 66 percent of Democrats strongly disapproved. As Gallup put it, 'Bush is the only president who has had more than 6 in 10 of his party's identifiers strongly approving of him at the same time that more than 6 in 10 of the other party's identifiers strongly disapprove of him'" (175–76). We therefore again have reasons to believe that partisanship, as well as an expectations gap, should be defining characteristics of the presidency of George W. Bush. We turn to an examination of the results of our analysis in the next two sections.

Testing the Expectations Gap

We begin with two basic questions: Is the expectations gap related to George W. Bush's approval ratings? If so, does it exert a deleterious impact on them? We do so by using the four leadership questions and the weighted gap measure we presented in chapter 4. We also examine our respondent's attitudes toward the state of the economy, as well as various measures of the war in Iraq and the war on terror and control for a variety of demographic and political factors, as well as for our respondents' evaluations of Congress. We include the latter because, at the time our survey was conducted, Bush governed during a period of divided government. We do not include a measure of income in the model because it greatly reduces the number of available observations without altering the model's main findings. Again, we analyze the data with an ordered probit model.

In the first column of table 8.1 we present the results with the four separate Bush gap measures. In the second column we then use the weighted gap measure. Both sound judgment in a crisis and an ability to work well with Congress are significant. The larger the gap on these two dimensions, the less likely that respondents will approve of the president's job performance (remember, the evaluations of the presidents are measured on a scale running from 1 = excellent to 4 = poor). Despite persistent concerns that the president and his administration had not been truthful in selling the Iraq War to the public, high ethical standards are not related to his approval ratings nor are perceptions of Bush's experience in foreign affairs—this, despite his

TABLE 8.1. George W. Bush's Expectations Gap with Presidential Approval as the Dependent Variable, 2007 Survey

	Presidential Approval	Presidential Approval
	Expectations Gap	
Sound judgment	.04***	—
	(.007)	
Experience in foreign affairs	−.006	—
	(.006)	
High ethical standards	.009	—
	(.006)	
Ability to work well with Congress	.02**	—
	(.006)	
Bush's weighted expectations gap	—	.06***
		(.01)
	Demographic Variables	
Age	.009	.01
	(.006)	(.006)
Education	.08	.08
	(.08)	(.08)
Latino	.73	.57
	(.82)	(.83)
African American	.34	.33
	(.46)	(.45)
Gender	.29	.29
	(.18)	(.17)
	Political Variables	
Democrat	.34	.37
	(.24)	(.23)
Ideology	−.12	−.10
	(.07)	(.07)
TV news	−.01	−.007
	(.02)	(.02)
Registered to vote	−.02	−.04
	(.35)	(.34)
	Economic Variables	
U.S. economy	−.20**	−.21**
	(.07)	(.07)
Pocketbook	.16	.17
	(.14)	(.14)
	War Variables	
Win war in Iraq	.06	.13
	(.23)	(.23)

TABLE 8.1.—*Continued*

	Presidential Approval	Presidential Approval
Commander in chief	1.49***	1.54***
	(.15)	(.15)
War on terror	.38**	.40**
	(.13)	(.13)
	Divided Government	
Congress	.53***	.50***
	(.13)	(.13)
N	856	856
Pseudo R^2	.49	.49

status as a foreign policy president. As we noted earlier in this chapter, when it comes to foreign policy considerations, sound judgment in a crisis appears to be more important to our respondents across our various surveys than actual, practical foreign policy experience. In the second column of table 8.1 we find that the weighted gap measure is significant and in the hypothesized direction. The broader the gap is, the less likely one is to approve of the president's job performance. Thus, while not all dimensions of presidential leadership are related to presidential approval ratings, the overall conclusion from our analysis, as with the evidence from the Clinton presidency, is that expectations matter.

It is interesting to note that none of the demographic variables and, more striking, none of the political variables are related to perceptions of Bush. Rather it is expectations and events that drive perceptions of the Bush presidency. The measure of the U.S. economy is significant in both models with stronger evaluations of the economy (1 = very poor to 7 = very good) related to more positive presidential approval ratings. As we found in most of our past analyses, pocketbook attitudes are not related to perceptions of the president.

Regarding the war in Iraq and the war on terror we find that there is a positive relationship between perceptions of Bush's performance as commander in chief and evaluations of his overall job performance. (In interpreting the coefficient, remember that both measures run from 1 = excellent to 4 = poor.) The same is true of evaluations of Bush's performance on the war on terror. Interestingly, perceptions of whether one believes we are winning the war in Iraq are not related to Bush's approval ratings. In a separate analysis not reported here we did examine the relationship between these same variables and Congress. We found that perceptions of whether we are

TABLE 8.2. Partisan Economic and Ethics Models

	Republicans	Democrats & Others	Republicans	Democrats & Others
Sociotropic attitudes	-.14	-.43***	-.03	-.38***
	(.09)	(.09)	(.10)	(.10)
Pocketbook attitudes	.10	-.09	.20	.07
	(.18)	(.16)	(.21)	(.17)
Bush's ethics gap	.07***	.06***	.04***	.03***
	(.008)	(.005)	(.009)	(.006)
Win war in Iraq	—	—	-.002	.51
			(.29)	(.34)
Commander in chief	—	—	1.74***	1.80***
			(.21)	(.20)
War on terror	—	—	.79***	.43**
			(.20)	(.17)
Gender	.24	.16	.12	.38*
	(.23)	(.20)	(.26)	(.23)
Age	.02**	.01*	.01	.015**
	(.007)	(.006)	(.008)	(.007)
Education	.06	.17*	-.05	.17
	(.12)	(.09)	(.13)	(.10)
African American	2.39***	-.36	1.89**	-0.05
	(.71)	(.45)	(.92)	(.50)
Latino	.89	.13	.16	.41
	(1.35)	(.82)	(1.69)	(.89)
TV news	-.01	-.002	-.30	-.004
	(.23)	(.21)	(.25)	(.23)
N	311	601	302	591
Pseudo R^2	.20	.29	.39	.44

Note: "Republicans" = "Strong Republican," "Republican," and "Lean Republican"; "Democrats & Others" = "Strong Democrat," "Democrat," "Lean Democrat," "Other Party," and "No Party."
*** significant at .01; ** significant at .05; * significant at .10.

winning the war were related to Congress's performance evaluations. These combined findings suggest that the opposition to the war had more of an impact on evaluations of Congress than on those of the president. Finally, with regard to divided government, we find that evaluations of Congress are related to those of the president, but that they are positive, indicating that increased approval of Congress is related to a similar inclination to approve of the president's performance. Remembering again that the gap measure for "an ability to work well with Congress" was significant, this may suggest that even though divided government prevailed, there was an inclination on the part of the public to favor cooperation over stalemate.

Partisan Effects

As we did in chapter 6 we again test for partisan effects related to the economy. We also include various measures of foreign policy. We present the results in table 8.2. While we found that all partisans gave President Clinton credit for a good economy, we find that the coefficient for sociotropic attitudes is significant only for Democrats and independents. The negative coefficient indicates that they gave the president greater credit for the good economy than Republicans (remember that the dependent variable runs from 1 = excellent to 4 = poor). This is a surprising finding. Perhaps under a Republican president Republicans expected even better economic performance. Whatever the explanation, it is the only finding that is not consistent with the performance-based assumption of the expectations gap thesis. Again, perceptions of Bush's ethics exert a broad-based effect. Likewise, the coefficients for the three foreign policy measures are consistent. The war in Iraq is not related to perceptions of the President Bush for either group, while perceptions of Bush's performance as commander in chief and on the war on terror have the same effects for both groups.

Conclusions

The combined evidence from chapters 6 and 8 suggests that there are some differences on the measure of the state of the economy, but not on ethics. There also is a broad consensus on foreign policy issues. And with regard to ethics, the public therefore has broad-based expectations of two different president's personal conduct. Since Clinton and Bush had very different personalities, and thus very different ethical behavior, the findings appear to be generalizable. All presidents should therefore be aware of the public's expectations in this realm.

CHAPTER 9

Barack Obama

The Candidate/Incumbent Expectations Gap

We're going to rely less on the collective wallet—we have to, to do
what I told you I want to do on the budget—less on the collective
wallet and more on the collective will. But this does not mean
lowering our sights or our expectations. It's just exactly the opposite
of that. In the era of tight budgets, we're not going to simply 'make
do with less.' We're going to learn how to do more with less—and do
it better. In the factory, you call it productivity. Across our country, I
call it the national spirit.

President George H. W. Bush, remarks to the
National Association of Manufacturers, March 23, 1989

As the George H. W. Bush quote suggests, at some point presidents are faced
with the realities of tight budgets or some other political reality that they
obfuscated during the previous election cycle but must confront head-on at
the governing stage. In this chapter we address the idea that presidents must
learn to deal with the realities of governance in comparison to the heighted
campaign promises that promote excessive and unrealistic public expectations. Consequently, this chapter deals with both public expectations and
the unrealistic expectations of an incumbent president.

With this point in mind, on August 1, 2008, presidential candidate
Barack Obama discussed a common theme of his campaign: the need for
change. Speaking to the Communications Workers of America via satellite,
Obama said:

Change is building an economy that rewards the work and workers who create it. Change is universal health care. Change is hav-

ing a president who's been an organizer, who knows what it's like to walk with you on that picket line and who lets unions do what they do best: organize our workers. But it's not going to be easy, CWA. And that's why I need your help. If you keep marching with me and knocking on those doors, and making those phone calls, and registering voters, and talking to your friends and co-workers and neighbors; and if you vote for me, then I promise you this: we will win the general election and then—you and I—together are going to change America and change this world.

If we deconstruct the language of this paragraph we learn that in these few short sentences, candidate Barack Obama promised (1) "to build an economy," presumably a prosperous one, (2) to secure universal health care, (3) inferred that because he had been a community organizer he presumably understood the needs of the members of the CWA, and (4) voiced his support for labor unions. These would have been sufficiently broad promises for any presidential candidate, but Obama promised (5) together we will change America and (6) together we will change the world!

When presidential candidates make promises during the heat of a campaign they are hoping to build a sufficiently large coalition of voters to elect them to office in November. They also, however, are laying the groundwork for voter expectations, which can affect their ability to govern once they are elected to office. In this regard the expectations for Barack Obama already were at "dizzying heights" (Sinclair 2012, 198). He was the first African American to be elected to the presidency. He replaced a highly unpopular president at a time when many people were looking for transformative change. The economy was on the verge of a depression and had already technically slipped into a recession. The financial industry, the auto industry, the housing market, and other vital sectors of the economy teetered on the brink of dysfunction and bankruptcy. To many Americans it looked indeed as if the sky were falling and Barack Obama represented the nation's hopes and dreams. As Suskind (2011, 33) writes, "[Obama] had officially become a vessel for hope, an emblem of the very comeback a bruised and battered nation, emerging from a dark decade, pined for. As his crowds began to swell, the question became one of whether this brilliant construct, a man who seemed to fuse together so many disparate elements of the wildly diverse country, could handle the waterfall of inchoate yearnings crashing down on him."

Yet, "the public's high expectations" combined with "the dire economic situation made the likely cost of not delivering exceedingly high" (Sinclair 2012, 202). The initial expectations might be useful in promoting support for some immediate policy changes, but the likely consequence over time is that the public will become disillusioned as an incumbent president struggles to satisfy excessive and often unrealistic demands for action. Obama's campaign rhetoric helped him win the White House, but it also fostered wildly unrealistic expectations. To promise to change America is one thing, but to promise to change the world! As grandiose campaign promises go, this one may be difficult to top.

Given the herculean scope of Obama's promises, it is not particularly surprising that after just one year in office the public already was showing signs that it believed Barack Obama had failed to satisfy their basic expectations. Based on the results of a *Washington Post* poll published on January 28, 2010, reporters Jon Cohen and Jennifer Agiesta concluded, "More than a third [of the poll's respondents] see the president as falling short of their expectations, about double the proportion saying so at the 100-day mark of Obama's presidency in April. At the time, 63 percent said the president had accomplished a 'great deal' or a 'good amount.' Now, the portion saying so has dropped to 47 percent."

These figures suggest that by the beginning of 2010 a substantial percentage of the American public believed that Barack Obama had not lived up to the lofty expectations engendered throughout the 2008 campaign. This sentiment had been reinforced in the fall of 2009 on a more humorous and biting satirical note by the popular television program *Saturday Night Live*. It opened with a skit portraying President Obama addressing the nation. In this faux presidential address the faux Obama declared, "It is very clear what I have done thus far, and that is nothing. Nada! Almost one year and nothing to show for it." He then listed a series of campaign promises. Had he closed Guantanamo Bay? No. Was the United States out of Iraq? No. Was the situation in Afghanistan better? Actually it was worse. Had he achieved health care reform? "Hell no!" Then he listed the promises he had made to liberals that he had not accomplished: global climate reform, immigration reform, gays in the military, limits on executive powers, and torture prosecutions. The faux Obama did take credit for two big accomplishments during his first year in office: "jack and squat."

Within a year of his inauguration why were there palpable signs of public discontent with President Obama's performance? One answer is that on a series of key promises, as the *Saturday Night Live* routine skillfully demonstrated, President Obama had come up short. Certainly the newly elected president had some very real and important policy accomplishments. He had convinced Congress to pass a massive stimulus bill that included funds to protect jobs at the local level, put money into infrastructure, and launched a major green energy initiative. He skillfully averted a potential depression and the economy was exhibiting at least tentative signs of growth. Still what many people saw was an unemployment rate of nearly 10 percent, with many more underemployed, a universal health care bill trapped in the mystifying congressional committee labyrinth, and other major reforms such as immigration reform and cap and trade either on the back burner or seemingly entirely forgotten. While the public still personally liked the president, and while his approval ratings hovered around the 50 percent mark, Americans did not see clear and convincing evidence of a changed America.

Instead, when they turned on cable TV news channels they saw the same partisan bickering they had witnessed during the George W. Bush presidency. In Congress, Republicans and Democrats still could not find common ground on almost any consequential issue. As anger coalesced, palpably expressed by the rising influence of the conservative Tea Party movement, the president discovered that independent voters were dissatisfied with the pervasive partisan tone, as well as with the massive and ever growing budget deficits. Therefore, in his January 26, 2010, State of the Union address President Obama pivoted, making budget reduction and fiscal discipline a key component of his speech, while health care had to wait thirty-two minutes before the president finally signaled his support for comprehensive reform.

What is of particular interest is that during his second year in office, Obama again was able to garner some impressive legislative achievements, including passage of the much vaunted national health care bill, a major overall of the financial system (the Dodd-Frank Act), the end of the Don't Ask, Don't Tell policy, an extension of unemployment benefits, credit card reform, changes to the student loan program, and the removal of combat troops from Iraq. Yet, surprisingly, his poll ratings continued to decline. Rather than reversing his downward trend in the polls, these major accomplishments largely were ignored by a public that seemed to see little progress on the economic front.

Expectations of Obama's performance continued to be a source of political difficulty as he reached the summer of his third year in office. Following the killing of Osama bin Laden, an event that galvanized and temporarily united a nation, as well as the systematic weakening of the al Qaeda terrorist network, Obama's approval ratings declined again, this time falling below the all important 50 percent mark, an indication that an incumbent is electorally vulnerable. In its analysis of a May 2011 *USA Today/Gallup* poll, Susan Page writes, "The soaring expectations that surrounded Obama's election haven't satisfied everyone. 24% say he's done worse as president than they expected; 14% better." The reason for these results: "On one critical measure, a majority now say they disagree with him on the issues that matter to most of them."

And by January 2012, 52 percent of the respondents to a *Washington Post* poll said that Obama had accomplished "not much" or "little or nothing." The president's approval rating was 48 percent. Interpreting these results, Dan Balz wrote, "The gap between what the president promised and the expectations he created in 2008 and his record of delivering will be at the heart of the Republican argument that he does not deserve a second term."[1] Hence, despite bringing about truly historic change, including a series of major accomplishments with the lame-duck Democratic Congress in December 2010, Barack Obama still was trying to satisfy a skeptical public's expectations. With a stubbornly floundering economy, the still personally popular incumbent (his likeability numbers remained high) found himself potentially vulnerable as he entered his 2012 reelection contest.

What is most striking about the Obama example is that it is not at all unusual. It illustrates several key factors relevant to the modern American presidency. In order to get elected presidential candidates have a strong political incentive to make bold promises during the campaign without worrying if those promises are realistic. Obama was not the first, and certainly will not be the last, presidential candidate to promise more than he possibly could deliver. For example, in 1988 George H. W. Bush famously promised American voters, "Read my lips, no new taxes." Once in office, however, he discovered that he had to raise taxes in order to corral runaway budget deficits. Political pundits often cited the violation of his no-new taxes pledge as a primary reason for Bush's 1992 reelection defeat, even though the tax deal he negotiated with a Congress controlled by Democrats likely played a vital role in the economy's robust recovery during the 1990s.

Barack Obama won reelection, though with a smaller popular vote and electoral vote margin than in 2008. Still, his experience with the presidency is not an aberrant case. It has become an all too common refrain for newly elected presidents, accompanied by a wave of initial unrealistic hopes and expectations, to later confront the cold realities of stalemate and bitter partisanship that characterizes our present unruly federal governmental system. Faced with the stark and unfriendly realities of governing, many of our modern presidents must confront what presidential scholars refer to as a gap between high and often unrealistic public expectations of presidential performance and the realities of what presidents actually and reasonably can accomplish once they enter the Oval Office. Barack Obama is not the first to learn this hard lesson, nor will he be the last president to do so. As many presidential pundits note, the expectations gap represents a continuing threat to the viability of the modern presidency. Combined with increased partisanship, it makes the president's job even that much more difficult.

President Obama's Expectations

Shortly after his 2008 election, president-elect Obama made the following optimistic statement:

> So I'm looking forward to meeting with both the Democrats and Republicans this afternoon. My expectation is that they will share the same sense of urgency [about the current fiscal situation] that I do, that we are going to move quickly, that we're not going to get bogged down in a lot of old-style politics on either side. There's not going to be a lot of finger-pointing or posturing. The American people need action now. That's what I intend to provide as president of the United States. (remarks to reporters, January 5, 2009)

Writing for the *New York Times Magazine,* Peter Baker later noted, "The biggest miscalculation in the minds of most Obama advisers was the assumption that he could bridge a polarized capital and forge genuinely bipartisan coalitions."[2] The American public elected Obama in large part because they were looking for a leader who could bridge the seemingly endless partisan divisions between Democrats and Republicans. Yet while the president-elect's statement may have been widely praised by the public at the time, its optimism reflected more hope than reality. To put it another way, the newly elected president's own expectations appear to be unrealistic.

This raises another question about the expectations gap thesis. Does the public alone have unrealistic expectations or do presidents themselves enter office with impractical attitudes regarding what they actually can accomplish? If so, it may be that the expectations gap is a two-way street. Presidents would then send a series of unrealistic signals to the public, not only during the election campaign but even afterward as they begin to prepare to lead the nation. In his book on the Obama presidency, George Edwards (2012, 2) calls this "overreach." He explains that "[t]he concept of overreach refers to presidents proposing policies that lack support in the public or Congress, expecting to create opportunities for change by persuading a majority of the public and the Congress to support their policies." Edwards concludes that the Obama administration overreached on a variety of issues, including health care reform. Edwards also explains why the Obama administration misinterpreted its mandate from the 2008 election: "The White House anticipated that it could attract bipartisan support from Republicans. The foundations of this expectation were weak, however. Partisan polarization was at an historic high, and the Republican Party's locus in the economic and social conservatism of the South reinforced the disinclination of Republicans to offer support across the aisle" (Edwards 2013, 1086–87). In other words, Obama misread public opinion and underestimated the level of opposition from the Republican Party.

One reason for these miscalculations may be that although Obama was not a true outsider president, he entered office with little federal governing experience. Like many of the outsider presidents (e.g., Carter, Reagan, Clinton, George W. Bush) Obama came to the presidency with little actual experience working in Washington. While he may not have been a true outsider, his elected experiences consisted mostly of having served in the Illinois legislature and an incomplete term as a U.S. senator. Much of his time in the Senate was spent in pursuit of the presidency. Obama therefore had little time to learn how the wheels of Washington government actually function.

As all presidents eventually do, in time Obama learned the hard reality of Washington politics: it is not easily conducive to abrupt and radical change and the opposition party most often is not amenable to the persuasive powers of the incoming president. Rather than cooperation, congressional Republicans consistently refused to vote for proposals they previously had supported and in some cases had even introduced. The Senate became a stumbling block with Minority Leader Mitch McConnell (R-KY) threatening to filibuster virtually every aspect of Obama's domestic policy agenda. Senators placed holds on nominations for key positions, leaving many posts in such critical departments as Treasury unfilled during a key point in the Obama presidency. Stalemate and gridlock thrived despite the new president's most earnest efforts.

Again, all this might have been forgotten since during his first two years in office Obama had a number of major legislative accomplishments, marking him as one of the most successful presidents in getting his preferred legislation passed by Congress. His stimulus package was dollar-wise the largest energy bill in U.S. history. It was among the largest expenditures ever for education and the environment. It also provided Americans with a substantial tax cut. In fact, in absolute terms, Obama cut taxes more than any previous president, including Ronald Reagan. This was followed by historic legislation on health care and financial reform, as well as the reform of the student loan process, new credit card protections, a bold initiative that preserved the U.S. auto industry, the repeal of Don't Ask, Don't Tell, pay equity legislation for women, and a new arms control treaty with Russia. Looking at these numerous accomplishments one can argue that Obama was a highly successful and perhaps in some ways even a transformative president. One can also argue that were it not for Obama's aggressive, activist economic policies (such as his unpopular decision to bail out the auto industry and the almost equally unpopular stimulus bill), the U.S. economy might have tipped into an actual depression. Yet despite these many extraordinary accomplishments, more than a year and a half into his presidency Peter Baker noted, "The president who muscled through Congress perhaps the most ambitious domestic agenda in a generation finds himself vilified by the right, castigated by the left and abandoned by the middle."

What did Obama learn from this political baptism by fire? According to Baker, "He has learned that, for all his anti-Washington rhetoric, he has to play by Washington rules if he wants to win in Washington. It is not enough to be supremely sure that he is right if no one else agrees with him." Obama commented: "I think anybody who's occupied this office has to remember that success is determined by an intersection in policy and politics and that you can't be neglecting of marketing and P.R. and public opinion."

During Obama's second year in office Baker noted that "[o]n the campaign trail lately, Obama has been confronted by disillusionment . . . Perhaps that should have come as no surprise. When Obama secured the Democratic nomination in June 2008, he told an admiring crowd that someday 'we will be able to look back and tell our children that this was the moment when the rise of the oceans began to slow and our planet began to heal; this was the moment when we ended a war and secured our nation and restored our image as the last, best hope on earth.'" When Baker read this line from the 2008 acceptance speech to Obama, who was now president, he responded, "It sounds ambitious. But you know we've made progress on each of those fronts." Yet few Americans were familiar with this progress. A *New York Times/CBS News* poll found that less than 10 percent were even aware that they had received a tax cut from President Obama.[3] Far fewer knew that Obama had cut taxes more than any other president.

Philosophically, Obama noted, "It would be hard for people to look back and say, You know what, Obama didn't do what he's promised. I think they could say, On a bunch of fronts he still has an incomplete. But I keep a checklist of what we committed to doing, and we've accomplished 70 percent of the things that we talked about during the campaign." When reminded that his rhetoric in the campaign was high flying, Obama responded, "I make no apologies for having set high expectations for myself and for the country, because I think we can meet those expectations. Now, the one thing that I will say—which I anticipated and can be tough—is the fact that in a big, messy democracy like this, everything takes time. And we're not a culture that's build on patience."

In time, however, Obama came to see how inflated expectations played a critical role in the drubbing the Democratic Party received in the 2010 congressional midterm elections. As *Washington Post* columnist Anne Cornblut wrote following the midterm election, "After nearly two weeks of introspection, President Obama's top advisers have concluded that the 'shellacking' Democrats took on Election Day [2010] was caused in large part by their own failure to live up to expectations set during the 2008 campaign, not merely the typical political cycles and poor messaging they pointed to at first."[4]

Other members of the Obama administration shared their thoughts with Baker. Peter Rouse, who would serve briefly as Obama's second chief of staff, said, "He [Obama] got here, and the expectations for what he could accomplish were very high and probably unrealistic." Baker added, "Yet even if the White House saw it coming, this is an administration that feels shellshocked." In defense, Joel Benenson, Obama's pollster, noted that the president's approval rating was higher than that of Congress, the media, and the banks. He then added, "We are in a time when the American public is highly suspect of any institution and President Obama still stands above that."

Still, Baker unmasked a spirit of deep skepticism inside the White House. He writes, "In their darkest moments, White House aides wonder aloud whether it is even possible for a modern president to succeed. . . . Everything seems to conspire against the idea: an implacable opposition with little if any real interest in collaboration, a news media saturated with triviality and conflict, a culture that demands solutions yesterday, a societal cynicism that hold leadership in low regard. . . . In this environment, they have increasingly concluded, it may be that every modern president is going to be, at best, average." What went wrong? Baker writes, "From the start, Obama has been surprised by all sorts of challenges that have made it hard for him to govern—not just the big problems that he knew about, like the economy and wars, but also the myriad little ones that hindered his progress, like one nominee after another brought down by unpaid taxes. Obama trusted his judgment and seemed to have assumed impressive people in his own party must have a certain basic sense of integrity—and that impressive people in the other party must want to work with him."

In sum, an incumbent president's own expectations upon entering the presidential office were in many ways no more realistic than those of the public. The experiences of presidents such as Carter and Obama raise yet another potential dimension of the expectations gap: the candidate/incumbent expectations gap. This expectations gap represents the difference between the expectations engendered by an individual when he or she is running for office (including the candidate's own overinflated sense of the personal skills he brings to governing) and what it actually takes to govern. As a series of outsider presidents arrive in Washington with limited knowledge of the federal system, with high hopes and expectations based on a national election and their own hubris, they find that the political system is nothing like what they expected it to be. They too are disillusioned and must react to their own excessive and unrealistic expectations of what they can accomplish. Carter found Washington to be nothing like he expected. Bill Clinton had to learn on the job and did so by transforming his presidency into one in which he triangulated between liberal Democrats and conservative Republicans. He also downsized his own expectations, tackling smaller issues rather than large ones such as health care. In the end, his new expectations better matched the ability of a modern president to govern effectively. On the other hand, Carter was unable to adjust to expectations and served but one term. It is interesting, when one of the authors of this book visited the Jimmy Carter Library in the 1990s, an entire section of the library was dedicated to expectations. Carter learned the hard way the lessons of excessive and unrealistic expectations. Consequently, the expectations gap reaches not only down into the electorate but rises up into the very center of political gravity, the president and the White House staff. Expectations are unrealistic everywhere and the end result is disillusionment everywhere. As Baker concludes:

> Four of the five presidents previous to Obama were governors who came to Washington vowing to fix it, only to realize that Washington defies the easy, and often hollow, rhetoric of change. While Obama was a senator when he set off on the campaign trail, he made the same pledges and has encountered the same reality. "The story of the first two years is the inherent conflict between a guy who ran from the outside to change Washington, gets here and the situation was even worse than we thought it was," a senior aide told me. "Here's a guy who ran as an outsider to change Washington who all of a sudden realized that just to deal with these issues, we were going to have to work with Washington to fix that."

Obama officials were left to complain that the system is "not on the level." This means, "Republicans, the news media, the lobbyists, the whole Washington culture is not serious about solving problems." As this reality became apparent to the now more seasoned and experienced president, by August 2011 Obama's rhetoric reflected a more realistic expectation of the American political process. At a birthday celebration in Chicago he told an audience, "When I said, 'Change we can believe in,' I didn't say, 'Change we can believe in tomorrow.'" As David Nakamura of the *Washington Post* writes:

> The paring back of expectations has been an increasingly necessary part of Obama's rhetoric, given the economic and political realities that have beset his presidency. But as the president prepares for his reelection campaign, his triumphant 2008 message of "hope and change" has undergone a radical transformation, from messianic to just plain messy. The candidate who once dazzled audiences with his soaring rhetoric is still searching for a compelling sales pitch to persuade voters to give him more time to accomplish his goals.[5]

As the empirical results from this book demonstrate, presidents should be aware that they face a buzz saw of excessive and often unrealistic expectations as soon as they take the presidential oath of office. The public, its expectations heightened by the high rhetoric of the 2008 campaign, was disillusioned once the messy process of government kicked in. Obama therefore found it necessary to pivot to new ground, claiming that he was a warrior for the middle class, as he prepared for his 2012 reelection campaign against yet another outsider candidate, Republican Willard Mitt Romney.

Disillusionment

An illustration of how expectations influence perceptions of presidential performance is provided by an examination of how one constituency's attitudes toward Barack Obama's changed following the election of 2008. By February 2010, *CNN* and other organizations reported greater disenchantment and disillusionment among younger voters:

> It is clear that the economic environment and the president's response have a direct effect on the political ties of an entire generation. Obama should consider himself warned. A new *Rasmussen* poll shows

that a vast majority of young adults aged 18–29 believe the nation is headed in the wrong direction. By a 68% to 23% margin young adults believe the United States is on the wrong track rather than the right direction—the highest margin of any age group polled. During the campaign Barack Obama appeared as if he was going to capture the hearts of a generation. Hope and change resonated with young adults who were completely fed up by a Washington removed from their cares and concerns. But President Obama is not the same as Campaign Obama and Republicans stand ready to reap the rewards.[6]

And it did not help that among young Americans in particular Obama developed a unique cult of personality, seemingly rising above mere politics. As Jonathan Alter (2010, xii) writes, "The expectations of Obama had been widely inflated all along, as he knew. But they came from a deep and sincere place in the American character, and their dashing would complicate his task." Alter (xv) continues: "It wasn't just that the rhetoric of campaigning and the reality of governing were at odds; that's always true in politics. The difference this time was that millions more people than usual took the rhetoric to heart, then turned on the television to see the ugly reality more vividly than they expected."

In his often critical book about the Obama presidency, Ron Suskind (2011, 8–9) remarks that "[t]he administration's strategy is to emphasize that the distance between the hopes of Grant Park [where Obama famously addressed an enthusiastic crowd on election night 2008] and the trimmed ambitions of legislative pragmatism is not a fissure, or acquiescence, but rather the hard reality of governing in a partisan era." When Barack Obama took center stage before Congress in September 2011 it was not to ask Congress to pass a job's bill, it was a demand for action. The president who had tried to work within the system had discovered the hard way that he had to use all of the tools of the presidency to defang his political opposition. For many of the president's long-time supporters it was a key moment, one where the president rejected his optimistic version of democracy and directly entered the fray of polarized partisan politics. Suskind (2011, 11–12) also discussed the president's learning curve. He notes that Obama is "not getting what he needs to manage this daunting task, and some advisers have become convinced that his lack of experience, especially managerial, may be his undoing; that, at a time of peril, the president may simply not be up to the demands of the moment."

One factor that can mitigate the expectations gap is presidential learning. There is no school for presidents. Presidents learn on the job. Those who are the most successful surround themselves with talented advisers and then learn how to manipulate the ropes of government. By the fall of 2011, with his poll numbers in the high 30s and low 40s, Barack Obama appeared to be a wiser president. The question was whether he had learned the job too slowly or if the damage done by a weak economy would be too late to preserve his presidency. But as a veritable Washington outsider he was showing signs that he understood the expectations gap dilemma and was working to address it by entering the principal fray of battle, engaging in partisan politics head-on. As Suskind (2011, 260) notes, "What the administration was finding . . . were the distinctions between campaign talk and governance. In government there was a system—albeit an imperfect one to 'price' expectations, and equally to negotiate, in a step-by-step process, the new laws of the land." As White House adviser David Axelrod explained, it is surprisingly difficult to translate the demands of the White House into effective and coherent action. Speaking for the president, Axelrod called it a "Sisyphean task" and yet "we haven't dropped the boulder yet" (quoted in Suskind 2011, 284).

By the fall of 2011 President Obama appeared to have learned this hard lesson and he secured reelection. But the key questions were whether the nation as a whole still had the opportunity to profit from this renewed wisdom. If not, there always will be another president ready to come along to face the same challenges, though history shows us that they are likely to arrive in Washington with the same unrealistic expectations that Obama carried to the White House on January 20, 2009. Presidents must not only overcome the public expectations gap, they must develop more realistic expectations of their own abilities.

CHAPTER 10

Micro- and Macro-Level Models of the Expectations Gap

> We know all too well from past experience that negotiations with the
> Soviet Union must be carefully prepared. We can't afford to repeat
> past mistakes—to arrive hastily at an arms control process that sends
> hopes soaring, only to end in dashed expectations.
>
> President Ronald Reagan, news conference, March 31, 1982

In the first nine chapters we have identified the expectations gap problem, defined the concept, and provided multiple means of operationalizing and testing the gap thesis. While this represents an important contribution to the understanding of a mainstay concept of the presidential literature, we still have another important task to perform. Although in the past chapters we provided empirical evidence related to the gap and its effects, we still do not know why the gap exists. Two intriguing possibilities exist: (1) the gap may have a partisan component, and (2) it may be related to diminished public trust in America's leaders. Support for both of these findings would suggest a broader theoretical placement of the expectations gap, beyond a mere presidency-centric concept to one that may have important implications for other American political institutions.

Given these intriguing possibilities, in this chapter we analyze two national surveys conducted in 1998 and 1999 to identify the actual determinants of the expectations gap. Some qualitative studies have shown that the gap may derive from lower levels of trust generated by such events as Vietnam and Watergate (Rose 1997) or from partisan polarization. In this chapter we take the analysis a step further by providing a direct test of the impact of partisanship, trust (particularly as it relates to our leaders), and then tie it back to the concept of a presidential expectations gap. To accomplish this objective, we test three micro- and two macro-level explanations for the presence of the gap. It is important to note that when we discuss micro- and macro-level explanations of the expectations gap in this chapter, we do not use the terms *micro* and *macro* in the same manner that public opinion scholars do. Rather, we consider micro-level explanations as focusing on the presidency, while macro-level explanations relate to broader perceptions of the entire governmental system. For example, partisanship and trust in government are macro level constructs that also may be important determinants of the gap.

Micro- and Macro-Level Explanations

We derive three micro-level explanations for the gap's existence from the presidential literature: that is, explanations that focus on a direct connection between the public and the president. These explanations generally refer to the larger political environment only when they discuss the president's inability to influence macro-level phenomena, such as the state of the economy or when scholars examine the consequences of the gap, such as the idea that the gap makes it harder for presidents to work with Congress (see Mezey 1989; Seligman and Covington 1989). Largely missing from the presidential literature are macro-level explanations for the gap's existence, that is, explanations that focus on the relationship between the broader governmental context and the public's perception of presidents (though see Waterman 2010). Since empirical evidence now indicates that a gap exists for both the Congress (Kimball and Patterson 1997) and the presidency, it is possible that public expectations may be related to macro-level factors such as public perceptions of the trustworthiness of government and its leaders, individuals' perceptions of their own political efficacy, and general partisan political attitudes. Our objective therefore is to identify and test three micro and two macro-level explanations for the gap's existence. We turn first to a delineation of the micro-level explanations.

The first micro-level explanation involves a relationship between the gap and expectations of presidential performance. The argument is that competent presidential performance on a wide range of issues is necessary to satisfy public expectations. It may be, for example, that attitudes reflect excessive and unrealistic public expectations of presidential performance—the second micro-level explanation for the existence of the expectations gap. As Moe (1985, 24) writes, "The president is burdened by expectations that far exceed his capacity for effective action. . . . The result is an institutional system that does indeed contain forces that push it toward greater congruence, but whose constraints guarantee that adjustments will be halting, highly imperfect, and nowhere near sufficient (at least for the foreseeable future) to alleviate the massive imbalance between expectations and capacity." A number of presidential scholars have echoed this idea that public expectations are not realistic (see Brownlow 1969; Cronin 1974; Buchanan 1978; George 1980; Destler 1981; Light 1983; Lowi 1985; Stuckey 1991; Bond and Fleisher 1990).

The proposition that public expectations are excessive and unrealistic is related to a third formulation of the expectations gap: the idea that the public looks first to the White House for political leadership. This presidential prototype formulation of the gap initially derived from the idea that Franklin Roosevelt transformed the presidential office and in so doing permanently altered public expectations of the president's legitimate role in our governmental system (Hess 1976). Other political actors also contribute to this propensity to look to the president. Iyengar and Kinder (1987) and Kinder and Fiske (1986) contend that the media portray the president as the central political actor in our governmental system, while Hargrove and Nelson (1984) argue, "The constitutional nature of the presidency assures that to the extent the federal government is the object of public demands for political change, the presidency will be the center of the American political system."

Women and ethnic minorities, who disproportionately benefit from the federal government on issues such as affirmative action, civil rights protection, and abortion rights, provide an example of the look-to-the-White-House thesis. The elderly also disproportionately depend on governmental assistance and federal action, as do the poor. Hence, these groups may be more likely than other groups to look to the White House for leadership, particularly during a Democratic president's term of office. During Republican administrations, other groups (e.g., business interests) may be more likely to look to the White House. The implication is that such groups will expect more from presidents and the federal government, and hence exhibit a broader set of expectations.

The three micro-level explanations for the expectations gap are interrelated. The public expects successful presidential performance on a wide range of issues. Due, however, to the limited capacities of presidents, such expectations tend to be both excessive and unrealistic. Presidents (and candidates for president) exacerbate these unrealistic expectations by actively encouraging the public to look first to the White House for leadership. Thus, we can conceptualize these three micro-level explanations as three parts of a cycle in which expectations are continually ratcheted up.

Whether we consider them as separate or interrelated explanations for the existence of the gap, the defining characteristic of these micro-level explanations is that they are based almost entirely on the relationship between public perceptions of the presidency and the ability of various presidents to meet those expectations.

There is a second way to think about the expectations gap: with public perceptions related not merely to the presidency but rather as a symptom of dysfunctions in the larger political process. In other words, we can also consider macro-level explanations for the existence of the presidential expectations gap. Recent research provides empirical evidence that an expectations gap exists for both Congress and the presidency (Kimball and Patterson 1997; Waterman, Jenkins-Smith, and Silva 1999). This suggests that the expectations gap is not limited to one particular federal political actor, but may involve broader public attitudes toward the governmental system. For example, perceptions of trust and efficacy may be related to the development of an expectations gap. Presidential scholars note the deleterious effects of Watergate, the Vietnam War, the Nixon pardon, the Iran-contra scandal, and the Clinton impeachment on the presidency (see Genovese 2002; Rose 1997). Our analysis of impeachment in chapter 7 also provided some insight on this matter. These events may contribute to diminishing levels of trust and an expanded expectations gap. Indirect empirical support for such a relationship is evident in that presidential approval ratings and perceptions of presidential character are linked to trust in government and, in turn, trust in government is related to the presidential vote between 1969 and 1996 (Citrin 1974; Citrin and Green 1986; and Hetherington 1998, 1999). It is possible then that individuals with lower levels of trust in government also exhibit a wider expectations gap.

Trust in government is only one aspect of the complex array associated with feelings of public estrangement from the U.S. governmental system. Political efficacy or whether an individual believes she can have an impact on government also may be related to the existence of an expectations gap. Two types of political efficacy are identified in the literature. Internal efficacy refers "to beliefs about one's own competence to understand and to participate effectively in politics," while external efficacy refers "to beliefs about the responsiveness of governmental authorities and institutions to citizen demands" (Craig, Niemi, and Silver 1990, 290). It is possible that the less efficacious one perceives oneself to be, internally or externally, the broader their gap will be between their perceptions of a hypothetical "excellent" and an incumbent president.

Another possible macro-level explanation is that the gap may be driven by each individual's political attitudes. Many presidential scholars describe the gap as a construct that affects all presidents equally, while others believe that the deleterious impact of the gap increases over the course of an individual presidential term. Neither conceptualization of the gap, however, considers the influence of political attitudes.

We know that such factors as political party affiliation and ideology are related to presidential approval ratings and vote choice in presidential elections. We also know from the work of Kimball and Patterson (1997) and Waterman, Jenkins-Smith, and Silva (1999) that there are variations in individual perceptions of the expectations gap. Therefore, just as a Democratic president can anticipate greater political support from his own party members, Democratic partisans may give a Democratic president the benefit of the doubt even if the incumbent is not living up to their overall expectations. Thus Democrats might exhibit a narrower expectations gap for President Clinton than Republicans and independents who, having invested less of their political capital in the incumbent president's success, may be quicker to blame the president for anything and everything that goes wrong. Moreover, in a period of divided government these political expectations may be influenced by the public's evaluations of the performance of the U.S. Congress. Those individuals who have more positive evaluations of Congress may be more likely to blame the president when stalemate emerges and thus exhibit a broader expectations gap.

In sum, we argue that the presidential expectations gap is influenced by two main types of factors—micro- and macro-level beliefs. To test the micro and macro explanations we analyze individual-level data. The data were generated specifically for this book because we need to compare individual perceptions of the presidential office and an incumbent president along comparable leadership dimensions. Although existing studies provide data on public attitudes about presidential incumbents, they do not provide a basis for comparing the presidential office to an incumbent.

The Dependent Variables

There are a number of ways of conceptualizing the expectations gap. Many scholars conceptualize it in a time-serial fashion, with presidential approval ratings declining and the gap's impact increasing over time. Such an analysis requires time-serial data. Since our data are cross-sectional, we instead follow Kimball and Patterson's (1997) method. We compare expectations for an excellent or ideal president with those of an incumbent president. As we have noted earlier in this book, theoretically this specification is based on the logic of the presidential prototype literature, which derives from social psychology and examines how people use ideal images of a group to establish expectations of the group's members (see Bem and McConnell 1970). We provided a description of how we operationalized these measures in chapter 4.

We then develop several measures pertaining to the expectations gap. The first represents the mean of the four excellent president questions, while the second is the average of the four incumbent president questions (in both cases, the range is from zero to ten). These measures allow us to separately model the determinants of expectations of an ideal president—in essence a surrogate for expectations of the presidential office—and an incumbent president. Third, we calculate a measure of the expectations gap for the incumbent president, Bill Clinton, on each of the four separate leadership questions. Since 10 is the highest possible rating one could give for Clinton's leadership on each dimension and 0 is the lowest, we calculated the incumbent gap measure for each of the four leadership questions by subtracting the actual rating each individual gave President Clinton from 10. Hence, if an individual ranked Clinton's performance on sound judgment in a crisis as a 6, his/her gap measure would be $10 - 6 = 4$. A 10 is the highest possible gap measure for each question and a 0 indicates that an individual perceived Clinton as having no gap whatsoever. Our fourth measure directly employs the logic of the presidential "prototype" literature comparing an incumbent to an excellent or ideal president:

Excellent President Evaluation – Clinton Evaluation

This measure is calculated for all four leadership qualities, with a range of possible values from 10 to –10. Higher values reflect a larger expectations gap, zero represents no gap whatsoever, and negative values indicate that some individuals gave Clinton a higher rating than they would have expected of a hypothetical "excellent" or ideal president. As one would expect, relatively few respondents rated Clinton above the expected performance of an ideal president. Less than 5 percent gave Clinton a higher rating on "sound judgment" than they did an ideal or "excellent president," 13.9 percent did so on the experience in foreign affairs questions, 6.6 percent on the high ethical standards questions, and 8.3 percent on the ability to work well with Congress questions. Our final measure of the gap is a hybrid that combines elements of our first two measures. It incorporates the incumbent gap by subtracting Clinton's rating from ten, the highest possible score that he could have achieved on any question. We then incorporate the logic of the presidential prototype or ideal president model by weighting these results by how each individual ranked their expectations for an "excellent" president:

(10 – Clinton Rating) ∗ Rating of Excellent President

In table 10.1 we provide the summary statistics for the various gap measures.

The Independent Variables

Although a description of how we operationalized the independent variables is included in appendix B, a few words about our choice of measures are in order. To measure performance expectations, we asked individuals about their perceptions of the state of the U.S. economy (a sociotropic concern) and about the state of their personal finances (a pocketbook concern). We include both measures, even though the literature suggests that sociotropic concerns predominate, because while scholars have examined their relationship to public approval ratings, there is no comparable analysis of the effect

TABLE 10.1. Summary Statistic for the Expectation Gap Measures, 1998 and 1999 Surveys

	Mean 1998	Standard Deviation 1998	Mean 1999	Standard Deviation 1999
Averages				
Four excellent president questions	8.88	1.09	8.60	1.25
Incumbent president questions	5.76	2.43	5.33	2.30
Incumbent Gap				
Sound judgment in a crisis	3.30	2.90	3.76	2.72
Experience in foreign affairs	3.41	2.70	3.85	2.55
High ethical standards	6.40	3.16	6.78	2.98
Work well with Congress	3.83	2.52	4.25	2.44
Ideal President Gap				
Sound judgment in a crisis	2.88	3.08	3.03	3.07
Experience in foreign affairs	1.94	3.04	1.81	2.86
High ethical standards	5.11	4.10	5.59	3.91
Work well with Congress	2.57	2.82	2.61	2.88
Weighted ideal gap	37.63	23.47	40.43	21.39

of economic attitudes on the expectations gap. Therefore it is possible that either sociotropic or pocketbook attitudes could contribute to the gap. This leads to our first hypothesis.

HI: The more favorably one rates the state of the economy or one's own personal finances, the more satisfied one will be with the president's performance and hence the narrower will be one's expectations gap.

To test the excessive and unrealistic expectations thesis we begin with an admittedly rough indicator, education. The idea is that the more educated one is, the more one should know about the American political system. Krause (1997) uses a similar measure. The logic is that because one is more likely to understand the constitutional and political limits of presidential power, one should not expect presidents to be capable of doing something about everything, which in turn should translate into a narrower expectations gap. Another measure of knowledge is the primary source individuals use to get their news and information. While there is a plethora of news coverage on television, and some of it (e.g., the "News Hour" on PBS) is quite informative, empirical studies have typically found that on the whole those who rely primarily on television news rather than the print media are less knowledgeable about politics (see, e.g., Delli Carpini and Keeter 1996, 185; but also see Price and Zaller 1993). If those who get their information predominantly from TV are less knowledgeable about the presidency and its powers, then they are also more likely to have unrealistic expectations of the presidency and a wider expectations gap. To test for such an effect, we include a dummy variable for whether TV news is the respondent's primary source of information.

Participation in the political process also should increase one's knowledge of that process and its institutions, and thus make one's expectations more realistic. One basic measure of participation is whether an individual is registered to vote. Those who are not registered are much less likely to get involved in politics, and hence are likely to be less knowledgeable about how the political system functions. Thus, for each of the measures of unrealistic expectations the theoretical focus is on the relationship between knowledge about politics and the resulting expectations.

H2: We posit the more knowledgeable one is, or the more one participates politically, the more realistic one's expectations will be, and the narrower one's expectations gap will be.

To measure the "look first to the White House for leadership" thesis, we include measures for those groups most likely to look to the federal government during a Democratic administration, since the focus of our study is President Clinton: we include dummy variables for women, African Americans, and Latinos. Also, we include a measure of the age of our respondents because the older one is the more one is likely to expect from a Democratic president on issues such as Social Security and Medicare. Age is operationalized as the number of years a respondent has lived, and therefore as a continuous variable, with the idea being that the older one is, the more likely they are to look to the White House. We also examined other means of operationalizing age including using a dummy variable for those who were 62 and over and squaring the age of the respondent. We also include a measure of income because poorer individuals are more likely to look to the White House for leadership during a Democratic administration. We expect:

H3: These various groups will exhibit broader expectations gaps than nonmembers since they should look to the White House and expect a Democratic president to take the lead on issues of importance to them. There is, however, a second possibility: all of these groups are key constituencies of the Democratic Party. If, therefore, we find that they exhibit lower expectations this will be evidence for the political attitudes hypothesis (H5, which we develop later).

These variables allow us to test micro-level explanations. We also need to examine the potential influence of macro-level phenomena. For the 1998 survey, we asked respondents a battery of questions related to trust:

- Whatever its faults may be, the American form of government is still the best for us.
- There is not much about our form of government to be proud of.
- It may be necessary to make some major changes in our form of government in order to solve the problems facing our country.
- Unless we keep close watch on them, many of our elected leaders will look out for special interests rather than for all the people.
- When government leaders make statements to the American people on television or in the newspapers, they are usually telling the truth.
- You can generally trust the people who run our government to do what is right.

All of these statements were aligned along a scale running from one (strongly agree) to four (strongly disagree). For consistency purposes, before we analyzed the set of six responses, we flipped the scales for the best government, truthful leaders, and trust the people who run our government questions. Hence, lower values equal lower levels of trust and vice versa. For the 1999 survey we only have data on the last two questions, which again are aligned so that lower values equal lower levels of trust. To determine whether responses to all six statements were tapping into the same dimension of trust, we conducted a principal component analysis for the extraction method, and Varimax with Kaiser normalization for the rotation method (see table 10.1).

Our principal component analysis indicates that our measures of trust load on two distinct measures. The first grouping consists of these questions:

- Whatever its faults may be the American form of government is still the best for us [Best Gov. (scale reversed)].
- There is not much about our form of government to be proud of [Not Proud].
- It may be necessary to make some major changes in our form of government in order to solve the problems facing our country [Change Gov.].

The second set consists of these items:

- Unless we keep close watch on them, many of our elected leaders will look out for special interests rather than for all the people [Trust Scale (reversed)].
- When government leaders make statements to the American people on television or in the newspapers, they are usually telling the truth [Truthful Scale (reversed)].
- You can generally trust the people who run our government to do what is right [Special Interests].

Conceptually, trust in government is not a monolithic construct. Rather, there is a meaningful differentiation between how people trust government in general and how they trust their leaders. We think this is an important distinction, particularly since the expectations gap is related to perceptions of both a governmental office (the presidency) and a governmental leader (an incumbent president).

The variable loading was quite clean on the two factors. This analysis was repeated using alternative extraction methods (Principal Axis Factoring) and alternative rotation methods (Quartimax, Equimax). Despite some variation in factor scores, in every case the pattern of factor loadings was similar to the results shown in the table. To measure trust for the 1998 survey we use two scales combining the three government questions and then the three leadership questions. For the 1999 survey we use a scale combining the two leadership trust questions.

For political efficacy we follow Craig, Niemi, and Silver's (1990) method and measure the concept in two ways. To measure internal efficacy we asked, "Sometimes politics and government seem so complicated that a person like me can not really understand what's going on." We also asked, "I feel I could do as good a job in public office as most other people." Both questions were based on a four-point scale from strongly agree to strongly disagree. The second question was recoded (flipped) so that the scales of the two variables were consistent, then the two were aggregated to form the internal efficacy variable.

To measure external efficacy we asked respondents to respond to the following: "Voting is the only way people like me can have any say about how the government runs things" and "people like me do not have a say about what government does." Again the responses ranged from strongly agree to strongly disagree on a four-point scale. The two were aggregated to form the external efficacy variable. Our research expectation for trust and efficacy is as follows:

H4: The lower one's levels of trust in government or its leaders the broader one's expectations gap should be. Likewise, the less efficacious (internal or external) one's perceptions are, the broader will be one's expectations gap.

As for the political attitudes hypothesis, respondents were asked with which political party they identify, and then how strongly they identify with it. Using these two questions a seven-point scale was created that provides a measure of both partisan identification and the strength of their attachment to that party. We use this scale because we are interested in providing a more nuanced measure of partisanship than we have used in past chapters. Respondents also were asked to place themselves on a seven-point ideological scale ranging from very liberal to very conservative, and were asked to rate the job that the U.S. Congress was doing on a scale from one to four (with one "excellent," two "good," three "fair," and four "poor"). Because our surveys were conducted during the Clinton presidency, we hypothesize:

H5: The more strongly one identifies with the Democratic Party the narrower will be that individual's expectations gap. Likewise, the more liberal one is the narrower their gap will be. In both cases Democrats should be more likely to give Clinton the benefit of the doubt. Mitigating in the opposite direction, since the legislative branch was in Republican hands in 1998 and 1999 when our surveys were conducted, we hypothesize that individuals who have a more favorable evaluation of Congress will exhibit a wider expectations gap.

Because past research demonstrates that the president's approval rating is related to expectations, perceptions of trust in government, and the performance of the U.S. economy, we controlled for Clinton's approval rating using a four-point scale from excellent to poor. Past research also demonstrates that there is a connection between election results, the expectations gap, and trust in government (Hetherington 1999). For 1998, an election year, we therefore controlled for the respondent's expected vote in the upcoming midterm House election.

Finally, since the first survey was conducted during the impeachment crisis we control for it with a dummy variable measuring support for Clinton's impeachment. We also examined other measures related to impeachment, including support for Clinton's resignation or for his censure. The results using each measure were similar, thus we present only the models using impeachment here. This measure, however, does not allay our concerns that 1998 was a unique political year. Because we want to determine whether trust in government relates to evaluations of the presidential office and an incumbent president, we need to do more to control for impeachment and its effects. We therefore conducted a second survey in late 1999, after the resolution of the impeachment crisis. This provides us with an ability to compare the results both during and after the constitutional crisis to see if such factors as political trust and efficacy, as well as political attitudes, have a differential impact on individual perceptions of the expectations gap.

H6: We hypothesize broader expectations gaps for those who favored impeachment, did not approve of the president's job performance, and were more likely to vote Republican in the 1998 midterm election.

For the 1999 survey, we control only for the president's approval rating.

Comparing Expectations Gaps

The gap generally is hypothesized to have systemic effects that are the same for all presidents, such as the idea that unrealistic expectations always lead to lower approval ratings and declining reelection success. It also is possible, however, that the impact of the gap varies across different presidencies; that is, Carter, with high inflation, unemployment, and interest rates, had a more difficult time satisfying public expectations of presidential performance than Clinton, who governed in plush economic times. In identifying its determinants, then, we need to consider the gap's possible multidimensional nature. We did so by asking respondents to evaluate the office of the president and how important they thought certain qualities were for a hypothetical "excellent" president. We then asked them to evaluate Clinton's performance on the same four leadership dimensions. By comparing perceptions of the presidential office with evaluations of Clinton's performance we not only can identify the factors that drive public expectations, we can determine whether the same factors influence perceptions of the office and an incumbent in the same way.

In table 10.2 our dependent variables are the four leadership questions for "excellent" presidents and the evaluations of Bill Clinton on the same questions. The scale ranges from 0 to 10 with higher values meaning that respondents consider the four qualities to be more important for excellent presidents and higher values indicating greater approval of Clinton's job performance. For 1998, which was a midterm election year, perceptions of the economy are related to expectations of the *presidential office* (the more positively one views the economy's performance, the lower one's expectations are). Contrarily, more positive evaluations of the economy promote higher *evaluations of Clinton's job performance* (second column, table 10.3). Thus, a healthy economy promotes a narrower expectations gap by both reducing public expectations of the presidential office and encouraging higher presidential evaluations of the incumbent; a cross-pressuring effect.

A number of other factors also exhibit this cross-pressuring effect. For those who favored impeachment, expectations of the presidential office were higher, while evaluations of Clinton's performance were lower. In this manner, impeachment exacerbated Clinton's expectation gap. Likewise, greater trust in leadership leads to lower expectations of the presidency and higher evaluations of the president, thus decreasing the expectations gap. We find the same effect for our measure of partisan identification/party strength. On the other hand, higher expectations and lower evaluations of Clinton's performance can be found for those individuals who voted (or intended to vote) Republican in the 1998 midterm election. Ideology and President Clinton's approval rating also exhibit cross-pressuring effects. Thus during a midterm election year, and one politicized by the impeachment crisis, we find evidence of cross-pressuring effects in a variety of macro-level variables. The same pattern, however, is less prevalent in 1999, a year without presiden-

TABLE 10.2. Factor Analysis Communalities

	Initial	Extraction
Best gov. (scale reversed)	1.000	.604
Not proud	1.000	.557
Change govt.	1.000	.488
Trust scale (reversed)	1.000	.511
Truthful scale (reversed)	1.000	.584
Special interests	1.000	.610

Total Variance Explained

Component	Initial Eigenvalues			Extraction Sums of Squared Loadings			Rotation Sums of Squared Loadings		
	Total	% of Variance	Cumulative %	Total	% of Variance	Cumulative %	Total	% of Variance	Cumulative %
1	2.102	35.028	35.028	2.102	35.028	35.028	1.687	28.123	28.123
2	1.253	20.883	55.911	1.253	20.883	55.911	1.667	27.788	55.911
3	.858	14.293	70.204						
4	.642	10.694	80.897						
5	.628	10.465	91.362						
6	.518	8.638	100.000						

Rotated Component Matrix

Component		
	1	2
Best gov. (scale reversed)	.773	
Not proud	.733	.143
Change govt.	.666	.211
Trust scale (reversed)	.236	.745
Truthful scale (reversed)	.199	.738
Special interests	-.118	.705

Component Transformation Matrix

Component	1	2
	.715	.699
	-.699	.715

TABLE 10.3. Multiple Regression Analysis with Presidential Office and Incumbent President as the Dependent Variables, 1998 and 1999 Surveys

	Presidential Office/ Excellent President	Presidential Office/ Excellent President	Incumbent President/ Bill Clinton	Incumbent President/ Bill Clinton
	1998	1999	1998	1999
Constant	9.32	7.99	8.84	11.05
	(20.25)	(14.00)	(13.85)	(14.92)
Micro variables: Performance gap				
Sociotropic	−0.02	0.05	0.14	0.004
	(0.56)	(1.02)	(2.70)	(0.68)
Pocketbook	0.15	0.03	0.19	0.29
	(2.16)	(0.34)	(2.03)	(2.69)
Unrealistic expectations				
Education	−0.04	−0.04	−0.12	−0.08
	(0.88)	(0.73)	(2.04)	(1.12)
TV news	−0.005	0.08	−0.004	0.08
	(0.84)	(0.78)	(0.49)	(0.56)
Registered to vote	−0.05	0.008	−0.03	−0.06
	(0.39)	(.05)	(0.14)	(0.28)
Look first to the White House				
Age	0.009	0.006	0.007	−0.008
	(3.21)	(1.81)	(1.88)	(1.81)
Gender	−0.30	−0.32	−0.19	−0.04
	(3.73)	(3.10)	(1.70)	(0.32)
African American	−0.03	−0.25	1.15	0.76
	(0.20)	(1.14)	(4.90)	(2.72)
Latino	0.11	0.33	0.52	0.46
	(0.63)	(1.12)	(2.16)	(1.20)
Income	−0.006	0.03	−0.04	−0.01
	(0.37)	(1.45)	(1.66)	(0.34)
Macro variables: Trust/Efficacy				
Trust scale: Leadership	−0.02	−0.002	0.14	0.16
	(0.72)	(0.5)	(3.47)	(2.84)
Trust scale: Government	−0.05	—	−0.10	—
	(1.80)		(2.71)	
Internal efficacy	−0.01	0.03	−0.09	−0.34
	(0.41)	(0.69)	(1.89)	(2.45)
External efficacy	−0.05	−0.04	−0.005	0.02
	(1.33)	(0.89)	(0.11)	(0.20)

TABLE 10.3.—*Continued*

	Presidential Office/ Excellent President 1998	Presidential Office/ Excellent President 1999	Incumbent President/ Bill Clinton 1998	Incumbent President/ Bill Clinton 1999
Political attitudes				
Party ID/Strength	-0.01	0.01	0.08	0.16
	(0.51)	(0.43)	(2.03)	(3.78)
Ideology	0.07	0.03	-0.08	-0.17
	(2.24)	(0.82)	(1.98)	(3.50)
U.S. Congress approval	-0.09	-0.10	0.06	-0.17
	(1.79)	(1.41)	(0.85)	(1.84)
Control variables				
Clinton approval	0.04	0.13	-1.13	-1.14
	(0.82)	(1.98)	(15.17)	(13.86)
Impeachment	0.19	—	-1.10	—
	(1.66)		(7.02)	
Midterm vote Republican	0.05	—	-0.19	—
	(0.46)		(1.14)	
N	712	582	708	573
Adjusted R^2	.08	.03	.68	.55

Note: The unstandardized regression coefficient and its corresponding *t*-value (in parentheses) are presented.

tial or congressional elections—though we do find cross-pressured effects among Clinton's approval rating, both internal and external efficacy, and ideology.

With regard to the determinants of the mean excellent president questions, in 1998 pocketbook concerns, age, gender, ideology, and perceptions of the U.S. Congress meet the standard of significance, with impeachment and trust in government significant at the one-tailed level. With regard to trust in government the more one trusts the government the less one expects from an excellent president. Interestingly, evaluations of Clinton's approval rating are not related to perceptions of the presidency for 1998, though they are for the 1999 model; the higher Clinton's ratings are the more one expects from an excellent president. In 1999, age and gender are related to perceptions of the office, but only at a one-tailed significance level. Most important, the evidence from the two surveys indicates that macro-level factors were less likely to exhibit cross-pressuring effects once America moved beyond such politicizing events as a midterm election and impeachment.

Perhaps the most interesting result is that the leadership trust scale is related and in the expected direction for both years, while government trust exhibits a negative impact on Clinton's evaluations (meaning the more highly one trusts the government, the lower one's evaluation of Clinton will be). This is an unexpected finding, for it suggests higher levels of trust are related to lower presidential ratings. What explains this result?

Testing Micro and Macro Models of the Expectations Gap

We have hypothesized that macro-level factors are important determinants of the expectations gap. The results from tables 10.4, 10.5, and 10.6 demonstrate that expectations are strongly influenced by perceptions of trust. As hypothesized (H4), for 1998 and 1999 higher levels of trust in our political leaders are associated with a narrower expectations gap. For 1998 this is the case in three of the four incumbent gap models, three of the four ideal-incumbent gap models, and in the weighted gap model. In fact, the only instance where there is no relationship between the leadership trust scale and the expectations gap concerns the president's "ability to work well with Congress," a somewhat surprising finding since the members of Congress, like the president, are political leaders. For 1999 the trust measure, which consists of two leadership-related questions, is related to sound judgment in a crisis and high ethical standards in both the incumbent gap and ideal-incumbent gap models. It also is related to the weighted expectations gap measure. Thus, despite somewhat different scales (we have only two of the three leadership questions for 1999), the evidence from the 1998 and 1999 surveys are quite consistent.

For the 1998 survey we also can examine a second dimension of governmental trust. While the variable is related to expectations in four of the nine models, the coefficients in each case are positive. This result indicates that the more one trusts government, the larger one's expectations gap will be. Rather than providing support for our trust in government thesis, these results are more consistent with the look-first-to-the-White-House thesis. In other words, the more one trusts government, the more likely one is to look to the White House for leadership, the higher one's expectations will be, and thus the greater the potential for an expectations gap to emerge.

Hence, the mechanisms under which these two dimensions of trust operate are quite different in terms of how they affect the expectations gap. Our results therefore underscore a theoretical reason for examining different dimensions of trust in government. Trust in leaders and trust in government are not related to the expectations gap in the same way. When we focus on leaders, greater trust means that we are more likely to be satisfied with presidential leadership, while greater trust in government appears to mean that individuals are more motivated to seek rewards from the presidency and the government (perhaps even to favor a more activist government). It is precisely those with the greatest wide-eyed trust in government that the expectations gap thesis warns are most likely to ultimately be disappointed in the president's performance, and hence will inevitably exhibit a broader expectations gap.

Interestingly, the analysis of internal political efficacy also is consistent with the look-first-to-the-White-House micro-level thesis. We had hypothesized that the less efficacious (internal or external) one is, the broader their expectations gap will be (H4). The efficacy variables are measured such that increases on the eight-point scale correspond to higher levels of perceived internal and external efficacy. With regard to internal efficacy, then, in five of the nine models in tables 10.4 through 10.6 the positive coefficient indicates that higher levels of efficacy are related to a wider expectations gap. Interestingly, for both the 1998 and 1999 surveys, internal efficacy is related only to sound judgment in a crisis and to experience in foreign affairs. As noted, of the four qualities we consider, these most directly relate to the president as crisis manager and commander in chief, certainly among the president's most significant leadership responsibilities. As for external efficacy it is related to the various expectations gaps in only one of nine models. It is in the hypothesized direction for one model for 1998 and none of the models for 1999.

Three of the four trust/efficacy measures, then, provide support for the idea that macro-level variables are related to the expectations gap, even though the analysis of two of them is more consistent with a micro-level theory. The evidence with regard to political attitudes is, however, more consistent with the macro-level political attitudes hypothesis (H5).

When we control for the president's approval rating, support for impeachment, and expected vote in the 1998 midterm elections, we find the first two are significant in all models, the last in none, which provides support for two of our H6 hypotheses. We also find that the strength of partisan identification is related to the gap in one of the 1998 incumbent gap models and all four of the 1999 models. It also is related to two of the 1998 and 1999 ideal-incumbent gap models, as well as the weighted gap measures for 1998 and 1999. In all cases the effect is in the expected direction, meaning that the more strongly one identifies with the Democratic Party the lower Bill Clinton's expectation gap will be.

TABLE 10.4. Multiple Regression with the Incumbent Gap as the Dependent Variable, 1998 and 1999 Surveys

	Sound Judgment 1998	Sound Judgment 1999	Experience in Foreign Affairs 1998	Experience in Foreign Affairs 1999	High Ethical Standards 1998	High Ethical Standards 1999	Works well with Congress 1998	Works well with Congress 1999
Constant	-0.05 (0.05)	-2.26 (2.27)	-0.13 (0.15)	-0.79 (0.83)	2.24 (2.35)	0.28 (0.26)	2.11 (2.47)	-1.59 (1.64)
Micro: Performance gap								
Sociotropic	-0.18 (2.48)	-0.04 (0.47)	-0.14 (2.06)	-0.02 (0.30)	-0.03 (0.38)	-0.01 (0.12)	-0.19 (2.65)	0.09 (1.11)
Pocketbook	-0.11 (0.84)	-0.31 (2.14)	-0.25 (1.99)	-0.33 (2.39)	-0.03 (0.21)	-0.29 (1.92)	-0.34 (2.71)	-0.27 (1.89)
Unrealistic expectations								
Education	0.02 (0.21)	0.08 (0.79)	0.14 (1.80)	0.09 (1.05)	0.15 (1.81)	0.15 (1.53)	0.15 (1.95)	-0.005 (0.06)
TV news	0.005 (0.46)	-0.05 (0.29)	-0.001 (0.06)	-0.28 (1.71)	-0.005 (0.39)	0.17 (0.93)	0.02 (1.54)	-0.07 (0.43)
Registered to vote	0.31 (1.18)	-0.17 (0.58)	0.20 (0.81)	-0.23 (0.81)	0.12 (0.42)	0.66 (2.15)	-0.47 (1.88)	-0.05 (0.19)
Look to White House								
Age	-0.006 (1.24)	-0.002 (0.26)	-0.004 (0.86)	0.05 (0.83)	-0.007 (1.28)	0.01 (2.16)	-0.01 (2.03)	0.01 (2.54)
Gender	0.20 (1.28)	0.12 (0.66)	0.36 (2.46)	-0.05 (0.27)	-.08 (0.48)	-0.006 (0.03)	0.26 (1.78)	0.07 (0.40)
African American	-0.78 (2.35)	-0.55 (1.49)	-0.81 (2.54)	-0.24 (0.68)	-1.77 (4.99)	-1.90 (4.77)	-1.23 (3.88)	-0.27 (0.75)
Latino	0.38 (1.12)	-0.36 (0.71)	-0.51 (1.54)	0.45 (0.93)	-0.48 (1.30)	-1.71 (3.12)	-0.73 (2.21)	-0.17 (0.33)

Income	0.007	0.01	0.03	-0.16	0.08	0.05	0.02	0.0005
	(0.24)	(0.28)	(1.17)	(0.50)	(2.59)	(1.31)	(0.62)	(0.01)
Macro variables: Trust/Efficacy								
Trust scale: Leadership	-0.11	-0.18	-0.14	-0.11	-0.22	-0.22	-0.07	-0.11
	(1.97)	(2.42)	(2.67)	(1.53)	(3.77)	(2.77)	(1.24)	(1.51)
Trust scale: Government	0.07	—	0.12	—	0.16	—	0.06	—
	(1.35)		(2.88)		(2.86)		(1.19)	
Internal efficacy	0.15	0.23	0.19	0.23	-0.06	0.05	0.11	0.04
	(2.09)	(3.15)	(2.78)	(3.19)	(0.75)	(0.63)	(1.57)	(0.60)
External efficacy	0.01	-0.05	-0.01	-0.10	0.08	0.07	-.07	0.04
	(0.22)	(0.77)	(0.17)	(1.47)	(1.08)	(0.89)	(1.14)	(0.64)
Political attitudes								
Party ID/Strength	-0.09	-0.13	-0.11	-0.20	-0.09	-0.22	-0.03	-0.10
	(1.56)	(2.34)	(2.13)	(3.78)	(1.63)	(3.64)	(0.47)	(1.91)
Ideology	0.06	0.24	0.10	0.19	0.11	0.15	0.05	0.12
	(1.02)	(3.72)	(1.74)	(3.04)	(1.73)	(2.16)	(0.94)	(1.94)
U.S. Congress approval	-0.14	0.09	-0.13	0.21	-0.06	0.07	0.10	0.32
	(1.38)	(0.78)	(1.40)	(1.84)	(0.54)	(0.55)	(1.05)	(2.69)
Control variables								
Clinton approval	1.32	1.33	1.01	1.02	1.20	1.10	1.02	1.08
	(12.56)	(12.06)	(9.98)	(9.72)	(10.65)	(9.38)	(10.08)	(10.04)
Impeach	1.08	—	0.80	—	1.45	—	1.06	—
	(4.87)		(3.79)		(6.15)		(5.00)	
Midterm vote Republican	0.27	—	0.15	—	0.30	—	0.03	—
	(1.14)		(0.70)		(1.19)		(0.14)	
N	712	583	714	581	714	582	713	581
Adjusted R^2	.54	.45	.50	.40	.55	.44	.46	.34

Note: The unstandardized regression coefficient and its corresponding *t*-value (in parentheses) are presented.

TABLE 10.5. Multiple Regression with the Ideal – Incumbent Gap as the Dependent Variable, 1998 and 1999 Surveys

	Sound Judgment		Experience in Foreign Affairs		High Ethical Standards		Works well with Congress	
	1998	1999	1998	1999	1998	1999	1998	1999
Constant	-0.94	-4.43	-0.01	-2.18	1.09	-3.38	1.66	-2.58
	(0.95)	(3.97)	(0.01)	(1.87)	(0.90)	(2.47)	(1.59)	(2.10)
Micro variables: Performance gap								
Sociotropic	-0.25	0.07	-0.14	-0.01	-0.08	0.03	-0.15	0.15
	(3.13)	(0.73)	(1.60)	(0.13)	(0.80)	(0.30)	(1.75)	(1.51)
Pocketbook	-0.02	-0.40	-0.01	-0.28	0.03	-0.22	-0.18	-0.23
	(0.11)	(2.47)	(0.06)	(1.62)	(0.15)	(1.11)	(1.17)	(1.27)
Unrealistic expectations								
Education	0.04	0.17	0.09	-0.005	0.17	0.13	0.02	-0.12
	(0.45)	(1.65)	(0.96)	(0.05)	(1.57)	(1.01)	(0.20)	(1.21)
TV news	0.001	-0.14	0.001	-0.11	-0.03	0.20	0.03	0.06
	(0.11)	(0.70)	(0.07)	(0.56)	(2.05)	(0.83)	(1.95)	(0.26)
Registered to vote	0.39	-0.07	-0.03	-0.26	-0.01	1.00	-0.40	-0.45
	(1.35)	(0.23)	(0.08)	(0.75)	(0.25)	(2.50)	(1.30)	(1.26)
Look to White House								
Age	0.004	0.003	0.001	0.01	0.002	0.02	-0.0004	0.02
	(0.75)	(0.41)	(0.20)	(1.84)	(0.24)	(2.30)	(0.07)	(2.92)
Gender	0.02	-0.17	0.02	-0.48	-0.43	-0.22	-0.02	-0.33
	(0.11)	(0.88)	(0.10)	(2.31)	(2.07)	(0.90)	(0.11)	(1.50)
African American	-1.40	-1.07	-0.53	-0.40	-1.76	-2.10	-1.06	-0.65
	(3.82)	(2.58)	(1.31)	(0.92)	(3.90)	(4.07)	(2.72)	(1.43)
Latino	-0.40	0.007	-0.25	0.90	-0.67	-1.27	-0.35	-0.07
	(1.07)	(0.01)	(0.60)	(1.49)	(1.43)	(1.80)	(0.87)	(0.13)

	(1)	(2)	(3)	(4)	(5)	(6)	(7)	(8)
Income	0.02 (0.64)	0.06 (1.61)	0.02 (0.45)	-0.05 (1.19)	0.08 (1.92)	0.09 (1.84)	-0.0002 (0.01)	0.04 (1.03)
Macro variables: Trust/Efficacy								
Trust scale: Leadership	-0.15 (2.39)	-0.20 (2.34)	-0.17 (2.50)	-0.04 (0.38)	-0.26 (3.41)	-0.22 (2.10)	-0.04 (0.71)	-0.15 (1.60)
Trust scale: Government	0.11 (1.89)	—	0.01 (0.18)	—	0.13 (1.78)	—	-0.04 (0.65)	—
Internal efficacy	0.18 (2.29)	0.30 (3.57)	0.16 (1.86)	0.26 (2.97)	-0.12 (1.30)	0.12 (1.17)	0.11 (1.30)	-0.03 (0.32)
External efficacy	-0.01 (0.12)	-0.12 (1.55)	-0.12 (1.47)	-0.07 (0.90)	0.08 (0.93)	0.03 (0.28)	-0.14 (1.75)	0.005 (0.05)
Political attitudes								
Party ID	-0.06 (1.06)	-0.10 (1.59)	-0.11 (1.71)	-0.19 (2.85)	-0.13 (1.71)	-0.21 (2.67)	-0.07 (1.18)	-0.07 (1.03)
Ideology	0.09 (1.40)	0.23 (3.15)	0.15 (2.12)	0.20 (2.58)	0.27 (3.44)	0.23 (2.54)	0.07 (0.98)	0.17 (2.14)
U.S. Congress approval	-0.18 (1.65)	0.20 (1.44)	-0.15 (1.20)	0.11 (0.76)	-0.29 (2.12)	-0.11 (0.64)	0.02 (0.19)	0.15 (1.02)
Control variables								
Clinton approval	1.29 (11.15)	1.38 (11.22)	0.97 (7.53)	0.96 (7.43)	1.45 (10.17)	1.68 (11.06)	0.99 (8.04)	1.08 (7.94)
Impeach	1.07 (4.38)	—	0.92 (3.40)	—	2.05 (6.81)	—	1.11 (4.28)	—
Midterm vote Republican	0.36 (1.39)	—	0.21 (0.75)	—	0.48 (1.50)	—	-0.11 (0.40)	—
N	711	582	711	581	713	580	712	580
Adjusted R^2	.51	.42	.35	.27	.56	.45	.33	.25

Note: The unstandardized regression coefficient and its corresponding t-value (in parentheses) are presented.

TABLE 10.6. Multiple Regression Analysis with the Weighted Gap as the Dependent Variable, 1998 and 1999 Surveys

| | Average Weighted Gap for All Four Leadership Dimensions | |
	1998	1999
Constant	13.12	−12.65
	(2.15)	(1.79)
Micro level variables: Performance based gap		
Sociotropic	−1.37	0.17
	(2.77)	(0.29)
Pocketbook	−1.29	−2.54
	(1.45)	(2.44)
Unrealistic expectations		
Education	0.76	0.71
	(1.40)	(1.10)
TV news	0.06	−0.49
	(0.76)	(0.40)
Registered to vote	0.46	−0.10
	(0.30)	(0.47)
Look first to the White House		
Age	−0.04	0.09
	(1.01)	(2.06)
Gender	0.33	−1.14
	(0.32)	(0.90)
African American	−10.17	−7.24
	(4.52)	(2.72)
Latino	−4.89	−2.88
	(2.11)	(0.79)
Income	0.35	0.23
	(1.69)	(0.94)
Macro level variables: Trust/Efficacy		
Trust scale: Leadership	−1.18	−1.26
	(3.13)	(2.36)
Trust scale: Government	0.51	—
	(1.42)	
Internal efficacy	0.83	1.24
	(1.74)	(2.35)
External efficacy	−0.17	−0.39
	(0.38)	(0.79)
Political attitudes		
Party ID/Strength	−0.86	−1.33
	(2.33)	(3.33)

TABLE 10.6.—*Continued*

	Average Weighted Gap for All Four Leadership Dimensions	
	1998	1999
Ideology	0.80	1.88
	(2.07)	(4.05)
U.S. Congress approval	-0.97	1.31
	(1.44)	(1.50)
Control variables		
Clinton approval	10.49	10.79
	(14.70)	(13.70)
Impeach	11.92	—
	(7.96)	
Midterm vote Republican	2.32	—
	(1.46)	
N	706	571
Adjusted R^2	.68	.54

Note: The unstandardized regression coefficient and its corresponding *t*-value (in parentheses) are presented.

Ideology is related to the gap in two of the 1998 incumbent gap and two ideal-incumbent models. Ideology also was related to the gap in the weighted gap model. For 1999 ideology is significant in all nine models. Perceptions of Congress were less important; they were significant in only two of nine models for both 1998 and 1999 (and the coefficients are negative for 1998 and positive for 1999). The partisanship and ideology measures, however, provide additional evidence that Clinton's expectations gaps were affected by macro-level political factors. What then is the evidence from our micro-level variables?

The strongest results are from the presidential performance variables. In 1998, in six of the nine models (three of the four incumbent models, two of the ideal-incumbent models, and the weighted gap model), perceptions of the U.S. economy (i.e., sociotropic attitudes) are related to the expectations gap. The more favorably one evaluates the performance of the economy, the lower Clinton's gap is. Pocketbook concerns have a lesser impact; they were significant in two instances (both of them incumbent models), but again the result was in the expected direction. More positive assessments of one's own personal finances were related to a narrower expectations gap. These results are consistent with much of the literature that argues that sociotropic attitudes are predominant over pocketbook attitudes.

The results from 1999—a nonelection year—provide an entirely different perspective. Sociotropic attitudes are significant in none of the nine models, while pocketbook attitudes are significantly related to expectations in six of nine models. It appears that, once the politicization of the election year passes, the public turns its primary attention from the state of the U.S. economy to their individual finances. This suggests an important difference between the determinants of the gap in an election and a nonelection year.

As noted, the macro-level results concerning trust in government provide support for the look-first-to-the-White-House thesis. Few of the coefficients for the measures of the groups most likely to look to the White House, however, provide support for this thesis. We find statistically significant coefficients for women (representing higher expectations of presidential performance) in three of the nine models for 1998. In two the result is consistent with the political attitudes thesis; women have lower expectations gaps; the one exception for 1998 is high ethical standards. Gilens (1988) also reports inconsistent findings with regard to the gender gap. He notes that military and social welfare issues exacerbated the gender gap, while environmental and women's issues had little effect. Since Clinton was accused of adultery with a much younger woman, this contrary result with regard to ethics is not particularly surprising. For 1999 gender is related to expectations in only one of nine models and not in the expected direction.

Income is positively related to the gap in three of nine models for 1998 and one of nine for 1999; meaning that poorer individuals have smaller expectations gap measures, rather than the larger ones that we hypothesized. Age is significantly related to expectations in only one of nine models for 1998 and again not in the expected direction; the older one is the lower one's expectations are. The evidence from 1999, however, is more compelling. The relationship is significant in six of nine models, and, as we anticipated, the older one is the higher one's expectations are likely to be. Likewise, in three of nine models for 1998, and one for 1999, the coefficient for Latinos is significant and negative, meaning that Latinos on the whole had a narrower expectations gap than did non-Latinos. We found the same result for African Americans; the results were significant in eight of the nine gap models for 1998 and four of nine for 1999.

Hence, the results are mixed. There is some support for the look-to-the-White- House thesis in these results, particularly among women in 1998 and with regard to age in 1999. The other look-to-the-White-House variables, however, are more consistent with the political attitudes thesis. African Americans and Latinos tend to be an important component of the Democratic constituency in presidential elections. With some exceptions, then, these findings point to a political attitudes interpretation of the expectations gap (H5).

Finally, there is little statistical support for the variables representing the unrealistic and excessive expectations model. Four of the coefficients for education are positive in 1998 (none in 1999), indicating that the more educated one is the higher one's expectations will be (which is contrary to H2). Registering to vote is related to lower expectations, as hypothesized, but only in one of nine models in 1998. For 1999, registering to vote is related to higher expectations in two of nine models. As for TV news, it is related to expectations in two 1998 models (but the coefficients are positive in one and negative in the other) and one 1999 model (and the coefficient is negative). This finding suggests that more research is required on the likely impact of TV along the lines of the work of Valentino, Hutchings, and White (2002) and Gilliam and Iyengar (2000).

In summary, our a priori theorizing led to some interesting results. First, two macro-level variables (trust in government and internal efficacy), while they are related to the expectations gap, provide better evidence for the micro-level "look first to the White House" hypothesis (H3). Second, increased trust in leadership is related to the gap as hypothesized (H4). Third, the evidence with regard to African Americans and to a lesser extent Latinos, when added to our measures of partisanship and ideology, provides convincing evidence that the gap is driven, to a considerable extent, by political attitudes (H5). Fourth, perceptions of economic performance (primarily sociotropic in 1998 and pocketbook concerns in 1999) are related to the gap and consistent with the performance-based assumption of the gap thesis (H1). Therefore, we find evidence that both macro and micro-level theoretical approaches address the determinants of the expectations gap. Furthermore, macro-level variables provide some of the strongest support for both the macro- and micro-level theories.

Conclusions

Presidential and congressional scholars have operationalized and tested a measure of the expectations gap, which, as hypothesized, is related to lower approval ratings and, in the case of the presidency, negatively related to vote choice for an incumbent president (Kimball and Patterson 1997; Waterman, Jenkins-Smith, and Silva 1999). In this book we also found a relationship between the expectations gap and vote choice in midterm elections. We also have contributed to this literature with the first comprehensive empirical analysis of the determinants of the expectations gap, examining the gap thesis from a variety of theoretical perspectives.

In this chapter our analysis incorporated both micro and macro-level explanations for why the gap exists. Importantly, we found that the gap is well explained with reference to macro-level political phenomena, such as perceptions of trust in leadership and government, internal political efficacy, and various measures of political attitudes. Ironically, the strongest evidence for the three micro-level theories of the presidency is provided by macro-level variables: trust in government and political efficacy.

Our findings also have implications for the trust in government literature. We show that trust exhibits differential impacts with regard to perceptions of government and its leaders.

Our analysis opens the door for research into expectations of other political actors across the governmental system, such as the courts, the media, interest groups, governors, state legislatures, and mayors, as well as the police and other civil servants. Only by examining the expectations gap over time and across different political institutions can we better understand how it is related to macro-level political variables. This line of research is theoretically and substantively important, for if the public expects too much from government in general, and is therefore most often disappointed in the results, it suggests that politicians need to make more credible promises when they run for office, the media has to do a better job of analyzing political news, and that the public needs to be better informed about the political process. A broadly based expectations gap across different governmental institutions therefore could provide a real threat to effective democratic government. We turn to this possibility in the final chapter.

The Expectations Gap in a Broader Theoretical Context

Poverty and hunger and disease are afflictions as old as man himself.
But in our time and in this age there has been a change. The change
is not so much in the realities of life, but in the hopes and the
expectations of the future.

President Lyndon Johnson, remarks to editors,
conference on foreign policy, April 21, 1964

For more than half a century presidential scholars of all stripes (including political scientists, historians, and biographers), journalists, pundits, political operatives, and bloggers have discussed the negative ramifications of the presidential expectations gap. As we demonstrate in this book, even presidents and their advisers have considered the double-edged possibilities of a gap. The expectations gap has been treated as a given, subject to rare and inadequate empirical analysis. Our book therefore represents the first comprehensive attempt to examine the gap and its effects. We have done so using a variety of measures of the gap, and while we certainly concur that much more work needs to be done to measure this thorny and complicated issue, we believe our initial work sheds substantial light on the dimensions of the gap problem, as well as demonstrating that we can directly test theories of the presidency using survey research techniques.

Still, presidential scholars tend to examine the gap as it relates only to the presidency. Yet our findings provide the first hint that the expectations gap is a larger and more formidable problem for American democracy. Not only do we find that the gap operates as has been long hypothesized, providing presidents with short-term benefits while threatening their long-term viability in terms of lower approval ratings, a lower probability of reelection success, and even a more damning verdict from the electorate at a president's midterm; we also show that the gap operates in a systematic fashion. Our findings can be extrapolated to suggest that the gap affects all modern presidents. Furthermore, there is no obvious solution to the gap problem. It is not enough for presidents to curtail expectations. The problem is endemic. The public has unrealistic and contradictory expectations of presidential performance that in time translate into disappointment and disillusionment.

Our Findings

First, we have demonstrated that the gap is not a monolith. Rather, it varies from individual to individual, with some people having higher expectations than others. As we found in the last chapter, the gap is related to partisan attitudes. In an age of increasing political polarization in Washington and among the electorate as a whole, these partisan impacts are proving toxic indeed. When Barack Obama tried to transcend partisanship he was derided as naïve and many of his signature policies were simply ignored. The Obama example shows that it simply is not enough to ignore partisanship. At certain critical periods in American history the electorate divides neatly into competing political camps. We are at such an impasse at present. Until the country decides to move in one direction or another, these partisan effects will continue to exert a deleterious impact on our political process. We contend that they will do so not only for the presidency, through the mediating factor of an expectations gap, but through impacts on other governmental institutions, as well. Hence, our findings with regard to partisanship suggest that the expectations gap, while it is important, is but one factor affecting evaluations of presidents and the presidency. Nor do we think that the gap is related only to the presidency. It may be appropriate to discuss an expectations gap in a larger context, one that affects our expectations of a wide variety of other policy actors, at all levels of government. In other words, the expectations gap may not be a presidency-centric concept at all, but rather a symptom of a larger dysfunction with American government.

A related finding from our work is that the expectations gap also is related to trust in government, but particularly to the issue of trust in our leaders. This finding also suggests that the expectations gap is not a solitary concept that is merely limited to the presidency alone. It ties into a larger trend, what we referred to in the last chapter as a macro-level phenomenon. Kimball and Patterson (1997) already demonstrated that there is evidence of a comparable gap in relation to the U.S. Congress. Our results in chapter 10 with regard to trust in government and its leaders likewise suggest that the expectations gap is related to a higher level of discontent with our governmental system. As such, it is evidence not merely of a dysfunction related to the presidency but quite possibly of a larger threat to our democratic institutions in general.

Trust Matters

Hetherington (2005, 8) writes that "the key change in American public opinion over the last 40 years" is that "Americans have lost faith in the federal government to implement and administer public policy." Declining levels of trust in government are important because scholars conclude that trust is related to perceptions of a variety of policy actors. In the last chapter we found that trust is related to perceptions of the presidential expectations gap. Trust also is related to perceptions of Congress.[1] And Blendon and colleagues (1997) show the public tends to trust state and local governments more than its federal counterpart.

Yet despite past work on the subject, we still do not know how extensive trust's impact is because most research on trust has been conducted with trust as the dependent variable.[2] While we therefore understand the determinants of trust (e.g., Citrin and Green 1986 show that it is related to economic performance; Patterson 1993 to negative coverage by the media), it is still unclear how extensively trust affects public perceptions of a variety of political actors and institutions.

To provide an initial test of the possibility that leadership trust and governmental trust are related to perceptions of various governmental actors at the federal and state level, as well as some nonpolitical service institutions, we analyzed individual-level data from two national surveys for 1998 and 1999. Since we are interested in trust in particular, a focus on both years allows us to put the passions of a midterm election year and the impeachment case (1998) into clearer perspective. By examining 1999 we can analyze perceptions after each of these events occurred (the election and the impeachment trial). We add a caveat at this point: the ordered probit models that we present are meant only as a preliminary analysis of the question of trust. While they are preliminary, however, the consistency of the results is striking and raises concerns about the long-term impact of trust and the expectations gap on our system of American democracy.

Evaluating Different Policy Actors

We are interested in the question of whether the expectations gap and trust are related to evaluations of the performance of government officials at all levels of government including federal-, state-, and local-level political actors. In addition, we want to know if trust is related to nonpolitical actors involved in service activities. We therefore have a series of dependent variables that are divided into three basic categories: federal actors—the federal government, the U.S. Congress, the incumbent president, Bill Clinton, and the incumbent vice president, Al Gore; state and local actors—state legislatures, governors, mayors, and, for 1999 only, school boards; and service institutions—police and public employees.

To gauge perceptions of these actors respondents were asked, "Using a scale of excellent, good, fair, or poor how would you rate the following:[3]

The performance of the U.S. Congress?
The job Bill Clinton is doing as President of the United States?
The job Al Gore is doing as Vice-President of the United States?
The performance of your state's Legislature?
The job your governor is doing?
The job your mayor is doing?
The job the school board in your area is doing? [for the 1999 survey only]
The performance of your state's public employees?
The performance of the police in your area?

Respondents were then asked, "Overall, would you say that the federal government is doing an excellent, good, fair or poor job of governing the U.S.?" The scale for all our dependent variables is therefore a four-point ordinal scale. To ease the interpretation of the results, we have reversed the order of the scale so that 4 = excellent, 3 = good, 2 = fair, and 1 = poor. Because all of our dependent variables are ordinal we employed an ordered probit analysis.

In table 11.1 we present the results of the 1998 and 1999 evaluations (in percentages) for each policy actor. There are similarities in the ratings of the various policy actors across the two surveys, though every single actor received a lower rating in 1999 than in 1998. When we combine "excellent" and "good" responses for 1998 we find that the police had the highest approval ratings (74.6%), followed by mayors (63.3%), governors (63.1%), the president (55.2%), public employees (52.9%), state legislatures (47.9%), the federal government (46.3%), the vice president (44.9%), and the U.S. Congress (35.3%). Thus, executives received some of the highest ratings, while legislators received some of the lowest. Since conventional wisdom suggests that people are generally dissatisfied with the federal government, it is a bit surprising that 46.3% rank it as "excellent" or "good." That the vice president and Congress have even lower ratings, however, is even more surprising.

For 1999 the police again have the highest approval rating (a combined 72.4%), followed by mayors (59.7%), governors (58.3%), school boards (53.1%), public employees (48.7%), state legislatures (48.7%), the president (44.6%), the federal government (37.7%), the U.S. Congress (28.1%), and the vice president (27.7%). The order of the rankings is similar to 1998, with executives again rated higher than legislatures. Again, the U.S. Congress and the vice president have lower ratings than the federal government, suggesting one reason why Al Gore did not do better in the 2000 presidential election, despite a robust economy.

Although there are patterns in the data, when we look across the three broad categories of policy actors (federal, state and local, and service actors) we find that the president is the most highly rated of the federal actors, but that the other three federal actors (the federal government, the U.S. Congress, and the vice president) rank toward the bottom of the list. Among the state and local actors state legislatures rank markedly lower than the mayors, governors, and school boards. The only area where all actors receive high evaluations is in the service area. The police rank well above all other actors in both surveys, while public employees are just over 50 percent in 1998 and just under 50 percent in 1999. The data show that executives have more posi-

TABLE 11.1. Job Approval Ratings for Federal, State, Local and Service Positions, 1998 and 1999 Surveys

	1998				1999			
	Excellent	Good	Fair	Poor	Excellent	Good	Fair	Poor
Federal government	4.5	41.8	40.6	13.1	1.9	35.8	43.1	19.2
U.S. Congress	3.0	32.3	45.4	19.3	1.3	26.8	49.2	22.8
President	16.6	38.6	22.1	22.6	11.0	33.6	29.4	26.0
Vice president	9.2	35.7	35.9	19.2	3.7	24.0	43.4	28.8
State legislatures	3.4	44.0	42.6	10.0	1.9	40.7	45.5	12.0
Governors	16.0	47.1	27.8	9.0	9.9	48.4	32.4	9.3
Mayors	13.5	49.8	28.4	8.3	12.2	47.5	29.0	11.2
Public employees	4.9	48.0	39.1	8.0	3.2	45.5	42.1	9.2
Police	21.8	52.8	18.8	6.7	19.3	53.1	20.0	7.7
School boards	—	—	—	—	11.2	41.9	29.9	17.0

tive evaluations than legislative institutions and reveal that there is considerable variation across the evaluations of the ten policy actors.

Federal Policy Actors

In the following tables we use a series of ordered logit models to examine whether trust is related to perceptions of the ten policy actors. We urge caution in interpreting the results, due to the often small pseudo r-squares. Still, as can be seen in table 11.2, of the two measures of trust in government, the leadership trust measure is related to three of the four federal policy actors for both 1998 and 1999. The higher one's level of trust in governmental leaders, the more likely one is to approve of the performance of the federal government, the U.S. Congress, and Vice President Al Gore. Leadership trust is not related to President Clinton's approval ratings, though it is related to Clinton's expectations gap. In fact, when we remove the expectations gap from the model, leadership trust is related to Clinton's job approval rating. This again suggests an interesting finding: that leadership trust is related to the public perceptions of the president's expectations gap, which in turn has a deleterious affect on the president's job approval rating. As for the government trust scale, it is related only to perceptions of the performance of the federal government in 1998—we do not have this measure for 1999. As we would expect, the more one trusts the government, the more likely one is to approve of the federal government. Therefore, the evidence from the eight federal models is consistent with our past finding that trust matters, particularly trust in leaders.

What then of the president's expectations gap? We hypothesize that it is related to other federal policy actors, as well as to other politicians holding executive positions. Not surprisingly, the gap is related to President Clinton's job approval ratings. The gap is also related to two other policy actors: perceptions of the federal government and Vice President Al Gore's job approval ratings. In both cases, the larger the president's expectations gap, the less likely one is to approve of the performance of these federal actors. Contrary to our hypothesis, the president's expectations gap is not related to evaluations of the job performance of the U.S. Congress.[4] Interestingly, for the 1998 models, other than the leadership trust scale and impeachment, no other variable is significantly related to evaluations of all four federal actors. Internal efficacy is related only to the vice president (and not in the expected direction), while external efficacy is not significant in any of the four models. Evaluations of the national economy (sociotropic perceptions) are related to evaluations of the federal government and the president, but not the vice president or Congress. Pocketbook perceptions are not related to any of the federal policy actors.[5]

As for the 1999 results, the leadership trust measure is related to evaluations of three federal actors in the expected direction, as is the president's expectations gap. Internal efficacy is related to evaluations of Congress in the hypothesized direction, while perceptions of external efficacy are not related to any of the four federal policy actors. Sociotropic attitudes are related to evaluations of the federal government and the president, while pocketbook attitudes are related to the federal government.[6]

While these results present some interesting insights, the most striking conclusion from the analysis of the federal actors is that perceptions of leadership trust are related to perceptions of federal actors in six out of eight models. In all cases, the higher the level of trust in leaders, the more likely one is to approve of the performance of the two federal institutions (the federal government and Congress) and Vice President Gore. But given the finding of Blendon et al. (1997) that the public has higher levels of trust in state and local governments than in the federal government, we also need to examine the effect of trust at the state and local level.

State and Local Policy Actors

The models for state and local institutions are presented in table 11.3.[7] The only variable that is related to all three state or local elective institutions (state legislatures, governors, and mayors) for 1998 and all four (including school boards) in the 1999 surveys is leadership trust. In each case, higher levels of trust are related to more positive evaluations for all three state and local policy actors. For 1998, the trust in government scale is related only to state legislatures in one of three models and only at the one-tailed level of significance. Still, as we found in the case of national institutions, trust in leadership matters.[8]

With regard to the expectations gap and other executive politicians the results are quite interesting. The president's expectations gap is related to the job performance rating of the 50 U.S. governors in 1998. Not only is the effect significant but also the broader the president's expectations gap is the more likely one is to have a favorable impression of the performance of one's governor. This suggests that the public may be more willing to blame executive failures on the president, rather than on their own governor. The evidence with regard to mayors bolsters this interpretation. The expectations

TABLE 11.2. Approval Ratings of Various Federal Positions as the Dependent Variable, 1998 and 1999 Surveys

	Federal Government 1998	Congress 1998	President 1998	Vice President 1998	Federal Government 1999	Congress 1999	President 1999	Vice President 1999
Expectations gap	.02*** (.005)	-.005 (.004)	.08*** (.006)	.05*** (.005)	.02*** (.006)	.009 (.05)	.09*** (.01)	.04*** (.01)
Leadership trust	-.47*** (.05)	-.41*** (.05)	-.04 (.06)	-.20*** (.05)	-.54*** (.08)	-.49*** (.08)	-.06 (.08)	-.24*** (.08)
Government trust	-.15*** (.05)	-.01 (.05)	-.10 (.05)	-.06 (.05)	—	—	—	—
Internal efficacy	-.03 (.07)	.09 (.06)	-.10 (.07)	-.13* (.07)	.09 (.09)	.16* (.04)	-.03 (.09)	-.02 (.09)
External efficacy	.06 (.06)	.01 (.06)	.04 (.07)	.04 (.06)	-.12 (.07)	.12 (.07)	.0005 (.08)	-.03 (.08)
Sociotropic perceptions	-.32*** (.07)	-.03 (.07)	-.24*** (.07)	-.06 (.07)	-.17* (.08)	-.05 (.08)	-.21* (.09)	.04 (.08)
Pocketbook perceptions	-.16 (.12)	-.06 (.12)	-.11 (.13)	-.10 (.12)	-.37* (.15)	.01 (.15)	-.001 (.16)	-.12 (.16)
Education	.06 (.07)	.10 (.07)	.09 (.08)	-.08 (.07)	.06 (.09)	.05 (.09)	-.07 (.10)	-.02 (.10)
Age	.01*** (.005)	.015* (.005)	.0005 (.005)	-.004 (.005)	.01 (.01)	.03*** (.01)	-.01 (.01)	-.01 (.01)
Gender	.48*** (.14)	.35** (.14)	.12 (.15)	.44** (.15)	.46** (.19)	.56** (.19)	.42* (.20)	.42* (.20)
African American	.08 (.31)	-.01 (.29)	-.90*** (.34)	.04 (.30)	-.60 (.40)	.11 (.39)	-.35 (.40)	.28 (.40)
Latino	-.95*** (.37)	-.25 (.34)	-.09 (.35)	.17 (.35)	-.68 (.58)	-1.49** (.57)	.80 (.64)	-.18 (.29)

Ideology	.004	-.15***	.01	.17***	.05	-.12	.04	1.16
	(.05)	(.05)	(.06)	(.05)	(.03)	(.07)	(.07)	(.64)
Democrats	-.31	.16	-.39**	-.43**	.24	.60***	-1.47	-.49*
	(.16)	(.15)	(.17)	(.16)	(.24)	(.24)	(.26)	(.25)
Registered to vote	-.31	.20	.08	.23	.40	-.09	.46	.61
	(.26)	(.24)	(.26)	(.25)	(.35)	(.33)	(.35)	(.34)
TV news	-.005	-.01	-.01	-.01	.15	-.09	.03	-.37**
	(.01)	(.01)	(.01)	(.01)	(.19)	(.18)	(.19)	(.19)
Support for impeachment	-.17	-.55***	1.52***	-.03	—	—	—	—
	(.20)	(.19)	(.12)	(.20)				
N	834	830	837	787	496	487	497	460
Probability > chi-square	.000	.000	.000	.000	.000	.000	.000	.000
Pseudo R^2	.14	.07	.37	.17	.14	.09	.33	.14

*** significant at the .001 level; ** significant at the .05 level; * significant at the .10 level.

TABLE 11.3. Approval Ratings of State and Local Positions as the Dependent Variable, 1998 and 1999 Surveys

	State Legislatures 1998	Governors 1998	Mayors 1998	State Legislatures 1999	Governors 1999	Mayors 1999	School Boards 1999
Expectations gap	−.004	−.01*	.008	.01	.003	.003	−.002
	(.005)	(.004)	(.005)	(.006)	(.005)	(.005)	(.01)
Leadership trust	−.36***	−.17***	−.17***	−.53***	−.16*	−.23**	−.21**
	(.05)	(.05)	(.05)	(.08)	(.08)	(.08)	(.08)
Government trust	−.09	−.05	−.06	—	—	—	—
	(.05)	(.05)	(.05)				
Internal efficacy	.09	−.01	.03	−.02	.09	.08	−.07
	(.07)	(.06)	(.07)	(.09)	(.08)	(.09)	(.08)
External efficacy	.14*	−.03	.16*	.01	−.06	−.01	−.15*
	(.06)	(.06)	(.06)	(.07)	(.07)	(.08)	(.07)
Sociotropic perceptions	−.09	−.17**	−.15*	−.05	−.16*	−.18*	−.02
	(.07)	(.07)	(.07)	(.09)	(.08)	(.09)	(.08)
Pocketbook perceptions	−.13	−.04	−.12	.11	.34*	−.03	.02
	(.07)	(.11)	(.12)	(.16)	(.15)	(.15)	(.15)
Education	.16*	.08	−.04	−.004	.06	−.02	.08
	(.07)	(.07)	(.07)	(.09)	(.09)	(.09)	(.09)
Age	.003	−.003*	−.005	.0003	−.01	−.002	−.01
	(.005)	(.005)	(.005)	(.006)	(.01)	(.01)	(.006)
Gender	.81***	.28*	.41**	.81***	−.02	−.09	.19
	(.15)	(.14)	(.14)	(.20)	(.18)	(.19)	(.19)
African American	.13	.28	−.13	−.09	−.12	−.51	.49
	(.31)	(.29)	(.30)	(.38)	(.36)	(.37)	(.35)
Latino	.17	−.04	−.82*	−.43	.09	.22	−.77
	(.36)	(.33)	(.34)	(.58)	(.55)	(.54)	(.58)
Registered to vote	−.51*	−.16	−.07	.28	−.09	−.24	.26
	(.26)	(.24)	(.25)	(.15)	(.32)	(.33)	(.32)
TV news	−.01	−.02*	−.01	−.11	−.42**	.20	−.16
	(.01)	(.01)	(.01)	(.19)	(.18)	(.19)	(.18)
Support for impeachment	−.07	.09	−.36	—	—	—	—
	(.20)	(.18)	(.20)				
N	808	827	773	480	491	445	469
Probability > chi-square	.000	.000	.000	.000	.015	.065	.028
Pseudo R^2	.07	.03	.03	.07	.03	.03	.02

*** significant at the .001 level; ** significant at the .05 level; * significant at the .10 level.

gap just falls short of statistical significance at the two-tailed level (t = 1.90) but is significant at the .10 level. In addition, the broader the president's expectations gap is, the more likely a person is to have a positive evaluation of their mayor's job performance.

What is particularly interesting is that there is no relationship between the president's expectations gap and governor and mayor evaluations in our 1999 survey. A midterm election occurred in 1998. As Erikson (1988) notes, midterm elections serve as a "referendum on the presidency." Consequently, the political opposition demonizes the White House in an attempt to elect more of its own officials. Although the president is not on the ballot, midterm elections therefore reflect public evaluations of the president. In 1999, which was not a national election year, the rhetoric is far different, focusing instead on the next presidential election. Without the constant drumbeat of attention on the president, the public was less inclined to draw a direct connection between the performance of other executive officials and that of the president. In sum, the midterm election provided a focusing event (see Kingdon 1997). By focusing attention directly on President Clinton, his evaluations had a more general impact on the evaluations of other executive branch officials. Once that focusing event was removed (that is, in a nonnational election year) the public no longer drew a direct comparison between the performance of their governor or mayor and that of the president.[9]

On the other hand, we find some support for the idea that perceptions of individual political efficacy are related to job-performance evaluations. Whereas internal efficacy is not related to any of the state or local actors, external efficacy is related to evaluations of the state legislatures and mayors, but only in 1998. Likewise, the economy is related to evaluations of governors and mayors. The more positive one's assessment of the economy, the more likely one is to approve of these political officials' job performance. This is the case for both surveys, though for governors in 1999 the relationship falls just short (1.93) of two-tailed statistical significance. As for pocketbook attitudes the better one is personally doing, financially speaking, the less likely they are to approve of their governor, but only in our 1999 survey.[10]

Again, the main finding from the state and local models is that leadership trust matters and that the presidential expectations gap is related to job approval ratings of mayors and governors, but only during a midterm election year. In both cases, more negative evaluations of the president are related to more positive assessments of these elected officials at the state and local levels. This suggests that governors and mayors may be well served by blaming many of their state and local problems on Washington and on the leadership faults of the president.

Service Policy Actors

In table 11.4 we present the models for public employees and the police for 1998. Again, the leadership-trust scale is related to evaluations of all service actors. The higher one's personal level of trust in leaders, the more positive one's evaluations of public employees or the police (in both 1998 and 1999) are likely to be. For 1999, perceptions of external efficacy are related to evaluations of public employees and the police, with higher levels of efficacy leading to more positive evaluations of both policy actors.

These combined findings demonstrate that leadership trust is related to all of the federal, state, local, and service actors our respondents were asked to evaluate, with the exception of the president of the United States, and we find evidence of an indirect effect in that case. As for the governmental trust scale, it is not related to evaluations of public employees, but it is just shy of two-tailed statistical significance (1.90) in relation to the police. The more favorably one rates the performance of the U.S. government the more likely one is to approve of the performance of the police. This provides further evidence that while trust matters, trust in leaders is a more consistently important determinant of evaluations of a wide variety of policy actors than is trust in government. Why is this so?

Since respondents were asked to evaluate individual leaders (their president, vice president, governor, and mayor) and institutions (the federal government, Congress, state legislatures, school boards, police), as well as the broad category of public employees, this finding is not merely an artifact of our asking respondents to evaluate similar types of leaders. In addition, leadership trust is related to institutions and policy actors at the federal, state, and local level. Hence the explanation cannot be that leadership trust is more likely to influence perceptions at any one level of government. Finally, trust in leaders is related to elected officials, as well as to those performing service activities (such as the police and public employees). Thus, it affects all sorts of governmental actors, not merely those who are elected. It also affects institutions that make policy with national implications (e.g., the federal government) and institutions that make policy narrowly and at the local level (e.g., school boards). That even evaluations of policy actors at the local level performing in highly specific issue policy areas are related to leadership trust is a palpable demonstration of trust's broad impact.

Is trust in leadership merely an artifact of the impeachment case, then? Hetherington (2005) finds that even during the impeachment case, public trust in government increased. We also find no relationship between impeachment and leadership or government trust. In addition, while impeach-

TABLE 11.4. Approval Ratings of Service Institutions as the Dependent Variable, 1998 and 1999 Surveys

	Public Employees 1998	Police 1998	Public Employees 1999	Police 1999
Expectations gap	−.0004	−.001	.006	−.01
	(.004)	(.004)	(.006)	(.01)
Leadership trust	−.19***	−.17***	−.36***	−.25**
	(.05)	(.05)	(.08)	(.08)
Government trust	−.04	−.09	—	—
	(.05)	(.05)		
Internal efficacy	.11	.08	−.02	−.13
	(.07)	(.06)	(.08)	(.08)
External efficacy	−.02	−.01	−.17*	−.18*
	(.06)	(.06)	(.08)	(.08)
Sociotropic perceptions	−.09	−.05	−.06	−.25**
	(.07)	(.07)	(.09)	(.09)
Pocketbook perceptions	.02	−.13	.09	.02
	(.12)	(.12)	(.15)	(.15)
Education	−.07	−.10	−.04	−.01
	(.07)	(.07)	(.10)	(.01)
Age	.0005	−.01*	−.004	−.01
	(.005)	(.005)	(.006)	(.01)
Gender	.46***	.01	.21	.27
	(.14)	(.14)	(.19)	(.19)
African American	.46	1.16***	−.48	.67
	(.30)	(.30)	(.40)	(.37)
Latino	.85**	.77**	−.16	−.86
	(.35)	(.34)	(.30)	(.59)
Ideology	−.002	−.11*	−.06*	.01
	(.05)	(.05)	(.62)	(.07)
Democrats	−.03	.35*	.34	.29
	(.16)	(.15)	(.25)	(.24)
Registered to vote	.27	.15	−.19	−.43
	(.25)	(.25)	(.33)	(.33)
TV news	−.004	−.01	−.02	.20
	(.01)	(.01)	(.19)	(.19)
Support for impeachment	.25	.24	—	—
	(.19)	(.19)		
N	817	835	478	497
Probability > chi-square	.000	.000	.000	.000
Pseudo R^2	.03	.04	.05	.05

*** significant at the .001 level; ** significant at the .05 level; * significant at the .10 level.

ment was related to two federal actors, it was related to none of the state, local, or service actors. Finally, impeachment's impact is limited to the national level. It does not affect perceptions of all actors across the spectrum, as does leadership trust. And since Hetherington concludes that evaluations of trust were actually increasing during the period when our surveys were conducted, it is difficult to argue that trust in leaders is merely an artifact of the impeachment case.

On the other hand, we can speculate that when people consider the issue of trust in general, they may be more prone to think about individuals because it is our leaders who promise more than they can deliver and thus are sometimes caught lying or violating the law. In this sense, Clinton and impeachment are a personification of the leadership trust issue. Rather than perceiving the government as being at fault, it appears Americans are more prone to find fault with their leaders. Certainly, the broad effect of leadership trust suggests that people do differentiate between leadership and governmental trust in a meaningful way. This differentiation has important implications for evaluations of political and service actors across the governmental spectrum.

The expectations gap also has a broad impact, influencing perceptions of three of four federal actors, as well as governors and mayors during a midterm election year. Evaluations of the state of the national economy also show some broad-based effects.

A New Model of Expectations, Partisanship, and Trust

Although our findings in the previous sections are indeed preliminary, their consistency suggests that trust is an exceedingly important factor in explaining the determinants of the expectations gap. It also suggests that the problem is not merely limited to one political actor, the president, but rather that the effects of a gap in public trust of its leaders may be widespread.

To illustrate this wider effect, in figure 11.1 we provide a model of the expectations gap in a broader governmental context. In this sense the expectations gap is related to other dysfunctional elements of American politics. Politicians running for president have an incentive to make extravagant campaign promises. This helps them to secure their party's nomination and to win the presidency. The process, however, unreasonably heightens public expectations. When the public is not satisfied, its expectations are dashed. This disillusionment then translates into lower levels of trust in public officials. Since there is nothing particularly endemic to the idea that politicians

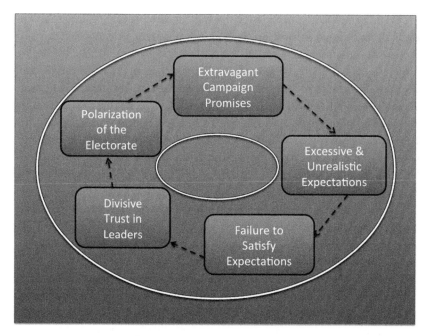

Fig. 11.1. Expectations Gap Process

overpromise and build up unrealistic expectations, we expect to see these same effects across the entire political spectrum, with levels of trust in government, particularly for leaders, plummeting. This process creates a toxic soup. Politicians ratchet up not only expectations, they then are forced to the partisanship well in an attempt to build a subsequent winning coalition. Since politicians typically promise more than they can deliver, partisanship and polarization ensure that the cycle of expectations, trust, and partisanship will begin anew.

What can be done to ameliorate the expectations gap? Unfortunately, as with most complex problems, there is no simple solution. To date most scholars recommend micro-level solutions involving changes only in the behavior of the presidency, such as toning down the rhetoric and the promises made in presidential campaigns or asking the media and voters to be more realistic in their appraisal of presidential candidates and presidential performance. Yet these proposals themselves are not realistic. Presidents will use whatever rhetoric they require to get elected and the voters are not likely to become more educated and involved regarding the nuances of our political system by listening to campaign rhetoric. Rather than fixing the mess, the mess in Washington appears to be getting murkier all the time.

During the Obama presidency the U.S. Senate became, at times, an entirely dysfunctional institution, leading the president to denounce our system as "dysfunctional government." Scholars and pundits also are becoming more concerned about the intrusion of politics into the realm of judicial decision making. Regrettably, at a time when partisanship and trust in leaders is a key problem, so-called cable networks have resuscitated the partisan press of the nineteenth century, with Fox News stridently representing the Republican point of view, while its owner News Corporation donated large sums of money to the Republican electoral cause. Meanwhile, MSNBC has become the place for liberal politics. As CNN watches its market share diminish it, too, has an incentive to join in the political fray.

As the public gives institutions from the Congress to the media ever poorer performance evaluations, it is apparent that the solution to the expectations gap dilemma is not merely to encourage presidents to promise less or for the public to be better informed or for the media to do a better job. Rather, as we move beyond a focus on expectations of the presidency, it is wise that we consider the problem of an expectations gap in a truly macro sense, affecting multiple institutions of government. Considered this way, the solutions involve deriving answers to the following questions:

- What can we do to make government work better?
- How can we increase the public's level of trust in its institutions and particularly in its leaders?
- How can we increase the public's sense of political efficacy?
- How can we reform elections to make them more accountable to the public? In particular, how can we shorten the electoral cycle that at present seems to be a continuous endeavor?

These questions and similar ones are fundamental to the very nature of democratic theory. We believe that it is only by providing answers to these macro-level questions that we can begin to unravel the puzzle of the presidential expectations gap. A focus on the presidency alone is but one place to start. But we cannot address the overall problem with a focus on the presidency. The expectations gap appears to be a wider and more destructive force in American politics than has previously been hypothesized. We therefore recommend that future research concentrate on its macro effects across the entire political spectrum. Only then can we begin to provide answers to the questions we have posed in this chapter.

Appendix A: Survey Methodology

We constructed and administered four surveys through the University of New Mexico's Institute for Public Policy. We conducted polls from January 21 through February 27, 1996, and October 30 through November 18, 1996. The timing of these two surveys was selected so that we could measure public expectations of the incumbent president, Bill Clinton, his main rival (Senator Bob Dole of Kansas), and an ideal president at both the beginning and the end of a presidential election year. A total of 564 adults from the state of New Mexico were interviewed for the first survey, while 624 were interviewed for the second one.

The surveys were pretested and applied, using a randomdigit dialing approach, to a random sample of households. Once a household was contacted, the respondent was chosen at random by selecting the household member over the age of seventeen who had the most recent birthday. The surveys were administered through a computer-assisted telephone interviewing system, through which phone numbers were called up to 12 times, at different times of day and days of the week, before being excluded from the sample. The survey cooperation rate (completed interviews divided by completes plus refusals) for the January-February survey was 67 percent. For the October-November survey the completion rate was 62 percent. Survey refusals were grouped into separate categories, including "hard refusals" and "reluctants," meaning those who have initially refused but who might be persuaded to cooperate after a "cooling off period" of several days. Both hard refusals and "unconverted" reluctants are treated as refusals for purposes of calculating the cooperation rate. A somewhat more conservative survey response calculation, generally referred to as a *response rate,* includes repeated "busy" numbers, no answers, and respondents who could not be interviewed due to language barriers or illness in the denominator. By this calculation, the survey response rate was 60 percent in the January-February survey and 59 percent in the October-November survey. The questions were included in the 30th and 33rd survey in a series of statewide New Mexico omnibus surveys, undertaken quarterly since 1988. The University of New Mexico's Institute for Public Policy sponsored the survey.

The data for two additional surveys in 1998 and 1999 also were generated specifically for this research project because we need to compare individual perceptions of the presidential office and an incumbent president along comparable leadership dimensions. Although existing studies provide data on public attitudes about presidential incumbents, they do not provide a basis for comparing the presidential office to an incumbent. Therefore, using the University of New Mexico's Institute for Public Policy computer-assisted telephone interviewing laboratory, we conducted two national surveys; 1,053 interviews were conducted between September 19 and October 20, 1998, and 824 interviews between October 26 and November 22, 1999. Each survey sample was drawn from a random digit-dialing frame.

The national RDD telephone list was purchased from Survey Sampling, Inc. The surveys were pretested and applied, using a randomdigit dialing approach, to a random sample of households. Once a household was contacted, the respondent was chosen at random by selecting the household member over the age of seventeen who had the most recent birthday. The surveys were administered through a computer-assisted telephone interviewing system, through which phone numbers were called up to 12 times, at different times of day and days of the week, before being excluded from the sample. For 1998 the response and cooperation rates were 54.3 percent and 59.4 percent, respectively, while for 1999 the rates were 56.5 percent and 60.9 percent (based on the *American Association for Public Opinion Research* [1998] standard definitions). The refusal rate was 37.1 percent for 1998 and 36.3 percent for 1999. Given the number of completed interviews, the estimated sampling error is approximately plus or minus 3.5 percent.

A survey also was conducted in 2007 specifically for this research project. The Public Policy Research Institute, PPRI, conducted a telephone survey on the topic of Presidential Expectations for the Bush School of Government and Public Service at Texas A&M University. The data collection started on May 24, 2007, and ended on July 18, 2007, and included a total of 1,021 completes. The Gap survey was conducted according to PPRI's standard data collection procedures. These protocols cover the entire interviewing process from recruiting interviewers to data delivery. The lab's standard survey process is outlined below in detail and any specific changes to standard protocol are explained. The following provides further detail on the survey conducted at the Bush School, but the University of New Mexico's Institute for Public Policy employed the same general parameters. Hence, it provides an overview of how the five surveys were conducted.

Sampling Methodology

The sample was a random digit sample of all telephone households in the United States. The sample was chosen to represent the general population of the area sampled in regards to demographic characteristics. Using listed telephone numbers, operating banks of telephone numbers were identified. A random sample was selected from among all numbers in the bank of numbers, whether listed or not. The sample was provided by Survey Sampling International.

Recruiting

New survey lab interviewers were recruited and selected utilizing our standard operating procedures. This process began with the announcement of new interviewer positions in local newspaper advertisements and student employment offices. A multistep screening process required potential interviewers to telephone our Survey Lab supervisor. Prospects were initially screened through this first contact telephone conversation. Those who failed to present themselves well on the phone were eliminated from further consideration. Those who passed the initial screening were asked to visit the Lab and complete an application form. Prospects whose applications were positively evaluated were interviewed face-to-face by the Survey Lab supervisor. In addition to providing standard employee information, the prospect was required to conduct a brief telephone interview with the supervisor using the project questionnaire.

The criteria for evaluation include:

- Evidence of reliability as an employee;
- Bilingual capability;
- Demonstrated articulation;
- Positive telephone "personality"; and
- Accuracy and attention to detail in reading the survey questionnaire, following instructions, and marking the responses.

Finally, new interviewers were carefully monitored during a trial period to identify and remedy problems immediately. This "on the job training" continued until the basic skills were mastered. At least six experienced shift supervisors were assigned to the project and trained along with the interviewers.

Training

Existing training manuals covering the standard operating procedures at PPRI as well as training material designed specifically for this project were used. In addition to the printed manuals, training materials included overhead slide presentations, worksheets, and example questionnaires.

The training session occurred on May 17, 2007, and covered the standard topics included in the training manual and was designed to encourage active participation of trainees and to familiarize them with the different types of respondents who would be interviewed. A large portion of the training session, like the training manual, was devoted to a question-by-question review of the survey instrument. Much of the training session involved didactic classroom sessions and practice interviewing.

Each trainee was observed and evaluated during the training session. Any trainees who did not perform satisfactorily were given additional individualized training or replaced, as necessary. The training session was designed to maximize the effectiveness of the interviewers. Topics covered in the training included:

- Background of the Gap survey including information on PPRI and random public opinion polls;
- Organization of the interviewing staff including responsibilities of supervisors, interviewers, and other staff;
- Standard management procedures including scheduling, logging in and out, payroll, sickness, absences, tardiness, etc.;
- Information on sampling: How it works in general; how the Gap sample was derived; what the interviewer must do; why the procedures must be followed exactly;
- General instructions on interviewing including interviewer preparation, how to establish contact, how to maximize response rates, how to deal with problems;
- Asking questions including maintaining neutrality, encouraging responses, probing, etc.;

- Specifics of the Gap survey including pronunciation, skips, allowable clarifications, etc.;
- Dealing with specific problems (such as concern about privacy); and
- Procedures for ensuring confidentiality.

Supervisors worked on an individual basis or in small groups with the trainees. Although some of the material was presented in a lecture format, much of it was presented by example, or through participation in exercises designed to replicate actual interviewing experiences. Finally, interviewers practiced interviewing each other using the actual iCATI equipment.

The training was conducted in a two-hour session, followed by a two-hour follow-up session. The first session covered general issues and instructors conducted specific training for this project. The two-hour follow-up was devoted to practicing the interview with the iCATI system.

At the end of the training session the prospective interviewers were tested for basic knowledge of the material and evaluated in a practical interviewing exercise. Trainees not meeting adequate standards were required to remedy their deficiencies before conducting project interviews.

Internet Computer-Assisted Telephone Interviewing System (iCATI)

The Internet computer-assisted telephone interviewing system in place in the Survey Laboratory represents the cutting edge of survey technology. With iCATI online, a computer manages the survey sample, displays prompt questions for the interviewer, and electronically records responses. The system also produces productivity reports, progress reports, interviewer time sheets, and telephone billing reports.

The iCATI prevents most mistakes from occurring by guiding the interviewer through the questionnaire and automatically skipping questions as appropriate, based on the respondent's answers. It also eliminates data entry errors that can occur as information is transferred from printed questionnaires into electronic format. The iCATI system allows the Survey Laboratory supervisor to monitor all interviewers from a central computer. Because the system is web-based, iCATI allows a survey to be conducted from anywhere where web access is available. A copy can also be installed on a laptop. This allows surveys to be conducted in remote locations with the data being uploaded at a later point.

The iCATI hardware used in PPRI's Survey Laboratory consists of a network of 40 desktop computers. The iCATI system is installed a Windows Server machine running Apache. The web pages were written in PHP with a MySQL database backend.

Each of the 40 available phone lines in the interview operation is linked to a central monitoring phone. A bank of call status lights indicates whether or not a phone is in use. Supervisors monitor a specific number of calls each shift using both the telephone monitoring and the interviewing computer-monitoring capability.

Phones are connected to the computers and the iCATI system provides automatic dialing of telephone numbers. This reduces the potential for error in dialing and speeds calling. It should be noted that PPRI does not use "presumptive" dialing, a commonly used method of using computers to dial numbers in anticipation that an interviewer will be available when a connection is made. Among other problems, this method results in the person answering the phone to experience at least a short delay before the interviewer begins, which reduces the probability of cooperation.

Survey Lab Capacity and Capabilities

The telephone survey facility consists of a monitoring and supervising office connected to a large room containing 40 interview stations. The stations are custom-built, sound-insulated cubicles that provide an effective interviewing environment.

The telephone interview facility keeps a very extensive schedule, operating a total of 84.5 hours per week. Interviews can be done anytime between 8:00 a.m. and 9:30 p.m. during the week, Saturday from 10:00 a.m. to 6:00 p.m., and 1:00 p.m. to 9:30 p.m. on Sunday. Interviewers can be very flexible in arranging attempts to call a respondent back or in receiving incoming calls. The interview facility is closed only on major holidays. The survey operation is open on all other days including other state and university holidays. A telephone answering machine is used to take messages during hours when the facility is closed.

Telephone Data Collection

The following describes the activities involved in the actual collection of the telephone data.

Interviewer Scheduling

Prior to each week of scheduled interviews, the supervisory staff determined the requisite number of interviewers to assign to each shift. Typically, for a project of this nature, 15 to 20 interviewers were assigned to this survey during evening (6:30–9:30) and weekend shifts (10:00–2:00 and 2:30–6:30 on Saturday and 1:30–5:30 on Sunday). Morning and afternoon shifts were scheduled with three or four interviewers due to the lower number of household contacts during these hours.

Daily Survey Activity. The survey program supervisory staff oversaw the preparation for interviewing each day. The following tasks were routinely part of that activity:

- Use the iCATI to produce sample status reports that could identify potential problems and establish priorities for interviewing during the shift;
- Use the iCATI to produce interviewer productivity reports that could identify problems; and
- Determine the appropriate response to refusals (e.g., scheduling another attempt) and other special situations.

Prior to each shift the shift supervisor:

- Allocated interview stations on the iCATI to interviewers;
- Assigned interviewers to special tasks, such as refusal conversion; and
- Determined which interviewers would be monitored (priority was given to new interviewers, interviewers with recognized problems, and interviewers who had not been monitored during their last four shifts).

During an interviewing session, shift supervisors had the responsibility for:

- Answering questions that arose and dealing with difficult situations with respondents;
- Monitoring interviews—at least 20 percent of the interviewers in a shift were monitored;
- Maintaining shift productivity; and
- Monitoring the iCATI system to make sure that appropriate allocations of the sample were made.

PPRI assigned a shift supervisor, an assistant supervisor, and an edit checker to the evening and weekend shifts. During morning and afternoon shifts, when fewer interviewers were working, a single shift supervisor was present.

Procedures for Contacting Respondents

Our standard procedure for attempting to contact a household was to place a call during each of five different shifts throughout the week. Four of these calls occurred during the evening or weekend hours when respondents were most likely to be at home. Numbers that were apparently disconnected were tried twice. Busy numbers were tried twice during the same shift, with repeated attempts during five different shifts. When a household had been reached, but the correct respondent was not available, as many as five more tries were made to reach the correct respondent.

PPRI attempted to convert virtually all refusals. The only refusals where conversions were not attempted were those where the respondent was extremely adamant that they did not want to be called again. Interviewers completed a special form when a refusal occurred that provided as much information as possible on the circumstances of the refusal. The respondent was then recontacted by interviewers specially trained to convert refusals.

Monitoring Interviews and Verification

Telephone interviewers were carefully supervised. One supervisor was on duty for every 10 interviewers. Interviews were regularly monitored from a central phone by supervisors who were required to monitor at least 20 percent of the interviews during a shift.

PPRI verified 5 percent of the interviews conducted by using the iCATI system to monitor all screen and keyboard activity at a workstation from a central terminal. A random procedure was specified for selecting interviews. Selection occurred throughout the entire shift.

Confidentiality

Several procedures ensured confidentiality during the interviewing process. PPRI is required to maintain confidentiality of records on a variety of projects, including ones in which records are maintained on identified individuals. The approaches include maintaining security, following specified procedures, and employee training and supervision.

The iCATI system enables control to be maintained over all files and records. Because all sample management and data collection were handled by computer, there were few printed materials that could compromise confidentiality. The computer system was secure. All areas where confidential material was stored were password protected and available only to a small group of staff who required access. Additionally, the premises and physical data were secured.

The most important procedural consideration in maintaining security was to make sure that the anonymity of the telephone interviews was not compromised. In the iCATI system, specific information (e.g., telephone number, first name of someone to be called back) was in a file separate from the collected data. These files could be linked, but they are not maintained in a linked form. As soon as the results were processed so there was no further need for access to telephone numbers and other identifying information, this data was destroyed.

All staff at PPRI are aware of the need for confidentiality. Highlighting its importance is part of all new employee training as well as the monitoring and supervision processes.

As for all research projects PPRI obtained permission to conduct research from the Texas A&M University Internal Review Board. This committee reviews all human subject research done on campus to ensure that the rights of respondents are protected.

Appendix B: Measurement of Our Independent Variables

The dependent variables are explained in the text, particularly in chapter 4. While we also discuss the independent variables at various points throughout the book, this appendix provides greater detail on how these questions were framed.

Micro-Level Theses

Performance Expectations. Sociotropic attitudes were measured by asking, "Using a scale of one to seven, where one means very poor and seven means very good, how would you rate the current performance of the U.S. economy?" Pocketbook attitudes were measured by asking, "Would you say that you and your family are financially better off, worse off, or about the same as you were a year ago?" Worse off was then coded as a 1, about the same as a 2, and better off as a 3.

Looking to the White House—Expectations. Gender, Latinos, and African Americans were measured as dummy variables (0 = female, 1 = male; 1 = Latino, and 0 = non-Latino; and 1 = African American, 0 = nonAfrican American). We measured income in increments of $10,000. Age was measured by asking, "How old are you?"

Excessive Expectations. Education was measured by asking, "What is the highest level of education you have completed?" This included (1) elementary or some high school; (2) high school graduate/GED and trade or vocational certificate; (3) some college/associates degree; (4) college graduate; or (5) post-grad degree. Source of news was measured in two ways. For 1998, respondents were asked what their primary source of news was. We then included a dummy variable—1 if they got their news primarily from TV and 0 otherwise. For 1999, we asked, how many times a week do you watch TV news? Basic political participation was measured by asking whether respondents were registered to vote (1 = yes, 0 = no). We then created a partisan measure by coding individuals who identified themselves as strongly identified with either the Republican or Democratic parties as a 3, Democratic and Republican identifiers as a 2, those leaning toward these parties as a 1, and those who identified themselves as independents or having no party as a 0.

Macro-Level Theses

Trust in Government/Political Efficacy. For the 1998 survey, respondents were asked, a series of six questions related to trust. All were on a scale of 1 = strongly agree, 2 = agree, 3 = disagree, and four = strongly disagree. People were then asked to respond to the following statements:

- Whatever its faults may be, the American form of government is still the best for us.
- There is not much about our form of government to be proud of.
- It may be necessary to make some major changes in our form of government in order to solve the problems facing our country.
- Unless we keep close watch on them, many of our elected leaders will look out for special interests rather than for all the people.
- When government leaders make statements to the American people on television or in the newspapers, they are usually telling the truth.
- You can generally trust the people who run our government to do what is right.

For consistency purposes the scales were switched/flipped for the best government, truthful leaders, and trust the people who run our government questions. To control for perceptions of the federal government we include the response to the following question, "Using a scale of excellent, good, fair, or poor how would you rate the job that the federal government is doing governing the U.S.?" Lower scores represent more satisfaction with government's approval and therefore should be associated with lower levels of trust.

To measure internal efficacy we asked whether the respondent agreed or disagreed with this statement: "Sometimes politics and government seem so complicated that a person like me can not really understand what's going on." We also asked, "I feel I could do as good a job in public office as most other people." Both questions were based on a four-point scale from strongly agree to strongly disagree. The second question was recoded so that the scales of the two variables were consistent, then the two were aggregated to form the internal efficacy variable. To measure external efficacy we asked respondents the following: "Voting is the only way people like me can have any say about how the government runs things" and "People like me do not have a say about what government does." Again the responses ranged from strongly agree to strongly disagree on a four-point scale. The two were aggregated to form the external efficacy variable.

Political Attitudes. Ideology was measured on a continuum from 1 = strongly liberal to 7 = strongly conservative. The strength of the partisan attachment is measured on the following scale: Democrats who "completely" identify with their party = 3, Democrats who "somewhat" identify with their party = 2, Democrats who "slightly" identify with their party = 1; nonparty identifiers or members of other parties = 0, Republicans who "slightly" identify with their party = 1, Republicans who "somewhat" identify with their party = 2, and Republicans who "completely" identify with their party = 3. Thus, the scale ranges from those who completely identify with the Democratic Party to those who completely identify with the Republican Party. Regarding impeachment, in the 1998 survey, respondents were asked, "Based on what you know about Bill Clinton, do you think that he should or should not be impeached and removed from office?" (1 = should be impeached and 0 = should not be impeached). Regarding Congress, evaluations were based on a scale of (1) excellent, (2) good, (3) fair, and (4) poor.

Clinton's Approval Rating. Evaluations of the incumbent president, Bill Clinton, also were based on a scale of (1) excellent, (2) good, (3) fair, and (4) poor.

The January-February 1996 survey was conducted immediately after the government shutdowns of December and January 1995–96. We therefore asked respondents whom they blamed for the shutdown, President Clinton, Congress, or both equally. Media exposure was measured by asking respondents their primary source of news. We then included a dummy variable—1 if they got their news primarily from TV and 0 otherwise. Political knowledge was gauged by asking whether the respondent watched the State of the Union address; this measure was only available for the January-February survey.

Notes

Chapter 3

1. See http://www.pollingreport.com/BushJob.htm. Also see "Bush's Final Approval Rating: 22 Percent," http://www.cbsnews.com/stories/2009/01/16/opinion/polls/main4728399.shtml.

Chapter 5

1. We note that the government shutdown variable was not significant in any of the models we ran in our earlier analysis of the same data (Waterman, Jenkins-Smith, and Silva 1999). In this chapter, we have different dependent variables and a different measure for political party support. We also have increased our sample size greatly by removing income from the model. As a result, some of the results related to the control variables are slightly different, though our conclusions about our main variables of interest—Clinton's and Dole's gap measures—remain the same as in our previously published work.

Chapter 8

1. See "Poll: Bush Still Blamed for Economy," http://politicalticker.blogs.cnn.com/2010/02/12/poll-bush-still-blamed-for-economy/?fbid=ttZ6MWPm7rv&hpt=Sbin.

Chapter 9

1. Dan Balz, "Obama Team Sees Romney Damaging Self with Independents for the Fall Campaign," *Washington Post,* January 25, 2012.
2. Unless otherwise identified, all subsequent quotes in this chapter are from Peter

Baker's "Education of a President," *New York Times Magazine,* October 17, 2010, http://www.nytimes.com/2010/10/17/magazine/17obama-t.html.

3. "Why Doesn't Obama Get Credit for Tax Cuts?" *The Week,* October 20, 2010, http://theweek.com/article/index/208375/why-doesnt-obama-get-credit-for-cutting-taxes.

4. Anne Kornblut, "Soul Searching Obama Aides: Democrats' Midterm Election Losses a Wakeup Call," *Washington Post* online, November 14, 2010, http://www.washingtonpost.com/wp-dyn/content/article/2010/11/13/AR2010111303260.html?hpid=topnews.

5. See David Nakamura, "Obama Offers 2012 Election Supporters Change They Can Believe In—Next Term," *Washington Post,* online, August 26, 2011, http://www.washingtonpost.com/politics/obama-offers-2012-election-supporters-change-they-can-believe-in—next-term/2011/08/25/gIQAJz9AhJ_story.html?hpid=z3.

6. See   http://www.redstate.com/brandongreife/2010/02/24/winning-a-new-generation-of-young-conservatives/, posted February 24, 2010.

Chapter 11

1. See Chanley, Rudolph, and Rahn 2000; Hetherington 1998; Williams 1985.

2. See Miller 1974; Weatherford 1984; Capella and Jamieson 1997; King 1997; Mansbridge 1997.

3. The order of these policy actors was randomly rotated so that respondents were not asked about these actors in the same order.

4. With regard to the control variables, the public's views on impeachment also are related to perceptions of the president and Congress, but not to the federal government and the vice president (for 1998). Those who support impeachment are less likely to approve of the president but are more likely to approve of the U.S. Congress. This finding underscores the political stakes of the impeachment issue, since it was a Republican-controlled Congress that impeached a Democratic president. Had impeachment undercut trust in government systematically across all institutions, we would expect to see negative coefficients for impeachment in each case. We also would expect to see impeachment driving perceptions of other governmental institutions. As we shall see when we examine state, local, and service institutions, this is not the case. Impeachment's effects are mostly limited to the federal policy actors.

5. Of the demographic variables gender is related to evaluations of federal institutions in three of the four models, age is significant in two of the models, and African Americans, and Latinos in one model each. In general, men have less positive evaluations of federal governmental actors than women. Interestingly, the one exception is the president. While the Clinton-Lewinsky scandal involved allegations of sexual impropriety, as well as perjury and obstruction of justice, there is no evidence that men or women evaluated Clinton's job performance differently. On the other hand, African Americans are more likely to approve of the president and Latinos are more likely to approve of the federal government's performance. With regard to our political variables, the more conservative one is the more likely one is to approve of Congress and the less likely one is to approve of the vice president. Democrats are more likely to approve of the president and the vice president.

6. The demographic variables again show considerable variation. Gender is related to all four policy actors for 1999. Latinos are more likely to approve of the performance of Congress. The older one is the less likely one is to approve of Congress. As for the political variables, the dummy variable for Democratic partisans is related to perceptions of the president, vice president, and Congress.

7. The models are similar to those for federal institutions. With federal institutions we had a Democratic president and a Republican-controlled Congress. Because control of governorships, state legislatures, and mayoral positions varies from state to state and locality to locality, controlling for ideology and partisanship is not as straightforward as it is in the federal case. We did run the models with ideology and the Democratic dummy, thus replicating the federal models. Neither variable was significant in the models. We also note that once we move to the state and local level, as well as service providers, the pseudo r-squares are small, with values of .07 or less.

8. As we move the analysis to the state, local, and service level we are now asking our respondents to evaluate their own state legislature and governor (of which there are 50), their own mayor, police, and school board (of which there are literally thousands).

9. As for the control variables, while impeachment was related to evaluations of two of the federal actors, support for impeachment is not related to any of the state or local actors. Whereas our results demonstrate that trust has an impact that transcends levels of government, the impeachment crisis did not. Its effects are limited to the national, not the state or local, level. This finding is further evidence that trust in 1998 exerted an independent impact on perceptions of policy actors beyond the details of the impeachment crisis.

10. Of the demographic variables, for 1998 gender is related to perceptions of all three policy actors, while in 1999 gender is related only to perceptions of state legislators. For 1998 the higher one's level of education the less likely one is to approve of the performance of one's state legislator and Latinos are more likely to approve of the job performance. For 1999 none of the other demographic factors are related to the performance evaluations. Of the political variables for 1998 whether one is registered to vote is related to evaluations of state legislatures, while whether one gets their news primarily from TV is related to governors. TV news also is related to governors in 1999. Finally, for 1999 Democrats are less likely to approve of their state legislature and their governor. Since the Republicans controlled most state legislatures and governorships at this time, this finding is not surprising.

References

Abramowitz, Alan I., Dan J. Lanoue, and Susan Remesh. 1988. "Economic Conditions, Causal Attributions, and Political Evaluations in the 1984 Presidential Election." *Journal of Politics* 50 (4): 849–63.

Alter, Jonathan. 2010. *The Promise: President Obama, Year One.* New York: Simon and Schuster.

American Association for Public Opinion Research. 1998. *Standard Definitions: Final Dispositions of Case Codes and Outcome Rates for RDD Telephone Surveys and In-Person Household Surveys.* Ann Arbor, MI: AAPOR.

Baker, Peter. 2010. "Education of a President." *New York Times Magazine,* October 17; http://www.nytimes.com/2010/10/17/magazine/17obama-t.html.

Bartels, Larry M. 2000. "Partisanship and Voting Behavior, 1952–1996." *American Journal of Political Science* 44 (1): 35–50.

Bartels, Larry M., and John Zaller. 2001. "Presidential Vote Models: A Recount." *PS: Political Science and Politics* 34 (1): 9–20.

Bem, Daryl J., and H. K. McConnell. 1970. "Testing the Self-Perception Explanation of Dissonance Phenomena: On the Salience of Premanipulation Attitudes." *Journal of Personality and Social Psychology* 14 (1): 23–31.

Bennet, James, with Janet Elder. 1998. "Public Ready to Forgive Clinton Private Failings." *New York Times,* February 24, A1, A14.

Blendon, Robert J., John M. Benson, Richard Morin, Drew E. Altman, Mollyann Bordie, Mario Brossard, and Matt James. 1997. "Changing Attitudes in America." In *Why People Don't Trust Government,* ed. Joseph S. Nye, Philip D. Zelikow, and David C. King. Cambridge: Harvard University Press.

Bloom, Harold, and H. Douglas Price. 1975. "Voter Response to Short-Run Economic Conditions: The Asymmetric Effect of Prosperity and Recession." *American Political Science Review* 69 (4): 1240–54.

Blumenthal, Sidney. 2003. *The Clinton Years.* New York: Farrar, Straus and Giroux.

Bond, Jon R., and Richard Fleisher. 1990. *The President in the Legislative Arena.* Chicago: University of Chicago Press.

Brace, Paul, and Barbara Hinckley. 1992. *Follow the Leader: Opinion Polls and the Modern Presidents.* New York: Basic Books.

Brady, David W., and Craig Volden. 2005. *Revolving Gridlock: Politics and Policy from Jimmy Carter to George W. Bush.* Boulder: Westview Press.

Branch, Taylor. 2009. *The Clinton Tapes: Wrestling History with the President.* New York: Simon and Schuster.

Brody, Richard A. 1991. *Assessing the President: The Media, Elite Opinion, and Public Support.* Stanford: Stanford University Press.

Brownlow, Louis. 1949. *The President and the Presidency.* Chicago: University of Chicago Press.

Brownlow, Louis. 1969. "What We Expect The President to Do." In *The Presidency*, ed. Aaron Wildavsky, 35–43. Boston: Little, Brown.

Buchanan, Bruce. 1978. *The Presidential Experience: What the Office Does to the Man.* Englewood Cliffs, NJ: Prentice-Hall.

Burns, James MacGregor. 1965. *Presidential Government: The Crucible of Leadership.* Boston: Houghton Mifflin.

Burns, James MacGregor. 1984. *Roosevelt: The Lion and the Fox.* New York: Harcourt, Brace, Jovanovich.

Canes-Wrone, Brandice. 2006. *Who Leads Whom?* Chicago: University of Chicago Press.

Capella, Joseph N., and Kathleen Hall Jamieson. 1997. *Spiral of Cynicism: The Press and the Public Good.* New York: Oxford University Press.

Carter, Jimmy. 2010. *White House Diaries.* New York: Farrar, Straus and Giroux.

Chanley, Virginia A., Thomas J. Rudolph, and Wendy M. Rahn. 2000. "The Origins and Consequences of Public Trust in Government: A Time Series Analysis." *Public Opinion Quarterly* 64 (3): 239–56.

Citrin, Jack. 1974. "Comment: The Political Relevance of Trust in Government." *American Political Science Review* 68 (3): 973–88.

Citrin, Jack, and Donald Philip Green. 1986. "Presidential Leadership and the Resurgence of Trust in Government." *British Journal of Political Science* 16 (4): 431–53.

Cohen, Jeffrey. 1997. *Presidential Responsiveness and Public Policy-Making: The Public and the Policies That Presidents Choose.* Ann Arbor: University of Michigan Press.

Cohen, Jeffrey. 2008. *The Presidency in the Era of 24-Hours News.* Princeton: Princeton University Press.

Coleman, John J. 1997. "The Importance of Being Republican: Forecasting Party Fortunes in House Midterm Elections." *Journal of Politics* 59 (2): 497–519.

Corwin, Edward S. 1984. *The President: Office and Powers.* New York: New York University Press.

Craig, Stephen C., Richard G. Niemi, and Glenn E. Silver. 1990. "Political Efficacy and Trust: A Report on the NES Pilot Study Items." *Political Behavior* 12 (3): 289–314.

Cronin, Thomas E. 1974. "The Textbook Presidency and Political Science." In *Perspectives on the Presidency*, ed. Stanley Bach and George T. Sulzner. Lexington, MA: D. C. Heath.

Cronin, Thomas E. 1980. *The State of the Presidency.* Boston: Little, Brown.

Cronin, Thomas E., and Michael A. Genovese. 1998. *The Paradoxes of the American Presidency.* New York: Oxford University Press.

Delli Carpini, Michael, and Scott Keeter. 1996. *What Americans Know about Politics and Why It Matters.* New Haven: Yale University Press.

Destler, I. M. 1981. "National Security II: The Rise of the Assistant (1961–1981)." In *The Illusion of Presidential Government*, ed. Hugh Heclo and Lester M. Salamon. Boulder: Westview Press.

Dobel, J. Patrick. 2010. "Prudence and Presidential Ethics: The Decisions on Iraq of the Two Presidents Bush." *Presidential Studies Quarterly* 40 (1): 57–75.

Druckman, James, and Justin Holmes. 2004. "Does Presidential Rhetoric Matter? Priming and Presidential Approval." *Presidential Studies Quarterly* 34 (4): 755–78.

Duch, Raymond. 2001. "A Developmental Model of Heterogeneous Economic Voting in New Democracies." *American Political Science Review* 95 (4): 895–910.

Duch, Raymond M., Harvey D. Palmer, and Christopher J. Anderson. 2000. "Heterogeneity in Perceptions of National Economic Conditions." *American Journal of Political Science* 44 (4): 635–52.

Durr, Robert H. 1993. "What Moves Policy Sentiment." *American Political Science Review* 87 (March): 158–70.

Edwards, George C., III. 1983. *The Public Presidency: The Pursuit of Popular Support.* New York: St. Martin's Press.

Edwards, George C., III. 2006. *On Deaf Ears: The Limits of the Bully Pulpit.* New Haven: Yale University Press.

Edwards, George C., III. 2009. *The Strategic President: Persuasion and Opportunity in Presidential Leadership.* Princeton: Princeton University Press.

Edwards, George C., III. 2012. *Overreach: Leadership in the Obama Presidency.* Princeton: Princeton University Press.

Edwards, George C., III. 2013. "Creating Opportunities? Bipartisanship in the Early Obama Presidency." *Social Science Quarterly* 93:1081–1100.

Edwards, George C., III, and Stephen J. Wayne. 1997. *Presidential Leadership: Politics and Policy Making.* New York: St. Martin's/Worth.

Ehrlich, Walter. 1974. *Presidential Impeachment: An American Dilemma.* Saint Charles, MO: Forum Press.

Erikson, Robert S. 1988. "The Puzzle of Midterm Loss." *Journal of Politics* 50 (4): 1011–29.

Erikson, Robert S. 1989. "Economic Conditions and the Presidential Vote." *American Political Science Review* 83 (2): 567–73.

Erikson, Robert S., Michael B. MacKuen, and James A. Stimson. 2002. *The Macro Polity.* New York: Cambridge University Press.

Farrand, Max, ed. 1966. *The Records of the Federal Convention of 1787.* New Haven: Yale University Press.

Feldman, Stanley. 1982. "Economic Self-Interest and Political Behavior." *American Journal of Political Science* 26 (3): 446–66.

Fiorina, Morris. 1981. *Retrospective Voting in American National Elections.* New Haven: Yale University Press.

Frolich, N., and J. A. Oppenheimer. 1978. *Modern Political Economy.* Englewood Cliffs, NJ: Prentice-Hall.

Fukuyama, Francis. 1995. *Trust: The Social Virtues and the Creation of Prosperity.* New York: Free Press.

Garand, James C., and James E. Campbell. 2000. *Before the Vote.* Beverly Hills, CA: Sage Press.

Genovese, Michael A. 1995. *The Presidential Dilemma: Leadership in the American System*. New York: HarperCollins.

Genovese, Michael A. 2002. *The Presidential Dilemma: Leadership in the American System*. New York: Longman.

George, Alexander. 1980. *Presidential Decisionmaking in Foreign Policy: The Effective Use of Information and Advice*. Boulder: Westview Press.

Gilens, Martin. 1988. "Gender Support for Reagan: A Comprehensive Model of Presidential Approval." *American Journal of Political Science* 32 (1): 19–49.

Gilliam, Franklin D., Jr., and Shanto Iyengar. 2000. "Prime Suspects: The Influence of Local Television News on the Viewing Public." *American Journal of Political Science* 44 (3): 560–573.

Goren, Paul. 2002. "Character Weakness, Partisan Bias, and Presidential Evaluation." *American Journal of Political Science* 46 (3): 627–41.

Greenstein, Fred I. 2009. *Inventing the Job of President: Leadership Style from George Washington to Andrew Jackson*. Princeton: Princeton University Press.

Hargrove, Erwin C., and Michael Nelson. 1984. *Presidents, Politics, and Policy*. New York: Alfred A. Knopf.

Haskin, Frederic J. 1923. *The American Government*. Washington, DC: Fred Haskin.

Hess, Stephen. 1976. *Organizing the Presidency*. Washington, DC: Brookings Institution.

Hetherington, Marc J. 1998. "The Political Relevance of Political Trust." *American Political Science Review* 92 (4): 791–808.

Hetherington, Marc J. 1999. "The Effect of Political Trust on the Presidential Vote, 1968–96." *American Political Science Review* 93 (2): 311–26.

Hetherington, Marc J. 2005. *Why Trust Matters: Declining Political Trust and the Demise of American Liberalism*. Princeton: Princeton University Press.

Hibbs, Douglas A. 1982. "The Dynamics of Political Support for American Presidents among Occupational and Partisan Groups." *American Journal of Political Science* 26 (May): 312–32.

Hibbs, Douglas A. 1987. *The American Political Economy: Macro Economics and Electoral Politics in the United States*. Cambridge: Harvard University Press.

Hinckley, Barbara. 1985. *Problems of the Presidency: A Text with Readings*. Glenview, IL: Scott, Foresman.

Hinckley, Barbara. 1990. *The Symbolic Presidency: How Presidents Portray Themselves*. New York: Routledge Press.

Howell, William. 2003. *Power without Persuasion: The Politics of Direct Political Action*. Princeton: Princeton University Press.

Iyengar, Shanto, and Donald R. Kinder. 1987. *News That Matters*. Chicago: University of Chicago Press.

James, Scott C. 2005. "The Evolution of the Presidency: Between the Promise and the Fear." In *The Executive Branch*, ed. Joel Aberbach and Mark A. Peterson, 3–40. New York: Oxford University Press.

Jenkins-Smith, Hank C., Carol L. Silva, and Richard W. Waterman. 2005. "Micro and Macro Models of the Presidential Expectations Gap." *Journal of Politics* 67 (August): 690–715.

Kernell, Samuel. 1978. "Explaining Presidential Popularity: How Ad Hoc Theorizing,

Misplaced Emphasis, and Insufficient Care in Measuring One's Variables Refuted Common Sense and Led Conventional Wisdom down the Path of Anomalies." *American Political Science Review* 72 (2): 506–22.

Kernell, Samuel. 1997. *Going Public: New Strategies of Presidential Leadership.* Washington, DC: Congressional Quarterly Press.

Key, V. O. 1958. *Politics, Parties, and Pressure Groups.* New York: Thomas Y. Crowell.

Kiewiet, D. Roderick. 1981. "Policy-Oriented Voting in Response to Economic Issues." *American Political Science Review* 75 (2): 448–59.

Kimball, David C., and Samuel C. Patterson. 1997. "Living Up to Expectations: Public Attitudes toward Congress." *Journal of Politics* 59 (3): 701–28.

Kinder, Donald R. 1986. "Presidential Character Revisited." In *Political Cognition: The 19th Annual Carnegie Symposium,* ed. Richard R. Lau and David O. Sears. Hillsdale, NJ: Lawrence Erlbaum.

Kinder, Donald R., Gordon S. Adams, and Paul W. Gronke. 1989. "Economics and Politics in the 1984 American Presidential Election." *American Journal of Political Science* 33 (2): 491–515.

Kinder, Donald R., and Susan Fiske. 1986. "Presidents in the Public Mind." In *Handbook of Political Psychology,* ed. Margaret G. Hermann, 193–218. San Francisco: Jossey-Bass.

Kinder, Donald R., and D. Roderick Kiewiet. 1979. "Economic Discontent and Political Behavior: The Role of Personal Grievances and Collective Economic Judgments in Congressional Voting." *American Journal of Political Science* 23 (3): 495–527.

Kinder, Donald R., and D. Roderick Kiewiet. 1981. "Sociotropic Politics: The American Case." *British Journal of Political Science* 11 (2): 126–61.

King, David C. 1997. "The Polarization of American Parties and Mistrust of Government." In *Why People Don't Trust Government,* ed. Joseph S. Nye, Philip D. Zelikow, and David C. King. Cambridge: Harvard University Press.

Kingdon, John. 1997. *Agendas, Alternatives, and Public Policies.* Boston: Little, Brown.

Kramer, Gerald. 1971. "Short-Term Fluctuations in U.S. Voting Behavior." *American Political Science Review* 65:131–43.

Krause, George A. 1997. "Voters, Information Heterogeneity, and the Dynamics of Aggregate Economic Expectations." *American Journal of Political Science* 41 (4): 1170–1200.

Lammers, William W., and Michael A. Genovese. 2000. *The Presidency and Domestic Policy: Comparing Leadership Styles, FDR to Clinton.* Washington, DC: CQ Press.

Leuchtenburg, William E. 1988. "Franklin D. Roosevelt: The First Modern President." In *Leadership in the Modern Presidency,* ed. Fred I. Greenstein, 7–40. Cambridge: Harvard University Press.

Lewis-Beck, Michael S. 1985. "Pocketbook Voting in U.S. National Election Studies: Fact or Artifact?" *American Journal of Political Science* 29 (2): 348–56.

Light, Paul C. 1983. *The President's Agenda: Domestic Policy Choice from Kennedy to Carter.* Baltimore: Johns Hopkins University Press.

Lowi, Theodore J. 1985. *The Personal President.* Ithaca: Cornell University Press.

Luhmann, Niklas. 1979. *Trust and Power: Two Works by Niklas Luhmann.* Chichester: John Wiley.

MacKuen, Michael. 1983. "Political Drama, Economic Conditions, and the Dynamics of Presidential Popularity." *American Journal of Political Science* 27:165–92.

MacKuen, Michael B., Robert S. Erikson, and James A. Stimson. 1992. "Peasants or Bankers? The American Electorate and the U.S. Economy." *American Political Science Review* 86 (3): 597–611.

Mansbridge, Jane. 1997. "Social and Cultural Causes of Dissatisfaction with US Government." In *Why People Don't Trust Government*, ed. Joseph S. Nye, Philip D. Zelikow, and David C. King. Cambridge: Harvard University Press.

Markus, Gregory B. 1988. "The Impact of Personal and National Economic Conditions on the Presidential Vote: A Pooled Cross-Sectional Analysis." *American Journal of Political Science* 32 (1):137–54.

Markus, Gregory B. 1992. "The Impact of Personal and National Economic Conditions on Presidential Voting, 1956–1988." *American Journal of Political Science* 36 (3): 829–34.

McCarty, Nolan, Keith T. Poole, and Howard Rosenthal. 2003. "Political Polarization and Income Inequality." January 27, Working paper, Princeton University. Available at SSRN: http://ssrn.com/abstract=1154098.

Mezey, Michael L. 1989. *Congress, the President, and Public Policy*. Boulder: Westview Press.

Milkis, Sidney M. 2009. *Theodore Roosevelt, the Progressive Party, and the Transformation of American Democracy*. Lawrence: University Press of Kansas.

Miller, Arthur H. 1974. "Political Issues and Trust in Government: 1964–1970." *American Political Science Review* 68 (3): 951–72.

Moe, Terry M. 1985. "The Politicized Presidency." In *New Directions in American Politics*, ed. John E. Chubb and Paul E. Peterson. Washington, DC: Brookings Institution.

Mueller, John. 1973. *War, Presidents, and Public Opinion*. New York: John Wiley.

Nadeau, Richard, Richard G. Niemi, David P. Fan, and Timothy Amato. 1999. "Elite Economic Forecasts, Economic News, Mass Economic Judgments, and Presidential Approval." *Journal of Politics* 61 (1): 109–35.

Neustadt, Richard E. 1980 [1960]. *Presidential Power: The Politics of Leadership from FDR to Carter*. New York: John Wiley and Sons.

Neustadt, Richard E. 1990. *Presidential Power and the Modern Presidents: The Politics of Leadership from Roosevelt to Reagan*. New York: Free Press.

Niekirk, William. 1999. "Pensive Senators Want Fast Trial: President's Approval Rating Makes Removal Unlikely." *Albuquerque Journal*, January 3, A1.

Norpoth, Helmut. 1996. "Presidents and the Prospective Voter." *Journal of Politics* 58 (3): 776–92.

Ostrom, Charles W., and Dennis M. Simon. 1985. "Promise and Performance: A Dynamic Model of Presidential Popularity." *American Political Science Review* 79 (2): 334–58.

Patterson, Thomas E. 1993. *Out of Order: How the Decline of the Political Parties and the Growing Power of the News Media Undermine the American Way of Electing Presidents*. New York: Alfred A. Knopf.

Pfiffner, James P. 1988. *The Strategic Presidency: Hitting the Ground Running*. Chicago: Dorsey Press.

Phelps, Glenn A. 1989. "George Washington: Precedent Setter." In *Inventing the American Presidency*, ed. Thomas E. Cronin, 259–81. Lawrence: University Press of Kansas.

Pious, Richard M. 1996. *The Presidency*. Boston: Allyn and Bacon.

Price, Vincent, and John Zaller. 1993. "Who Gets the News? Alternative Measures of News Reception and Their Implications for Research." *Public Opinion Quarterly* 57 (2): 133–64.

Raichur, Arvind, and Richard W. Waterman. 1993. "The Presidency, the Public, and the Expectations Gap." In *The Presidency Reconsidered*, ed. Richard W. Waterman, 1–21. Itasca, IL: Peacock Press.

Reeves, Richard. 2000. "Clinton Was Great in Goodbye Speech." *Albuquerque Journal*, August 18, A14.

Riker, William H. 1984. *The Theory of Political Coalitions*. New York: Praeger.

Rivers, Douglas. 1988. "Heterogeneity in Models of Electoral Choice." *American Journal of Political Science* 32 (3): 737–57.

Roosevelt, Theodore. 1913. *Theodore Roosevelt: An Autobiography*. New York: Charles Scribner's Sons.

Rose, Gary L. 1997. *The American Presidency under Siege*. Albany: State University of New York Press.

Schier, Steven. 2009. *Panorama of a President: How George W. Bush Acquired and Spent His Political Capital*. Armonk, NY: M. E. Sharpe.

Schier, Steven. 2011. "The Contemporary Presidency: The Presidential Authority Problem and the Political Power Trap." *Presidential Studies Quarterly* 41 (4): 793–808.

Schlesinger, Arthur, Jr. 1957. *The Crisis of the Old Order: The Age of Roosevelt*. Boston: Houghton Mifflin.

Schlesinger, Arthur, Jr. 1958. *The Coming of the New Deal: The Age of Roosevelt*. Boston: Houghton Mifflin.

Schlesinger, Arthur, Jr. 1960. *The Politics of Upheaval: The Age of Roosevelt*. Boston: Houghton Mifflin.

Schlesinger, Arthur, Jr. 1973. *The Imperial Presidency*. Boston: Houghton Mifflin.

Schneider, William. 1998. "It's a Values Thing. Or Not." *National Journal*, December 19: 3042.

Sigelman, Lee. 1991. "'If You Prick Us, Do We Not Bleed? If You Tickle Us, Do We Not Laugh?' Jews and Pocketbook Voting." *Journal of Politics* 53 (4): 977–92.

Seligman, Lester G., and Michael A. Baer. 1969. "Expectations of Presidential Leadership: Leadership in Decision-Making." In *The Presidency*, ed. Aaron Wildavsky, 18–35. Boston: Little, Brown.

Seligman, Lester G., and Cary R. Covington. 1989. *The Coalitional President*. Chicago: Dorsey Press.

Silva, Carol L., Richard W. Waterman, and Hank C. Jenkins-Smith. 2007. "Why Did Clinton Survive the Impeachment Crisis? A Test of Three Explanations." *Presidential Studies Quarterly* 37 (3): 468–85.

Simon, Dennis M. 2009. "Public Expectations of the President." In *The Oxford Handbook of the American Presidency*, ed. George C. Edwards III and William G. Howell, 135–59. New York: Oxford University Press.

Sinclair, Barbara. 2012. "Doing Big Things: Obama and the 111th Congress." In *The*

Obama Presidency: Appraisals and Prospects, ed. Bert A. Rockman, Andrew Rude-livige, and Colin Campbell, 198–222. Washington, DC: Congressional Quarterly Press.

Solomon, Burt. 2000. "Disunity for All." *National Journal* 51 (December 16): 3870–76.

Stimson, James A. 1976. "Public Support for American Presidents: A Cyclical Model." *Public Opinion Quarterly* 40 (Spring): 1–21.

Stimson, James A. 1976–77. "On Disillusionment with the Expectation/Disillusion Theory: A Rejoinder." *Public Opinion Quarterly* 40 (Winter): 541–43.

Stuckey, Mary. 1991. *The President as Interpreter-in-Chief.* Chatham, NJ: Chatham House.

Suskind, Ron. 2011. *Confidence Men: Wall Street, Washington, and the Education of a President.* New York: Harper.

Thach, Charles C., Jr. 1969. *The Creation of the Presidency, 1775–1789: A Study in Constitutional History.* Baltimore: Johns Hopkins University Press.

Thomas, Norman C., Joseph August Pika, and Richard Abernathy Watson. 1993. *The Politics of the Presidency.* Washington, DC: Congressional Quarterly Press.

Toobin, Jeffrey. 1999. *A Vast Conspiracy: The Real Story of the Sex Scandal That Nearly Brought Down a President.* New York: Simon and Schuster.

Tufte, Edward R. 1978. *Political Control of the Economy.* Princeton: Princeton University Press.

Valentino, Nicholas A., Vincent L. Hutchings, and Ismail K. White. 2002. "Cues That Matter: How Political Ads Prime Racial Attitudes during Campaigns." *American Political Science Review* 96 (1): 75–90.

Warren, Mark E. 1999. *Democracy and Trust.* New York: Cambridge University Press.

Waterman, Richard W. 2010. *The Changing American President: New Perspectives on Presidential Power.* 3rd ed. Cincinnati: Atomic Dog Publishers.

Waterman, Richard W., Hank C. Jenkins-Smith, and Carol L. Silva. 1999. "The Expectations Gap Thesis: Public Attitudes toward an Incumbent President." *Journal of Politics* 61 (November): 944–66.

Waterman, Richard W., Robert Wright, and Gilbert St. Clair. 1999. *The Image-Is-Everything Presidency: Dilemmas in American Leadership.* Boulder: Westview Press.

Wayne, Stephen. 1982. "Great Expectations: What People Want from Presidents." In *Rethinking the Presidency,* ed. Thomas E. Cronin. Boston: Little, Brown.

Weatherford, M. Stephen. 1978. "Economic Conditions and Electoral Outcomes: Class Differences in the Political Response to Recession." *American Journal of Political Science* 22 (4): 917–38.

Weatherford, M. Stephen. 1983. "Economic Voting and the 'Symbolic Politics' Argument: A Reinterpretation and Synthesis." *American Political Science Review* 77 (1): 158–74.

Weatherford, M. Stephen. 1984. "Economic 'Stagflation' and Public Support for the Political System." *British Journal of Political Science* 14 (2): 187–205.

Welsh, Susan, and John Hibbing. 1992. "Financial Conditions, Gender, and Voting in American National Elections." *Journal of Politics* 54 (1): 197–213.

White, Leonard D. 1958. *The Republican Era: A Study in Administrative History, 1869–1901.* New York: Macmillan.

Whitford, Andrew B., and Jeff Yates. 2009. *Presidential Rhetoric and the Public Agenda: Constructing the War on Drugs.* Baltimore: Johns Hopkins University Press.

Wiebe, Robert H. 1967. *The Search for Order: 1877–1920.* New York: Hill and Wang.

Williams, John T. 1985. "Systemic Influences on Political Trust: The Importance of Perceived Institutional Performance." *Political Methodology* 11 (1–2): 125–42.

Wood, B. Dan. 2007. *The Politics of Economic Leadership: The Causes and Consequences of Presidential Rhetoric.* Princeton: Princeton University Press.

Wood, B. Dan. 2009. *The Myth of Presidential Representation.* New York: Cambridge University Press.

Wood, B. Dan, Chris T. Owens, and Brandy M. Durham. 2005. "Presidential Rhetoric and the Economy." *Journal of Politics* 67 (3): 627–45.

Young, James S. 1966. *The Washington Community.* New York: Columbia University Press.

Zaller, John R. 1998. "Monica Lewinsky's Contribution to Political Science." *PS: Political Science and Politics* 31 (2): 182–89.

Index

Abramowitz, Alan, 76
Adams, Gordon, 76, 90
Adams, John Quincy, 8
Afghanistan, 16–17, 22, 104, 109–10, 122
Alter, Jonathan, 131
Anderson, Christopher, 78
approval ratings (presidential), 2–3, 5–7,
  14, 15, 19–20, 23, 25–26, 28–37, 43,
  46, 50–70, 73, 75–79, 81–88, 90–93,
  95–103, 108–9, 111, 114–18, 123–24,
  128, 136–37, 139, 144–45, 149, 151, 153,
  155, 157, 159, 161, 164–68, 189, 191n1
  (chap. 3)

Baer, Michael, 3–4, 12, 30
Baker, Peter, 125, 127–29, 191–92
Bartels, Larry, 77, 109
Bem, Daryl, 36, 138
Bin Laden, Osama, 31, 34, 104, 123
Blendon, Robert, 163, 167
Bloom, Harold, 75
Blumenthal, Sidney, 89, 91, 103
Bond, John, 135
Brace, Paul, 75, 90, 109
Brady, David, 76
Branch, Taylor, 41
Brody, Richard, 18, 75
Brownlow, Louis, 3, 4, 31, 72–74, 81, 83,
  105, 135
Buchanan, Bruce, 19, 135
Buchanan, James, 9

budget (budgeting), 1, 13, 16–17, 41, 90,
  104, 113, 120, 123–24
bully pulpit, 10
Burns, James MacGregor, 33
Bush, George Herbert Walker, 6, 12–13,
  17, 20–27, 32–35, 86, 120, 125
Bush, George Walker, 2, 5, 12–13, 17, 19,
  26–30, 32–34, 37, 40, 42–44, 46, 48–
  50, 86, 104–5, 108–19, 123, 126
Bush School, 178–79

Campbell, James, 75
candidate/incumbent gap, 14, 120, 129
Canes-Wrone, Brandice, 10
Carter, Jimmy (James Earl), 6, 12–14,
  16–18, 20–24, 26–27, 32–34, 86, 126,
  129, 145
censure (of the president), 85, 88, 90,
  95, 144
challenger gap, 47–48, 50, 57, 59, 62,
  64–66, 69
"chief magistrate," 8
Citrin, Jack, 136, 163
civil rights, 12, 32, 135
civil servants, 160
Civil War, 9
Cleveland, Grover, 9
Clinton, Hillary Rodham, 13, 91, 109
Clinton, William (Bill), 2, 5, 12–13, 17,
  19–29, 31–32, 34–35, 37, 39–49, 51–71,
  73–74, 76–93, 95–105, 109, 114, 117,

119, 126, 129, 136–39, 141, 143, 144–45,
148–51, 153, 156–58, 164, 166, 171, 174,
177, 189, 191n1 (chap. 5), 192n5 (chap.
11)
Cohen, Jeffrey, 18, 75
Cold War, 17, 40, 108
Coleman, John, 77
Commander in Chief, 104–6, 108, 111–
12, 117, 119, 151
Committee on Administrative Management (Brownlow Committee), 3, 11
Congress (congressional), 1, 6–8, 10, 12–
13, 14, 17–18, 23–25, 31, 36, 38–48, 51,
53–57, 59–64, 68–70, 84–86, 88–90,
92–93, 96–103, 105, 107, 112, 115–18,
122–28, 131, 134, 136–39, 143–44, 149–
50, 152–55, 157, 159, 163–68, 172, 176,
189, 192nn4–5 (chap. 11), 193nn6–7
Constitution (constitutional), 1, 4, 7–8,
17, 86–87, 92, 105, 106–7, 135, 140, 144
Corwin, Edward, 33
Covington, Cary, 34
Craig, Stephen, 136, 143
Croly, Herbert, 9
Cronin, Thomas, 3–4, 37, 135

Delli Carpini, Michael, 140
Destler, I. M., 135
divided government, 18, 24, 53, 105, 115,
117–18, 137
Dobel, Patrick, 110, 113
Dole, Robert, 24–25, 47–49, 52–55, 57–
60, 62–65, 177, 191n1 (chap. 5)
Druckman, James, 74
Duch, Raymond, 78
Durham, Brandy, 74
Durr, Robert, 75

economy, 3, 6–7, 9, 16–17, 28, 40, 43, 54,
62, 66–68, 70–83, 85, 89–90, 93, 96,
99–105, 109, 113–17, 119–21, 123–24,
127–28, 132, 134, 139–40, 144–45, 157–
58, 165–66, 171, 174, 187
Edwards, George, viii, 3, 16, 18, 35, 38–
39, 74, 77, 91, 112–15, 125–26
efficacy (political), 134, 136, 143–44,

149, 151, 159–60, 166–67, 171–72, 176,
188–89
Ehrlich, Walter, 86
Eisenhower, Dwight, 12, 20–24, 26, 32,
107
Erikson, Robert, 37, 67, 74–75, 90, 171
ethics (high ethical standards), 22–24,
38–46, 48–49, 54–55, 57, 59, 61–63,
68–70, 72–85, 88–89, 93, 96–103, 115–
16, 118–19, 139, 150, 152, 154, 158
excellent presidents, 39, 41, 49–50, 145

Farrand, Max, 106
Feldman, Stanley, 76, 79, 90
Fiorina, Morris, 76
Fiske, Susan, 36, 135
Fleisher, Richard, 135
Ford, Gerald, 6, 14, 17, 20–24, 31, 32–34,
51, 86
foreign affairs (experience in), 8, 10, 23,
38–46, 48, 54–55, 59, 62, 88, 100, 105–
9, 115, 138, 151
Frolich, N., 76

Garand, James, 75
Genovese, Michael, 3–4, 19, 136
George, Alexander, 135
Gilens, Martin, 158
Gilliam, Franklin, 159
Gingrich, Newt, 24–25
Gore, Al, 73, 164–66
Goren, Paul, 77
governors, 13, 129, 160, 164–65, 167, 170–
72, 174, 193nn7–8, 193n10
Grant, Ulysses, 9
Great Depression, 7, 10, 17, 113–14
Green, Donald, 136, 163
Green, John, 73
Greenstein, Fred, 8
Gronke, Paul, 76, 90

Hamilton, Alexander, 86–87, 102–3, 105
Hargrove, Erwin, 4, 135
Haskin, Frederic, 11
Hayes, Rutherford, 9
Hess, Stephen, 36, 135

Hetherington, Marc, 136, 144, 163, 172, 174, 192n1
Hibbing, John, 76
Hibbs, Douglas, 75, 77–78
Hinckley, Barbara, 7, 75, 90, 109
Holmes, Justin, 74
Hoover, Herbert, 6, 33
House of Representatives, 8, 46, 77–78, 85–88, 93, 96, 113
Howell, William, 4, 11
Hurricane Katrina, 17, 34, 43
Hussein, Saddam, 34, 113
Hutchings, Vincent, 159

ideal gap, 138–39
impeachment (impeach), 8, 24, 34–35, 43, 45–46, 66–68, 78, 83–88, 90–93, 95–100, 102–3, 136, 144–45, 149, 151, 153, 157, 163, 166, 169–70, 174, 189, 192n4 (chap. 11), 193n9
imperial presidency, 108
incumbent gap, 138–39, 150–52, 154, 157
Iran Contra Scandal, 34–35, 84, 86, 136
Iraq, 16, 34, 43, 86, 104, 109–19, 122–23
isolationism, 107–8
Iyengar, Shanto, 125, 159

James, Scott, 11
Jefferson, Thomas, 8
Johnson, Andrew, 9
Johnson, Lyndon, 6, 12, 20–24, 32–34, 84, 86, 107, 161
Jones, Charles, 18

Kennedy, John F., 1, 5, 12, 20–24, 26, 32, 107
Kernell, Samuel, 19, 75
Ketter, Scott, 140
Key, V. O., 9
Kiewiet, Roderick, 76, 79, 90
Kimball, David, 36, 134, 136–37, 159, 162
Kinder, Donald, 36, 76, 90, 135
Kingdon, John, 171
Korean War, 107
Kramer, Gerald, 75
Krause, George, 77–78, 140

Lammers, William, 4
Lanoue, Dan, 76
Leuchtenburg, William, 11
Lewinsky, Monica, 24, 34–35, 46, 86–87, 192n5
Lewis-Beck, Michael, 73, 76
Light, Paul, 31, 135
Lincoln, Abraham, 9, 37, 106
Lowi, Theodore, 4, 8, 12–13, 18, 31

MacKuen, Michael, 37, 74–75, 90
Madison, James, 106
Markus, Gregory, 66, 76, 90
mayors, 160, 164–65, 167, 170–72, 174, 193nn7–8
McCarty, Nolan, 76
McConnell, H. K., 36, 138
McKinley, William, 106
Mezey, Michael, 134
Milkis, Sidney, 10
Monroe, James, 6–7
Mueller, John, 31, 75, 109

Nadeau, Richard, 75
Nelson, Michael, 4, 134
Neustadt, Richard, 3, 5, 33
New Deal, 11
Niemi, Richard, 136, 143
Nixon, Richard, 12–14, 17–18, 20–24, 32, 34–36, 84, 86, 136
Norpoth, Helmut, 75

Obama, Barack, 2, 5, 12–14, 16–18, 28, 31–32, 34, 109, 113, 120–32, 176
Oppenheimer, J. A., 76
Ostrom, Charles, 75, 90
outsider presidents, 13–14, 126, 129–30, 132
Owens, Chris, 74

Palmer, Harvey, 78
Panic of 1819, 6
Panic of 1907, 7, 10
Patterson, Samuel, 36, 134, 136–37, 159, 162
Patterson, Thomas, 163

performance-based model, 30, 39, 71–77, 81, 85, 89–90, 93, 100, 102, 119, 159
Perot, Ross, 53–54
Phelps, Glenn, 8
Pierce, Franklin, 9
Piffner, James, 31
Pika, Joseph, 8
Pious, Richard, 35
pocketbook attitudes, 66–67, 75–77, 79–80, 82, 114, 118–19, 139–40, 148, 152, 154, 156–59, 166, 167–68, 170, 173, 187
police, 160, 164–65, 172–73, 193n8
political parties, 2, 5, 9, 13, 18, 37, 43, 87, 113, 188–89
Polk, James, 106
Poole, Keith, 76
presidential (ideal) prototype, 30, 33, 36, 39, 41, 72, 135, 138–39
Price, H. Douglas, 75
public employees, 164–65, 172
public opinion, 30, 31, 87, 90, 103, 109, 114, 126–27, 134, 163, 178, 180

Reagan, Ronald, 6–7, 12–14, 17, 20–23, 26–27, 32, 34–35, 84, 86, 126, 133
Reeves, Richard, 47
Remesh, Susan, 76
retrospective evaluations of the economy, 75
retrospective evaluations of presidents, 2, 5, 16–17, 19–21, 24, 26–28, 29, 49, 72, 83
Riker, William, 33
Rivers, Douglas, 77
Roosevelt, Franklin, 3, 10–12, 14, 29–30, 32–33, 36–37, 107, 135
Roosevelt, Theodore, 7, 10, 37, 106
Rose, Gary, 33–34, 85, 133, 136
Rosenthal, Howard, 76

scandal, 3, 14, 21, 24, 34–36, 43, 46, 83–87, 110–11, 136, 192n5 (chap. 11)
Schier, Steven, 4, 109–10
Schlesinger, Arthur, Jr., 33, 108
school boards, 164–65, 167, 172, 193n8

Seligman, Lester, 3–4, 12, 30, 34
Senate, 18, 43–44, 78, 85, 87, 126, 176
Senate Majority Leader, 24–25
shutdown (government), 41–42, 46, 53, 55–58, 60, 189, 191n1 (chap. 5)
Sigelman, Lee, 76
Silver, Glenn, 136, 143
Simon, Dennis, 5, 30, 39, 75, 90
sociotropic attitudes, 66–67, 75–77, 79–80, 81, 114, 118–19, 139–40, 148, 152, 154, 156–59, 166, 167–68, 170, 173, 187
"sound judgment in a crisis," 23, 38–46, 48, 54–59, 61–63, 67–70, 88, 96–98, 100, 109, 115–17, 138–39, 150–51
Spanish-American War, 9, 106
Speaker of the House, 24–25, 41
Square Deal, 10
Starr, Kenneth, 78, 85, 91–96, 98–99, 101–3
state legislatures, 160, 164–65, 167, 171–72, 193nn7–10
Stimson, James, 32, 37, 74–75
Stuckey, Mary, 135
Suskind, Ron, 112, 131–32

Taylor, Zachary, 9
textbook presidency, 36–37
Thach, Charles, 7
Thomas, Norman, 8
Toobin, Jeffrey, 91
Truman, Harry, 12, 30, 32, 107
trust in government (trust in leaders), 3, 5, 14–15, 21–22, 25, 28, 86, 133–34, 136, 141–51, 153, 155–56, 158–60, 162–64, 166–68, 170–76, 188, 192n4 (chap. 11), 193n9
Tufte, Edward, 32, 75, 90
Tyler, John, 8

Valentino, Nicholas, 159
veto, 4, 8
vice president, 22, 34, 73, 86, 164–67, 172, 192nn4–5 (chap. 11), 193n6
Vietnam War, 17, 21, 34, 84, 86, 107, 133, 136

Vietnam Watergate Era (period), 21–22, 28

Volden, Craig, 76

War of 1812, 106

War on Terror, 17, 104, 110, 114–15, 117–19

Washington, George, 8, 106

Watergate scandals, 21–22, 24, 34, 84, 86, 133, 136

Watson, Richard, 8

Wayne, Stephen, 3, 35

weapons of mass destruction, 34, 86, 104, 110–11, 113

Weatherford, M. Stephen, 75–77, 79, 192n2 (chap. 11)

weighted gap, 44–48, 50, 54–65, 67–70, 83, 89, 115–17, 150–51, 156–57

Welsh, Susan, 76

White, Ismail, 159

White, Leonard, 9

Whitford, Andrew, 10

Wiebe, Robert, 9

Wilson, Woodrow, 10, 37, 106

Wood, B. Dan, 31, 71, 73–74, 85

World War I, 106

World War II, 17, 106–8, 113

Yates, Jeff, 10

Young, James, 8

Zaller, John, 87, 90, 100, 109, 140

Printed and bound by CPI Group (UK) Ltd, Croydon, CR0 4YY

09/06/2025

14686143-0001